"*Soul Pilgrimage* is a clear-sighted primer to spiritual formation, a delightful invitation for the Christian curious about how their faith can move beyond mere creedal affirmation or pious living and delve deeper into a journey of soul transformation."

—Felicia Song
Professor of Sociology, Westmont College

"This is one of the more unique and compelling books I have read. Compelling, because it explores the core of who we are, what we were designed for, and what it means to walk with our Designer. Unique, because its theological and philosophical insights are provided by a trail mate (and his better half) who is simply . . . walking with us and unveiling the fruit of a remarkable pilgrimage. Happy trails!"

—Stan D. Gaede
President emeritus, Christian College Consortium

"*Soul Pilgrimage* is an act of hospitality. James and Jennifer generously invite you to step into their Camino de Santiago adventure, and at the same time, to embark on your own journey with a sacred goal. . . . Friendship with the Trinity is the destination the authors have in mind. And this, as Dallas Willard points out, is eternal living."

—Gary W. Moon
Founding Executive Director, Dallas Willard Center, Westmont College

"This is a rare book; it combines thoughtfulness of mind with depth of devotion. James Taylor guides us on a journey that will make you feel that you, too, have followed the way of the pilgrim on the Camino. Great learning on every page about the most important topic in the world."

—John Ortberg
Author of *Eternity Is Now in Session*

"Jim Taylor has effectively leveraged his experiences during a physical pilgrimage into a rich array of principles and themes that illuminate our spiritual journey in this soul-forming world. *Soul Pilgrimage* creatively integrates themes ranging from apologetics, theology, and biblical studies to meaningful applications from rich historical resources and time-tested practices. Jennifer's journal and the reflection questions make this accessible, attractive, and practical for all who struggle with identity, purpose, and hope."

—Kenneth Boa
President, Reflections Ministries

"*Soul Pilgrimage* takes you to some lovely places! First, a geographical journey, by way of Jennifer's thoughtful journaling. And then, Jim applies his years of academic study and personal experience to a different kind of journey, one that invites you 'higher up and further in.' You will be in good hands as you discover the joys and challenges of your own soul pilgrimage. I urge you to take up the challenge."

—Diana Trautwein
Spiritual Director and retired Pastor

"In this accessible and salient volume, James and Jennifer Taylor invite the readers to know God better in our day-to-day life by taking up a soul pilgrimage. Based on the insights from their physical pilgrimage, this rich spiritual guide shows the soul pilgrimage to be the transforming journey of fulfilling the great commandments of loving God and our neighbors. 'Take up and read.'"

—Helen Rhee
Professor of History of Christianity, Westmont College

"Imaginatively written and convincingly hopeful, *Soul Pilgrimage* encourages doubters, skeptics, and believers who aspire to get closer to God that it *is* possible to know God and to know him deeply. . . . If you're looking for honest answers to your questions and you relish being surprised by an unexpected friendship with God, I invite you to consider Jim and Jennifer Taylor to be your pathfinders."

—Beth Seversen
President, Academy for Evangelism in Theological Education

SOUL PILGRIMAGE

Soul Pilgrimage

Knowing God in Everyday Life

JAMES E. TAYLOR
and
JENNIFER MOE TAYLOR

CASCADE *Books* · Eugene, Oregon

SOUL PILGRIMAGE
Knowing God in Everyday Life

Copyright © 2022 Wipf and Stock. All rights reserved. Except for brief quotations in critical publications or reviews, no part of this book may be reproduced in any manner without prior written permission from the publisher. Write: Permissions, Wipf and Stock Publishers, 199 W. 8th Ave., Suite 3, Eugene, OR 97401.

Cascade Books
An Imprint of Wipf and Stock Publishers
199 W. 8th Ave., Suite 3
Eugene, OR 97401

www.wipfandstock.com

PAPERBACK ISBN: 978-1-7252-8084-7
HARDCOVER ISBN: 978-1-7252-8082-3
EBOOK ISBN: 978-1-7252-8085-4

Cataloguing-in-Publication data:

Names: Taylor, James E., author. | Taylor, Jennifer Moe, author.
Title: Soul pilgrimage : knowing God in everyday life / James E. Taylor and Jennifer Moe Taylor.
Description: Eugene, OR: Cascade Books, 2022 | Includes bibliographical references.
Identifiers: ISBN 978-1-7252-8084-7 (paperback) | ISBN 978-1-7252-8082-3 (hardcover) | ISBN 978-1-7252-8085-4 (ebook)
Subjects: LCSH: Spiritual life—Christianity. | Christian life. | Spiritual formation.
Classification: BV4501.3 S660 2022 (paperback) | BV4501.3 (ebook)

VERSION NUMBER 031122

All Scripture quotations, unless otherwise indicated, are from the New Revised Standard Version Bible, copyright © 1989 National Council of the Churches of Christ in the United States of America. Used by permission. All rights reserved worldwide.

To our children and grandchildren
—may your pilgrimages be blessed.

"Blessed are those whose strength is in you,
whose hearts are set on pilgrimage."

—Ps 84:5 (NIV)

Contents

Tables | viii
Acknowledgments | ix

Introduction: An Invitation to Christians Who Want to Know God Better | 1

I—This Is Eternal Life
1 The Promise: Why Does Knowing God Matter? | 11
2 The Possibility: Can You Really Know God? | 31
3 The Profile: What Does It Mean to Know God? | 46

II—My Own Know Me
4 God's Person: What Can You Know About God's Nature? | 67
5 God's Presence: What Are Signs of God's Presence in Your Life? | 86
6 God's Provision: How Can You Tell When God Guides and Empowers You? | 107

III—Growing in Grace and Knowledge
7 The Path: How in General Does Knowledge of God Grow? | 129
8 The Practices I: What Can You Do Alone to Know God Better? | 147
9 The Practices II: What Can You Do With Others to Know God Better? | 169

Conclusion: A Prayer for a Deeper Friendship with God (A Camino Prayer) | 188

Bibliography | 189
Scripture Index | 193

Tables

Table 1—Pilgrimage routines, stages, and practices

Acknowledgments

I'm grateful to the Westmont College Professional Development Committee for providing me with a sabbatical during the fall semester of 2018 with funding to support my trip to Northern Spain to walk the Camino de Santiago—and the time away from college responsibilities to start writing the book on my return. I also appreciate the valuable feedback I received from a number of people who read entire drafts of the book: Greg Spencer, Sameer Yadav, an anonymous reader, and the students in my spring 2019 and spring 2021 Philosophy Senior Seminar classes. In addition, my department colleagues Mark Nelson and David Vander Laan helped me process my ideas at an early stage. Finally, I'm especially thankful for my wife Jennifer's companionship, collaboration, encouragement, and assistance. Her loving friendship and partnership as a fellow pilgrim sustained me as we walked the Camino together and worked on the book together. She is the author of the Camino journal entries at the beginning of each chapter.

Introduction

An Invitation to Christians Who Want to Know God Better

September 21, 2018, Pamplona (from my wife Jennifer's journal)

Darkness greets us when Jim closes the door of the Hostal Navarra behind him. We flip on our flashlights. "This way," he points to the illumined street signs giving us the bearings we need. We step into the street in the direction of the Camino trailhead.

Walking to our *hostal* from the bus station the previous evening, we surveyed enough of Pamplona to take in its mix of historic city with modern metropolis. The combination thrilled me.

Now, in the early morning light, a human figure in hiking gear comes into view as we step onto a paved trail. When he passes by, I notice the symbolic scallop shell attached to his backpack. "A fellow pilgrim," I whisper.

Jim and I pause and look at each other. We laugh at the same time. At long last, we're embarking on our Camino adventure.

"Hey, look—another pilgrim symbol!" Jim's excitement matches my own. He points to a beautiful square of dark blue tile imbedded in the trail. It displays the yellow lines of a scallop shell, indicating all trails lead to Santiago de Compostela. The tile serves as our first marker, showing us that we are indeed on the Camino.

How many times have I pictured the Camino in my mind over the past year of planning? My head dances with images from *The Way* starring Martin Sheen.

I turn to Jim with my own epiphany. "In spite of all the information we've collected and planning we've done, we can't really *know* the pilgrim experience until we actually *walk in it*."

And so we step forward.

An Invitation to Pilgrimage

Jennifer captures the first moments of our Camino de Santiago pilgrimage well. With months of careful preparation behind us, we felt an exciting season of adventure drawing us forward. After an extended period imagining ourselves walking the Way of St. James, we were actually traversing the historic path together!

I chose to travel to northern Spain during a sabbatical from my philosophy professor job at a Christian liberal arts college to experience pilgrimage as an act of spiritual discipline. I wanted to see whether this age-old Christian practice would help me grow closer to Christ. What Jennifer and I discovered was that our physical pilgrimages would facilitate our spiritual pilgrimages only if our preparation involved ongoing interior soul work as well as bodily exercise and the right kind of hiking equipment. We learned this lesson together through our daily experiences and discussions on the trail.

Pilgrimages can be solo affairs. The backpack-toting human figure Jennifer mentions in her journal entry was hiking alone. But the best spiritual quests are pursued in the company of others who share the same goal (think of Frodo and Sam in Tolkien's *Lord of the Rings*). And the best religious journeys result in pilgrims better able to love and serve God and others. In other words, a pilgrimage is an activity that is ideally both *with* and *for* others. For that reason (and many others!), I'm glad I invited Jennifer to be my pilgrimage partner.

And now I'm happy to invite you—my reader—to go on a pilgrimage with me as well. You can join me just by reading this book and putting what you learn from it into practice. You may think that would be a strange kind of pilgrimage. But what is a pilgrimage? A pilgrimage is a journey that has a sacred goal. And a journey can be spiritual rather than geographical. The sacred goal I have in mind for you and me is *knowing God*. That's a goal you can strive to attain no matter where you are. Perhaps you're already on that pilgrimage. Perhaps you already know God. In that case, I invite you to join me in seeking to know God *better*.

A literal religious pilgrimage involves going to a *place*. In the Christian tradition, pilgrims have journeyed to such places as Jerusalem, Rome, and, like Jennifer and me, Santiago de Compostela. Going to these places requires moving your body to them—usually by walking (though sometimes by bicycling, horseback riding, or in the case of disabled pilgrims, using a wheelchair!).

But the pilgrimage I'm inviting you to start—or continue—is primarily a pilgrimage for your *soul*. Your main purpose on this pilgrimage will be to get your soul closer to God rather than to move your body closer to a sacred place.

Your soul is the deepest part of who you are. It's the eternal part of you that was created by God for relationship with him and fellow humans. It's the part of you that senses, thinks, feels, wills, and acts. It's the part of you that loves—or fails to love. In short, *you* are your soul. On a literal pilgrimage, your soul moves your body from one physical place to another. On a soul pilgrimage, your soul allows itself to be moved by God toward deeper intimacy with him.

A pilgrimage is something you *do*. In the case of a literal pilgrimage, you have to keep your body moving in the same direction for a long time. Doing so requires both using your body (e.g., walking, carrying, looking, and listening) and caring for your body (e.g., eating, drinking, resting, and sleeping).

In the case of a *soul* pilgrimage, you have to keep your soul directed toward God for a long time. Doing so requires the use and care of your soul by means of engaging in various *spiritual practices* (e.g., praying, worshiping, trusting, and obeying). These are practices that help soul pilgrims know God and grow in their knowledge of God.

A pilgrimage is not only something you do, it's also something you *learn* to do by doing it. Pilgrimage involves experimentation. It involves learning from your successes and your failures—trial and error. On a *literal* pilgrimage, you have to learn how to find your way without getting off on the wrong track. And you have to learn how much walking your body can handle before you need to rest and refuel.

The pilgrimage I'm recommending to you is a process of coming to know God better by doing things that require faith in God and then seeing what happens as a result. Along the way, you learn the way to God and you get to know God better. But you also learn about yourself—including how much risk you can stand and how much intimacy with God you can handle.

I hope you'll join me on this pilgrimage. I hope you'll take the steps of faith required to begin (or continue) walking on the soul pilgrimage path toward deeper knowledge of God. I hope you'll engage in this grand spiritual experiment with me.

My Personal Journey

Though I've been a follower of Christ for over fifty years, I haven't always thought the sort of soul pilgrimage I'm asking you to take with me would be both desirable and possible.

As I look back at my life, I realize now that there was a time, early on, when I was what I will call a "satisfied" Christian. Though I wasn't satisfied then with my knowledge *about* God (I wanted more), I was content with the lived experiences I had with God. It didn't occur to me then that it might be possible to *grow* in my direct personal knowledge of God.

Before I committed my life to Christ at the age of thirteen, I attended church weekly with my family. In Sunday school I learned Bible stories and memorized passages of Scripture. During worship services I became familiar with the elements of the liturgy and many of the great hymns of the Christian tradition. But I didn't have a desire to know God more deeply.

In eighth grade, I raised my hand when a visiting evangelist asked which of us junior high kids who heard him share the gospel wanted to accept Christ as our Savior and Lord. And I followed him to a nearby room where he told us new Christians we had become disciples of Jesus who needed to give our lives to him. But it didn't occur to me that I had just entered into a *friendship* with God.

Later that year, I read Norman Vincent Peale's *The Power of Positive Thinking* (which I had found on my grandmother's bookshelf), and was thrilled to discover that being a Christian could change your life for the better. But I had no idea at the time that genuine transformation would occur only as I received the resurrection life of Christ through prayerfully abiding in loving communion with him.

And in the summer between my sophomore and junior years in high school, I traveled with my church high school youth group to attend Campus Crusade's Explo '72 evangelistic conference in Dallas, Texas. It was exciting to be around so many (over seventy-five thousand!) fellow young believers and to hear famous Christian preachers (such as Billy Graham) and listen to popular Christian musical artists (such as Larry Norman).

But the main takeaway from the event was instruction on how to share the gospel by means of a pamphlet, written by Bill Bright (the founder of Campus Crusade for Christ), which contains "The Four Spiritual Laws."[1] The original version of this tract talks about a relationship with God (and even fellowship with God) resulting in an abundant life. But it doesn't stress

---

1. The four laws are: "(1) God loves you and offers a wonderful plan for your life; (2) Man is sinful and separated from God. Therefore, he cannot know and experience God's love and plan for his life; (3) Jesus Christ is God's only provision for man's sin. Through him you can know and experience God's love and plan for your life; and (4) We must individually receive Jesus Christ as Savior and Lord; then we can know and experience God's love and plan for our lives." Bright, *Have You Heard?* Interestingly, the updated version of the booklet containing these laws is entitled, *Would You Like to Know God Personally?* (it also uses inclusive language).

the need for individual Christians to undergo a lifelong process of *deepening* one's fellowship with God.

In sum, these early Christian experiences of mine (and many others) stimulated in me a desire to grow in my knowledge of the Bible, participate in regular worship, strengthen my faith in and commitment to Christ, read inspiring Christian books promising to improve my life, draw closer to my Christian friends, and become a more effective evangelist. But though I considered myself to have a relationship with God, I didn't hunger for a life of ever-deepening intimacy with him. In short, I was a satisfied Christian.

Satisfied Christians such as I used to be presuppose that ordinary humans can know God but also assume they already know God as much as they need or want to—at least in this life. Satisfied Christians may balk at accepting my invitation because they think a pilgrimage of soul wouldn't be worthwhile.

Later, I became what I'll call a "skeptical" Christian. Though I believed in God and had faith in God, I didn't think it possible to *know* that God exists or to have personal *knowledge* of God. And it seemed to me that I had been naïve to think, as a satisfied Christian, that humans could have any kind of knowledge concerning God (rather than mere *belief about* or *faith in* God).

As a skeptical Christian, I thought of myself as relatively sophisticated. I thought my philosophical and theological education had demonstrated that, though it's possible to grow in *faith*—and even *reasonable* faith—growth in knowledge about God and knowledge of God was impossible.

I transitioned from my satisfied stage to my skeptical stage in college. During the summer between my junior and senior years at a Christian liberal arts college, I suddenly began to experience serious and intense doubts about the existence of God. I remember waking up periodically during this time with a sick feeling in the pit of my stomach. I wanted very much to believe in God, but during that time I couldn't.

I was a philosophy major, and during my junior year I had taken courses covering the entire history of Western philosophy. One thing that struck me as a result of taking those courses was that if the great philosophical minds of history couldn't agree with one another about whether we could *know* that God exists (or even whether God *does* exist), then who was I to think I could figure it out?

Something happened in the spring semester of my senior year that eventually led to the dissolution of my doubts and the corresponding strengthening of my Christian conviction and commitment. It was a spring break trip to Mexico with a few hundred fellow students to lead vacation Bible school programs and evangelistic meetings in various neighborhoods around Ensenada. What I found during that trip was that the experience of Christian service, evangelism, worship, and fellowship revived my faith in God. This revival happened because through these experiences I had a strong sense of God's presence and activity.[2]

However, though I recovered my belief that God exists and my faith in God, I stopped short of concluding that *I knew* that God exists or even that *I knew God*. And this skeptical attitude of mine persisted even through the year I spent as a ministerial intern at a Presbyterian church and during the subsequent two-year period I took courses at a theological seminary for my master's degree in theology. I also remained skeptical concerning knowledge about (and of) God during my five-year PhD program in philosophy—though that's not surprising, since there were no Christians on the faculty, and the subculture was highly secular, naturalistic, and materialistic. My skepticism continued for a number of years after that while I taught at both a secular university and a Christian college.

Was my experience unusual? I don't think so. In spite of the persistent religiosity of our culture, it's become increasingly secular over the years. That secularism has affected even the subculture of the Christian church and Christian institutions of higher learning (whose faculty are usually trained in graduate programs at secular universities). And secularism breeds skepticism about God.

Recent experiences of mine with some faculty and students at my current institution have confirmed, anecdotally, that my previous skeptical attitude was not an anomaly. A number of fellow Christian faculty members from various disciplines told me during a faculty research retreat that they didn't think we can know *anything* (!)—including anything about God. And when I ask my Christian students each semester whether it's possible to *know* anything about God (as opposed to just believing things about God or having faith in God), many give a negative reply.

Skeptical Christians like these faculty, students, and my former self may hesitate to accept my invitation because they think my soul pilgrimage goal—knowing God and growing in the knowledge of God—can't be achieved.

In sum, one type of Christian (satisfied) may turn down my invitation on the ground that a pilgrimage aimed at knowing God isn't desirable, and another type of Christian (skeptical) may turn down my invitation on the ground that a pilgrimage aimed at knowing God isn't possible.

---

2. This and the previous two paragraphs are from a longer account of my story of doubt in my book *Introducing Apologetics*, 9–11.

I hope to show in the following pages that neither of these grounds is tenable. I hope to demonstrate that a soul pilgrimage toward deeper and deeper knowledge of God is not only possible and desirable but also the very pilgrimage of soul to which Jesus invites us when he bids us follow him and become citizens of the kingdom of God.

When I encountered the work of Dallas Willard in midlife, my skepticism about knowing God gradually disappeared and was replaced by a growing dissatisfaction with the quality of my relationship with God. Throughout his Christian books, Willard promotes the idea that knowing God is at the heart of the Christian life. His defense of the nature, importance, and possibility of knowing God is especially clear and cogent in *Knowing Christ Today: Why We Can Trust Spiritual Knowledge*. Willard convinced me that there is another and better type of Christian: not a satisfied Christian or a skeptical Christian but (what I will call) a *soul pilgrim Christian*.

Once I was persuaded that the soul goal of knowing God—and growing in knowledge of God—was both possible and desirable, I began to encourage others, especially my students, to pursue it. Though some were eager to do so, others were reluctant—either because they were satisfied with their current knowledge of God or skeptical that knowing God is possible. Some in the latter category questioned or abandoned their Christian identity. I had convinced them that Christians are people who know God through knowing Christ, and apparently their skepticism about knowing God, combined with this claim, led them to conclude that they weren't (or couldn't be) Christians.

In my attempts to persuade these students to hang onto their Christian faith, I urged them to reflect on their personal experiences throughout their lives and up to the present to identify their experiences of God. But some of them didn't think—or weren't sure—that they had ever *had* any experiences of God. And *I* wasn't sure what I could tell them to help them recognize an experience of God and distinguish it from experiences of other things.

My memory of a conversation with one of these students is especially poignant. Paul (not his real name) had grown up in a solid Christian home. And he had taken both my introductory philosophy course and my Christian apologetics class. Shortly before he graduated, we met in the front patio of my house to talk about his waning Christian commitment due to doubts about his ever having experienced God. Though I tried my best during our extended discussion to facilitate his recognition of such experiences, he remained unconvinced—and disappointed.

That's when I decided to write this book. In the process of preparing to do so, I've become convinced, on the basis of my own personal experience, the witness of Scripture, and the testimony of Christians throughout the ages—including Dallas Willard—that Christians can do things to put themselves in a position to experience God, to learn how to recognize their experiences of God *as* experiences of God, and to grow thereby in their knowledge of God.

These things that Christians can do are individual and corporate practices—Willard would call them "spiritual disciplines"[3]—that form Christians, over time, into people who are capable of discerning the presence, availability, and activity of God in their lives more and more effectively. But becoming proficient at the regular exercise of these practices, disciplines, or activities is a process, a journey, a *pilgrimage*. And the goal of this pilgrimage is an ever-deepening intimate loving union and communion with the Triune God.

I'm currently on this pilgrimage. Though I'm not a novice, I'm far from being a master. I'm instead an apprentice, student, or disciple. I'm learning what the journey is like and how to do it as I "walk" it day by day. My writing of this book is in some respects a *result* of this sojourn, to some extent a *part* of it, and, perhaps most of all, a *preparation* for it.

As I invite you, dear reader, on this pilgrimage of soul toward deeper knowledge of God, I ask you to join me as I seek, find, explore, and investigate new stretches and dimensions of the path. I'll share with you what I've experienced, what I'm currently in the process of discovering, and what I hope at some point to find out. To some extent, I'll be your pilgrimage guide. But as a soul pilgrim with much to learn, I'll constantly be looking to—and directing your attention to—our Heavenly Guide.

Whether you're a satisfied Christian, a skeptical Christian, a dissatisfied and non-skeptical but-for-some-reason-reluctant Christian—or already a soul pilgrim Christian, I encourage you to come with me as a fellow pilgrim, experimenter, and learner. I welcome you to accompany me on the journey. As Jennifer said in her journal entry, "we can't really *know* the pilgrim experience until we actually *walk in it.*" Will you step forward onto the path with me?

---

3. See for instance Willard, *The Spirit of the Disciplines*.

I

This Is Eternal Life

"And this is eternal life, that they may know you, the only true God, and Jesus Christ whom you have sent."

—John 17:3

I

The Promise

Why Does Knowing God Matter?

March 5, 2018, Santa Barbara (from Jennifer's journal)

When Jeanie agreed to meet with Jim and me to tell us about her Camino experience, we were eager to hear from a veteran pilgrim.

A septuagenarian and former missionary, Jeanie told us she had earned her *Compostela* a couple of years earlier on a solo walk along the Camino de Santiago.

"What's a *Compostela*, Jeanie?" My question exposed my ignorance.

"A *Compostela* is a Camino certificate of completion. To earn it, I gathered at least two stamps each day in my pilgrim's passport." We looked at her stamped *Credencial del Peregino* with awe. The dog-eared booklet showed wear due to the many stamps Jeanie had collected from the churches, hotels, and restaurants she'd visited along the way.

Jeanie reflected, "Arriving at the Santiago de Compostela Cathedral was the culmination of a dream. For years, my late husband and I had talked of walking the Camino together. When he died unexpectedly, I decided I could still realize our dream, but I would need to do it on my own."

The lovely *Compostela* Jeanie held in her hand proved she had completed her walk. As we talked, Jim and I learned she could have earned it with far less effort.

"Pilgrims can earn the *Compostela* by walking only the last sixty-two miles," she said. "But I'm so glad I chose to walk more." I took in Jeanie's petite size, delicate skin, and shy smile. I would not have picked her out of a crowd to take on such a challenge.

"You could have realized your dream with a lot less rigor," I said. "Instead, you walked four times the number of required miles. Why did you put in the extra effort? Why did it matter?"

Jeanie's response told me how much the process had meant in achieving her goal. "I had some grieving to do." She paused before she continued. "I needed to figure out what might come next in my life. As I collected information about the Camino, I felt encouraged. I decided more time on the trail would allow me space for contemplation and prayer. I became convinced it would be worth it. In the end, it was one of the hardest things I've ever done," she said quietly, "but really good for me."

Our visit with Jeanie prompted Jim and me to have our own conversation about the Camino later. What would make the experience worth the considerable effort? We both want to get away from obligations and distractions.

But we're seeking more. At my age, I know life can change quickly. A job can be terminated unexpectedly. A fire can burn up a house and all its contents within hours. A bad fall can take the life of a beloved family member without warning.

Now we have an opportunity that's too good to pass up. Jim's interest in the practice of pilgrimage propels him. I'm ready to partner with him in the adventure. Earning a *Compostela* is a wonderful goal, and like Jeanie, we want to have a meaningful *journey* too.

Our Camino Pilgrimage Story: The Value of Walking the Camino

As Jennifer and I were deliberating about whether to travel to northern Spain to walk the Camino Francés to Santiago de Compostela, we had to decide whether the trip would be worth it. Would the costs we would incur be outweighed by the benefits?

The costs were clear. We would be spending a fair amount of money, a month of my sabbatical, and time away from our family members and friends. We would need to purchase hiking equipment and arrange for accommodations and various means of travel (airplane, train, bus, and taxi). We would need to practice walking long distances in advance of our trip and then spend a lot of time walking during our trip. Jennifer wasn't surprised that I took these costs seriously. She knows I don't spend money easily and like my ordinary routines.

We were also aware of the risks in addition to the costs. What if we got injured or sick? What if we were delayed due to a cancellation? What if we didn't have the energy or strength to walk as far each day as we needed to reach our reserved accommodations? Since I tend to be risk averse in addition to being frugal, dwelling on these risks made me anxious. And my anxiety made me wonder if we should take the trip after all.

In the end, we realized it would be worth incurring these costs and taking on these risks if the rewards of walking the Camino compensated for them. But what would those rewards be?

We came to see that the valuable outcomes of a Camino pilgrimage were of two general sorts: (1) *completing* the journey by arriving in Santiago de Compostela so as to be qualified to receive a *Compostela* and (2) *experiencing* the journey itself from start to finish. So, the benefits can be thought of in terms of the *product* or the *process*—or both.

Some pilgrims value completing the journey more than the journey itself. A long time ago, the Camino was so full of hardships and dangers that many pilgrims saw walking it as merely a necessary means to reach the cathedral in Santiago where they could venerate the remains of St. James and receive a pardon for their sins from the Church.

More recently, many pilgrims have seen the experience of walking the Camino itself as at least as worthwhile as—and in some cases *more* worthwhile than—arriving in Santiago and being awarded a *Compostela*. Contemporary pilgrims take up the trail for various reasons, in some cases more spiritual than religious and in others more recreational than spiritual.

On the basis of the testimonies of other Camino pilgrims we know, we found ourselves motivated to go—in spite of the costs and risks—primarily to experience the Camino itself (and only secondarily to receive our *Compostela*). In spite of my money worries and fear of potential catastrophes along the way, my growing excitement about the promise of a Camino pilgrimage made me anxious to start our adventure!

The Value of Knowing God

A soul pilgrimage toward deeper personal and relational knowledge of God also involves costs and at least apparent risks. Ultimately, it costs your life. And to those who value their lives, it can seem like a risk to give one's life to God (what if surrendering my life to God doesn't pay off for me—or even makes me worse off in some way?). Perhaps you experience the decision about whether to embark on a soul pilgrimage as a *dilemma*—a choice that seems to have only bad consequences: either I lose my life or I lose God.

That's how I've sometimes experienced it—starting with my emotional reaction as a thirteen-year-old to the visiting evangelist I mentioned in the Introduction. You'll recall he told us converts we needed to "give our lives" to Christ—our *whole lives*! That seemed a scary idea to my eighth-grade self. What would my friends think? Would I still be able to have fun? My fears were alleviated to some extent when I overheard an adult during fellowship hour tell a friend her total dedication to the Lord gave her great joy.

But I continued to struggle with the decision nonetheless. The way I thought about it at the time was that though Jesus had become my *savior*, I hadn't yet decided to make him my *lord*. Little did I know then that I would continue to wrestle with the need to *surrender* myself to God. The problem persisted even though my specific attachments continued to change over time. And one of the reasons the dilemma dragged on is that I considered my sacrifices something I *had* to do to be a "committed Christian" rather than something I *wanted* to do to know God more deeply.

Is a soul pilgrimage involving knowing God worth the real costs and apparent risks that go along with it? Like pilgrims who have decided to walk the Camino because of the rewards one can hope to attain by doing so, many soul pilgrims—like me—have decided it would be worthwhile to cultivate personal knowledge of God. We've decided that knowing God personally *matters*.

Of course, many people have decided that knowing God personally *wouldn't* be worthwhile. These people can be compared to those who choose not to walk the Camino. Or they are like a young couple Jennifer and I met who decided early on to *stop* walking it.

We met Beth and Travis on a bus from Logroño to Nájera when we took a day off from walking so I could nurse a sore tendon. They told us they had started the Camino Francés with great enthusiasm at the traditional beginning of this route in Saint-Jean-Pied-de-Port, France. But the challenge of crossing the Pyrenees Mountains took a toll on them. After only a few days on the trail, they became disappointed with the Camino due to ongoing discomfort and injuries. They decided to abort their trek and spend time in a big city resting, dining, and shopping before heading back home to the States. The difficulties they encountered convinced them that sticking with their original plan to walk the whole Camino wasn't worth it. Jesus's parable of the sower features would-be soul pilgrims who give up their quest for similar reasons.

So, some think a soul pilgrimage would be worth it and others don't. But *why* does it matter whether or not a Christian has personal *knowledge* of God? Isn't it enough just to *believe in* God and *have faith in* God? After all, according to John 3:16, "For God so loved the world that he gave his only Son, so that everyone who *believes* in him may not perish but may have eternal life" (italics mine).

In reply, a broader reading of the Gospel of John reveals that eternal life involves *knowledge* of God. In chapter 17, Jesus affirms, in his prayer to the Father, that "this is eternal life, that they may *know* you, the only true God, and Jesus Christ whom you have sent" (v. 3; italics mine).

Jesus is clearly saying here that eternal life is *identical* with knowing God and knowing Jesus himself. (In 1 John 5:20, John says the Son of God, Jesus Christ, "is the true God *and eternal life*;" italics mine.)

What Jesus says about eternal life in John 17:3 means John 3:16 can be read as implying that everyone who believes in the Son may not perish but instead may enjoy a life characterized by knowing God. And the kind of knowledge in view here is not merely *head* knowledge (not just knowledge of facts about God) but *relational* knowledge (knowledge of God through a personal relationship with God).

So, the reason it matters whether a Christian has personal knowledge of God is that eternal life itself—the primary goal of the Christian life—*consists in* personal relational knowledge of God. In the same way, it matters whether a husband has personal knowledge of his wife (and vice versa), since married life—the primary reason for two people to enter into the covenant of marriage—consists in intimate loving union and communion.

The Scriptures make it clear, in various places, that the expression "eternal life" characterizes not merely a quantity of life (never-ending) but also a *quality* of life (abundant). It's the kind of life enjoyed by the Triune God. And for us humans, eternal life as personal knowledge of God is the sort of life that leads, not just to our continued existence, but also to our *fulfillment* as human beings—to full human life, health, and well-being.

The second-century theologian Irenaeus of Lyon (130–202) affirms this idea in a book he wrote to define central Christian teachings: "The glory of God is a human being fully alive, and the life of a human being consists in beholding God. If what the creation shows of God grants life to all living in the earth, then much more does that revelation of the Father which comes through the Word give life to those who see God."[1]

Irenaeus has two kinds of life in mind here: the uncreated eternal life of God (*zoe* in Greek) and the created earthly life of biological organisms (*bios* in Greek). God provided the latter to all living creatures. The former kind of life is available to humans through Jesus Christ, the living Word of God. It consists in a personal knowledge of God that will eventually involve

---

1. Payton, *Irenaeus*, 116.

actually beholding or seeing God after death. But even in this life, we can participate in this kind of life by knowing God through Christ.

> ### Soul Pilgrim Reflection Question
>
> How much do you desire and value knowing God
> —*friendship* with God?

Biblical Affirmations: The Prophets

The biblical prophets portray personal knowledge of God as desirable and valuable. Passages from Hosea, Jeremiah, and Isaiah confirm that this is the case.

In speaking to the people of Israel, who have been alienated from God, the prophet Hosea says, "Let us return to the Lord . . . let us know, let us press on to know the Lord" (6:1a, 3a). He also implies that God will respond favorably as they make an effort to know him: "his appearing is as sure as the dawn; he will come to us like the showers, like the spring rains that water the earth" (6:3b). And later in the same passage Hosea adopts the voice of God himself in saying, "I desire steadfast love and not sacrifice, the knowledge of God rather than burnt offerings" (6:6). Hosea implies that knowing God by way of a loving personal relationship is better than interacting with him by means of engaging in religious observances.

As a "satisfied" Christian in my pre-college years, I strove to grow in my faith and strengthen my Christian commitment. The means I used for these purposes were a daily "quiet time," the reading of Christian books, and regular attendance at midweek youth group meetings and Sunday services of worship. In retrospect, it seems to me now that my relationship with God at that time was characterized more by these religious practices than it was by knowing God personally. There was nothing wrong with the activities, of course, but I wasn't using them primarily to deepen my friendship with God. I wasn't following Hosea's exhortation to "press on to know the Lord." As a result, I wasn't refreshed by his appearing to me "like the spring rains that water the earth." I didn't fully realize, along with Hosea, that knowing God is better than the practices meant to facilitate that knowledge.

Moreover, what Jeremiah says implies that knowing God is better than human wisdom, strength, and wealth (all of which are good things): "Thus says the Lord: Do not let the wise boast in their wisdom, do not let the mighty boast in their might, do not let the wealthy boast in their wealth; but let those who boast boast in this, that they understand and know me, that I am the Lord; I act with steadfast love, justice, and righteousness in the earth, for in these things I delight, says the Lord" (Jer 9:23-24).

Knowing God and understanding the character of God as one who acts with (because he delights in) steadfast love, justice, and righteousness is to be in a valuable condition indeed.

I wish I had taken this passage in Jeremiah to heart as a "skeptical" Christian in my college and post-college years. Though I've never had enough money or power to be tempted to boast in wealth or might, as a graduate student and eventually a university and college professor caught up in various academic subcultures, I tended to value human wisdom more than I should have. And at the time, what passed for wisdom was that, even though it might be reasonable to *have faith* in God and to *believe* various things about God, it wasn't possible to *know* God or *know anything about* God. As a result of my assimilating this message, I was more likely to boast about this "wisdom" than I was to boast with Jeremiah about *understanding and knowing the Lord*!

In delivering God's judgment to Shallum, an unrighteous king of Judah who was guilty of many injustices, Jeremiah portrays God as comparing Shallum to his righteous and just father Josiah: "Did not your father eat and drink and do justice and righteousness? Then it was well with him. He judged the cause of the poor and needy; then it was well. Is not this to know me? says the Lord" (22:15-16).

Here the Lord implies that those who know him will be just and righteous—and that those who are not just and righteous do not know him. So, knowing God is not only valuable in itself but also worthwhile because people who know God become like God—and demonstrate their knowledge of God through their likeness to God—in being good people who engage characteristically in loving, righteous, and just behavior.

In both my satisfied Christian phase and my skeptical Christian period, I missed this connection between knowing God and being good. My earlier focus was on being forgiven by God for *not* being good. And my later orientation was to realize the importance of being loving, righteous, and just but without acknowledging that it would be possible for me to acquire these virtues only by knowing God.

Soul pilgrims should keep this connection between knowing God and being like God clearly in mind. I've defined the goal of a soul pilgrimage in terms of knowing God. Now we can see from the Jeremiah passage just cited that knowing God involves loving others as well. So, a soul pilgrimage is not merely about pilgrims getting closer to God. It's also about pilgrims taking care of their fellow human beings. People who know God love God, and those who love God love what God loves. Since God loves the world, those who know and love God will love the world too. Soul pilgrims who journey to the heart of God will also gain God's heart for others.

Isaiah implies the same sort of thing in a passage in which he prophesies the coming of One who will bring about an era in which "They will not hurt or destroy on all my holy mountain; for the earth will be full of the knowledge of the Lord as the waters cover the sea" (11:9). Why will there be no harm or destruction on God's holy mountain? Because everyone on earth will know the Lord, and knowing God makes people good. This verse from Isaiah not only connects knowing God with goodness and justice; it also provides a glimpse of a glorious future made possible by a universal knowledge of God. Such a vision can motivate soul pilgrims to keep to the path when they're tempted to give up.

When we got tired and hot during long stretches on the Camino, Jennifer and I often encouraged each other by talking about what we imagined it would be like when we finally arrived in Santiago. We pictured throngs of exultant fellow pilgrims celebrating in the Santiago Cathedral Square. And we visualized ourselves worshipping in the pews of the cathedral during the culminating pilgrims' mass. In the same way, soul pilgrims can meditate on a future in which the kingdom of God is fully realized in such a way that widespread friendship with God has brought about a just and peaceful world.

Knowing God in a personal loving relationship is such a good thing that God himself not only wants it for us but also promised to enable his people to experience it. Through the prophet Jeremiah, he said of the people of Judah who were in exile that, "I will give them a heart to know that I am the Lord; and they shall be my people and I will be their God, for they shall return to me with their whole heart" (24:7). As we'll see next, the New Testament makes it clear how God has fulfilled this promise in the person of Jesus Christ.

> ## Soul Pilgrim Reflection Questions
>
> Have these passages from Hosea, Isaiah, and Jeremiah motivated you to know God and grow in your knowledge of God? If so, in what ways?

Biblical Affirmations: The Gospel of John

We've already seen how Jesus identifies eternal life with knowing God "and Jesus Christ whom (God the Father) has sent" (John 17:3). The Gospel of John makes it clear what the benefits are of eternal life as knowing the Father and the Son. Knowing Jesus—and his word (his teaching)—enables you to "know the Father" (8:19) and to "know the truth... which will make you free" (8:31–32).

Those who love Jesus and obey him (keep his commandments) receive the "Spirit of truth"—the Holy Spirit—from the Father and the Son. Jesus tells his disciples that this Spirit is one "whom the world cannot receive, because it neither sees him nor knows him." But then he tells them, "You know him, because he abides with you, and he will be in you" (14:17). And he says this Spirit "will teach you everything, and remind you of all that I have said to you" (14:26).

Knowing Jesus, "abiding" in Jesus and his love, loving Jesus, knowing Jesus's teaching, and obeying Jesus lead to effective prayers, fruitfulness, complete joy, and peace (15:1–11; 16:33).

And Jesus asks the Father to bring about a relationship of mutual indwelling between those who believe in him and the Father and Son. This relationship is to be characterized by a loving unity so complete that not only will Jesus's followers be unified by it, but also the world will come to know about Jesus's divine origin and God's love by means of it (17:20–24). The benefits of knowing the Triune God are obviously numerous and far-reaching.

Our Camino experience gave us an imperfect but suggestive sense of the kind of community Jesus intends the church to be. Though the pilgrims we met in passing were strangers to us, we nonetheless shared a bond with them in virtue of having a common goal. We were all walking in the same direction to the same destination. And fellow pilgrims could be easily identified by their Camino equipment. All wore backpacks or knapsacks, and many had some version of at least one of the traditional pilgrim accessories (hat, water container, walking stick, and scallop shell). In addition to having the same goal and similar garb, pilgrims also used the same greeting: "¡Buen Camino!" ("Have a good walk!"). The feeling of unity created by these commonalities was especially meaningful, since Camino walkers are a diverse lot—young and old, religious and secular, and from many different nations, races, and ethnicities. Unity in diversity.

We soul pilgrims who are becoming increasingly united with God in loving friendship can also experience a growing unity with one another. Our common love for God, together with our having clothed ourselves with Christ, make us one in Christ Jesus in spite of our differences (Gal 3:27–28). And this common destiny and dress will dispose us to greet each other with generosity and hospitality as we walk the soul pilgrim's path together. As a result, we'll progressively come to hold each other in our hearts (Phil 1:7), thus deepening our mutual indwelling. Based on what Jesus prays in John 17, we can say that the goal of a soul pilgrimage is both union with God and with all who love God. What could be better than that?

> ## Soul Pilgrim Reflection Question
>
> Which benefits of knowing God mentioned in the Gospel of John have you experienced?

Biblical Affirmations: Paul

Paul clearly considered knowing God to be worthwhile. Toward the beginning of his letter to the church at Colossae, he tells them that since the day he heard about their faith in Jesus Christ and their love for all the saints, he and his companions "have not ceased praying for (them) and asking that (they) may be filled with the knowledge of God's will in all spiritual wisdom and understanding, so that (they) may lead lives worthy of the Lord, fully pleasing to him, as (they) bear fruit in every good work *and as (they) grow in the knowledge of God* (1:9–10; emphasis mine). Paul prayed not only that the Colossians would know God's will but also that they would know God and grow in their knowledge of God.

Paul also prayed that the Ephesians would know the *love* of God in Christ: "I pray that you may have the power to comprehend, with all the saints, what is the breadth and length and height and depth, and to know the love of Christ that surpasses knowledge, so that you may be filled with all the fullness of God" (Eph 3:18–19). An essential element of knowing God is knowing God's love. Notice that Paul characterizes the love of Christ as a love that "surpasses knowledge." I think what he means by this is that we cannot know God's love in such a way as to be able to fully *describe* or *explain* it. But we *can* know God's love insofar as we *experience* it—at least to some extent. And again, knowing God's love is an important part—and a valuable benefit—of knowing God.

Finally, Paul expressed his own longing to know God in Christ by telling the Philippians that he "want(s) to know Christ and the power of his resurrection" (3:10a). In doing so, he calls our attention to another worthwhile consequence of knowing Christ: the power (ability, capacity, strength) of Jesus's resurrection life—a life that God provides to those who are "in Christ" (as Paul would put it) as a result of their freely accepting God's offer of saving, new, and abundant life in Christ.

In sum, according to Paul, knowing God enables soul pilgrims to know God's will, to know God's love, and to know the power of Christ's resurrection. That is, knowing God can facilitate our experience of God's guidance, affirmation, and empowerment. And growing in the knowledge of God can deepen our experience of these things.

Paul's jubilant characterization of life with God in Christ contrasts starkly with what I experienced in a season of my life between my seventh-grade conversion and my tenth-grade summer trip to Explo '72. During ninth grade, my adolescent desire to be accepted by the popular kids at school overcame my aspiration to give my whole life over to Christ. As a result, I got in with the proverbial "wrong crowd," and lived a double life—acting one way at church and another at my junior high. I was acutely aware of my hypocrisy at the time, but was too weak-willed to follow my conscience.

Then one evening as I was sitting alone in the dark on the steps leading into the basement of our house, I found myself feeling overwhelmingly lost, lonely, and listless. And I had a strong sense of God's absence. I was terribly sad. And I cried out to God for help. God eventually answered my prayer when my dad's work transferred him to a new city, where I got to start my life over with a new set of friends—mostly through the youth group of our new church. Though that was a dark time, I'm grateful that my memory of it enables me to appreciate more fully Paul's picture of a life of knowing God, a life providing divine direction, affection, and help on the path to perfection.

> ## Soul Pilgrim Reflection Question
>
> Which of these three benefits of knowing God (orientation, encouragement, and enablement) do you currently need most on your soul pilgrimage?

Biblical Affirmations: Second Peter

Second Peter is another New Testament book that communicates the value of knowing God. The author expresses his desire that his readers have "grace and peace . . . in abundance *in the knowledge of God and of Jesus our Lord*" (2 Pet 1:2; italics mine). He also tells them that God's "divine power has given us everything needed for life and godliness, *through the knowledge of him* who called us by his own glory and goodness" (1:3; italics mine). Moreover, he says that among these things made possible by knowing God that are needed for life and godliness are God's "precious and very great promises" through which we "may become participants of the divine nature" (1:4).

In a nutshell, personal, relational knowledge of God yields abundant grace and peace, everything needed for life and godliness—including God's precious and very great promises—and ultimately, even *participation in the very nature of God!* If the combination of these things doesn't add up to an abundant life, it's hard to see what would!

In sum, the Bible treats knowing God as a very good thing. God wants us to know him, so he makes it possible for us by enabling us to know him. When we try to do so, God responds by rewarding us with his presence. Knowing God is better than any merely human good. Those who know God become like God in being loving, just, and peaceful. The best way to know God is to encounter God in and through Jesus Christ, who is God the Son incarnate as a human being. As we get to know God in Christ, we grow in knowledge, freedom, fruitfulness, joy, and peace. And those of us who know God through Christ are drawn together in love and also draw the world to God through God's love for us and our love for each other.

These biblical passages about knowing God played a central role in my personal decision to embark on a soul pilgrimage. I'm not sure how they escaped my attention earlier, but when it became clear to me that the overall witness of Scripture is that knowing God is not only possible and desirable but also the central purpose of human being and living, my earlier satisfaction and skepticism subsided, and I began to yearn for a deeper connection with God—and through God, with my fellow human beings.

> ## Soul Pilgrim Reflection Questions
> Has this biblical survey convinced you that a soul pilgrimage would be worth your while? Why or why not?

Historical Christian Testimonies

Many well-known Christians throughout the history of the church have manifested or expressed a desire to know God—a desire so strong as to show they value knowing God above everything else. Here are a few examples.

In his *Confessions*, St. Augustine (354–430) chronicles and reflects on his own soul pilgrimage. He wrote this spiritual autobiography as an extended prayer. At one point, he prays, "May I know you, who know me. May I 'know as I also am known' (1 Cor 13:12)"[2] Here Augustine asks God to enable him to know God as deeply and fully as God knows Augustine.

---

2. Augustine, *Confessions*, 179.

That's quite an aspiration! In another prayer—one that occurs in the very first paragraph of the work—Augustine reveals his motivation for knowing God: "you have made us for yourself, and our heart is restless until it rests in you."[3] Augustine believed that human fulfillment is possible only through knowing God. And the *Confessions* are full of his longing for complete knowledge of God.

Augustine tells a story that illustrates this desire of his. He and his mother Monica were staying in a house in Ostia on the River Tiber "where, far removed from the crowds, after the exhaustion of a long journey, we were recovering our strength" for an upcoming voyage. He says they were having an intimate conversation about "what quality of life the eternal life of the saints will have." They concluded that "the pleasure of the bodily senses . . . is seen by comparison with the life of eternity to be not even worth considering." At this point, writes Augustine, "our minds were lifted up by an ardent affection towards eternal being itself . . . We moved up beyond (created things) to attain to the region of inexhaustible abundance . . . And while we talked and panted after it, we touched it in some small degree by a moment of total concentration of the heart. And we sighed and left behind us 'the first fruits of the Spirit' (Rom. 8:23) bound to that higher world, as we returned to the noise of our human speech . . ."[4] Augustine cherished this experience of union with God in loving fellowship with his mother.

St. Thomas Aquinas (1225–1274) believed that the highest goal of human life was to experience a direct vision of God[5]. This perception of God is known as the "Beatific Vision." The Beatific Vision of God doesn't consist in merely "looking at" God. It's more like gazing into the eyes of your lover. It's a personal and intimate direct encounter with God made possible by the purity of your heart and by God's self-disclosure. So, it's like seeing a man (or woman)—and seeing him to some extent for who he really is—as opposed to merely hearing about him or merely seeing his body. Aquinas thought a person could have this experience of God only after death.

But shortly before he died, while he was celebrating mass in 1273 on the Feast of St. Nicholas, Thomas received a revelation from God that affected him so profoundly that he decided to stop writing. He told his friend and secretary Reginald that all of his writings were "like straw" compared to what God had revealed to him.[6] Though this revelation may not have

---

3. Augustine, *Confessions*, 3.

4. Augustine, *Confessions*, 170–71.

5. Aquinas, *Summa Theologiae*, Supplement to the Third Part, Question 92, Article 1.

6. Butler, *Butler's Lives*, 511.

been the Beatific Vision itself, it was apparently an encounter with God that Thomas treasured so much that he was willing to consider his life's theological work much less valuable in comparison.

Though the philosopher Rene Descartes (1596–1650) is typically considered a rationalist, he reveals a mystical side in the following paragraph of his *Meditations on First Philosophy* (a paragraph that occurs after he's constructed a couple of arguments for God's existence and then discussed some of God's attributes):

> I should like to pause here and spend some time in the contemplation of God; to reflect on his attributes, and to gaze with wonder and adoration on the beauty of this immense light, so far as the eye of my darkened intellect can bear it. For just as we believe through faith that the supreme happiness of the next life consists solely in the contemplation of the divine majesty, so experience tells us that this same contemplation, albeit much less perfect, enables us to know the greatest joy of which we are capable in this life.[7]

Descartes's language here ("gaze . . . on the beauty of this immense light") suggests knowledge *of* God rather than merely knowledge *about* God. Furthermore, he places the highest possible value on this experience (the "greatest joy" in this life and the "supreme happiness" in the next).

The mathematician, physicist, inventor, philosopher, and theologian Blaise Pascal (1623–1662) had a profound experience of God for two hours one night in November of 1654. This experience has come to be known as Pascal's "Night of Fire," since he starts his account of it by simply writing, "FIRE." Among the things he wrote in his record of the encounter are two quotations of Jesus from the Gospel of John: "The world has not known you, but I have known you" (John 17:25) and "This is eternal life, that they know you, the one true God, and the one that you sent, Jesus Christ" (John 17:3). Pascal considered his meeting with God to have involved *knowing* God and he characterized his knowing God to be *eternal life*. It's also clear that he treasured this experience deeply, since he sewed the document containing his reflections about it (now known as "Pascal's Memorial"[8]) into his jacket, so he would always have it with him—close to his heart.

It's worth pointing out that though these four people were intellectuals who prized the life of the mind highly, each of them nonetheless valued knowing God even more. What they found in their academic pursuits was

---

7. Descartes, *Meditations*, 36.
8. Pascal, *Pensées*, 309–10.

not enough to satisfy them. They weren't content with anything less than a personal encounter with the Triune God.

> ### Soul Pilgrim Reflection Questions
>
> Do these four examples inspire you? If so, which inspires you most?

Testimonies of Ordinary People

The four people featured in the previous section are famous, male, intellectual Christians from history, three of whom had relatively extraordinary experiences of God. But a soul pilgrimage is for all people who want to know God more deeply—including ordinary people of all kinds. Here are two testimonies from individuals in this category. They are taken from the pages of William James's *Varieties of Religious Experience*. Each account shows how much the person valued his or her experience of God.

The first is by a woman who was "the daughter of a man well known in his time as a writer against Christianity . . . She relates that she was brought up in entire ignorance of Christian doctrine, but, when in Germany, after being talked to by Christian friends, she read the Bible and prayed, and finally the plan of salvation flashed upon her like a stream of light." Here's what she says in her own words about her conversion:

> The very instant I heard my Father's cry calling unto me, my heart bounded in recognition. I ran, I stretched forth my arms, I cried aloud, "Here, here I am, my Father." Oh, happy child, what should I do? "Love me," answered my God. "I do, I do," I cried passionately. "Come unto me," called my Father. "I will," my heart panted . . . I was satisfied. Had I not found my God and my Father? Did he not love me? Had he not called me? Was there not a Church into which I might enter?[9]

This woman was delighted when she recognized her heavenly Father's call even though her earthly father had not only neglected to prepare her to know God but had also criticized the Christian faith. Her innate need for God overrode the secular orientation she had acquired from her upbringing. Knowing and loving God meant so much to her that she immediately set aside her family's values to devote her life to God.

---

9. James, *Varieties*, 68–69.

The second is from a forty-nine-year-old man about his ordinary life with God. James uses it as an example of someone who has a "habitual and so to speak chronic sense of God's presence":

> God is more real to me than any thought or thing or person. I feel his presence positively, and the more as I live in closer harmony with his laws as written in my body and mind. I feel him in the sunshine or rain; and awe mingled with a delicious restfulness most nearly describes my feelings. I talk to him as to a companion in prayer and praise, and our communion is delightful. He answers me again and again, often in words so clearly spoken that it seems my outer ear must have carried the tone, but generally in strong mental impressions. Usually a text of Scripture, unfolding some new view of him and his love for me, and care for my safety. I could give hundreds of instances, in school matters, social problems, financial difficulties, etc. That he is mine and I am his never leaves me, it is an abiding joy. Without it life would be a blank, a desert, a shoreless, trackless waste.[10]

To these two I'll add my own account of a special experience with God. During the summer before our Camino, I spent a fair amount of time memorizing passages of Scripture. I would go over these sections of the Bible while I walked a three-mile loop on the Jesusita Trail close to our house in Santa Barbara. On one such occasion, close to the end of the summer, I found myself reciting various passages of Scripture out loud in the form of prayers. It's hard to express the joy and satisfaction I experienced as the verses I spoke took on new life for me, and I found myself feeling a strong sense of companionship with God. God had spoken his word to me in the Bible, and I had spoken portions of it back to him with gratitude for its life-giving richness. That particular walk—which I took in preparation for much walking to come on my literal pilgrimage—was also a highlight of my *soul* pilgrimage!

Soul Pilgrim Reflection Questions

Do you find these ordinary testimonies appealing? Why or why not?

---

10. James, *Varieties*, 70.

Eternal Life as Knowledge of God

It's clear from all these testimonies that eternal life as personal knowledge of God is a kind of life available *now* and not one for which we need to wait until after we've died (though there are aspects of it we won't be able to experience until the afterlife when we will "know fully" instead of "only in part"—1 Cor 13:12). That's because it's possible for us to know God, in personal relationship—at least to some extent—in this life (I'll defend this claim in chapter 2 against skeptical arguments to the contrary).

And, as I said above, personal knowledge comes in degrees. That's why Paul could pray that the Colossians would "*grow* in (their) knowledge of God" (Col 1:10) and Peter could urge his readers to "*grow* in the grace and knowledge of our Lord and Savior Jesus Christ" (2 Pet 3:18; italics mine).

In sum, eternal life as knowledge of God is a kind of life that contributes to our well-being, is available to us even now, and can be experienced by us more fully as time goes on. The Bible portrays it as a kind of life that is maximally desirable, immediately possible, and progressively improvable.

Eternal life as knowledge of God is *maximally desirable* because God made us human beings to be fulfilled by our knowing him personally in a relationship of loving communion with him. And God made us in such a way that we can be fulfilled *only if* we have this kind of relationship with him. Created things can contribute to our fulfillment, but we can't be fulfilled by them alone. Rather, they benefit us most when we see them as gifts God has given us that point to him as the Giver.

The moments on the Camino I enjoyed most were those in which the beauty of a scene or the kindness of a fellow pilgrim made me grateful to God for his handiwork and grace. Those experiences became opportunities to delight in God's creation and in God himself. One such occasion that stands out in my mind took place during the morning of our longest and steepest walk. Having left the little farming community of Las Herrerías in the coolness of a pre-dawn October morning, we ascended toward the quaint Tolkienesque mountain hamlet of O'Cebreiro in the province of Galicia. On the way, we witnessed a spectacular sunrise that gradually revealed a gorgeous verdant and hilly vista that reminded us of scenes from our childhoods in the American Northwest. The wind was blowing softly, and we paused in the quietness to drink in the natural beauty and to thank God for filling us to overflowing with his extravagant artistry.

That experience reminded me that we need to know God to be fulfilled. And since we have that need, it makes sense that the more we know God, the better off we'll be. Knowing God *more and more deeply* is the ultimate goal of a soul pilgrimage of the sort I'm recommending to you. And since knowing God as fully as we can is necessary for ongoing increasing degrees of human fulfillment, we must embark on and persist in a soul pilgrimage toward deeper knowledge of God in order to have any hope of enjoying progressively richer well-being.

Eternal life as knowledge of God is *immediately possible* in the sense that it's always possible at any time in one's life to come to know God personally—at least to some extent and in certain ways. God has extended an invitation to each individual human being to know him personally through Jesus Christ, and God has provided each individual human being with all the resources required to respond affirmatively to his invitation. Therefore, a soul pilgrimage both begins and ends with the same aim: to know God. The only difference is the degree to which and the ways in which one knows God at different points in time.

Similarly, it's always possible to embark on a pilgrimage on the Camino de Santiago—just by walking out your front door with the intention of heading in that direction! If Santiago is your goal, every step you take towards it counts as progress on your pilgrimage. Of course, you must delay gratification on a literal physical pilgrimage; you don't achieve your goal until you've reached the Cathedral of Saint James. But as I said in the previous paragraph, on a soul pilgrimage, you can realize your objective to some extent right off the bat, since your friendship with God begins as soon as you choose to follow Jesus.

Finally, eternal life as knowledge of God is *progressively improvable*. From the beginning of one's soul pilgrimage and in every subsequent stage, you can always cooperate with God in such a way as to let God help you grow to know God more deeply. Of course, it's also possible at any time to refrain from cooperating with God for this purpose and, as a result, either to fail to grow in knowledge of God or even to come to know God less (to be more alienated from God rather than more intimately united with God in friendship).

The parallel with a literal pilgrimage is that, if you keep walking with the right resources and in the right direction, you'll keep getting closer and closer to your ultimate destination. But if you decide to stay in a particular town on the way for an extended period, you won't make progress. And if you abort your journey—the way the young couple I mentioned earlier did—you may never reach your goal.

> **Soul Pilgrim Reflection Questions**
>
> Which of these three truths about eternal life do you need most to act on at this point? Do you need to make knowing God your top priority in life? Do you need to start knowing God personally? Do you need to deepen your knowledge of God?

Knowing God and Enjoying Knowing God

Each of the stages of a soul pilgrimage—the beginning, the middle, and the end—has the same object: to know God. The stages differ only in the quantity and quality of one's knowledge of God. Soul pilgrimages differ from literal physical pilgrimages in this way. On a literal physical pilgrimage, the experience of walking toward the sacred place (which is one's ultimate pilgrimage destination) has rewards that differ from the reward of reaching the sacred place itself (though along the way, pilgrims can be rewarded by sharing an attitude of hopeful anticipation of eventually reaching the sacred place together). But on a soul pilgrimage of the sort I'm recommending, the reward of the journey and of the journey's end are the same: knowing God. What changes over time is the extent to which one is capable of *enjoying* this reward in virtue of how well one knows God at any given time.

And enjoying God is key. According to the Westminster Shorter Catechism, which I learned about in my Presbyterian church confirmation class in seventh grade, the "chief end" of human beings is to "Glorify God and enjoy him forever."[11] And according to Aquinas, this activity and experience will eventually involve "total immersion in absolute goodness forever."[12]

Since our enjoyment of God—and the personal fulfillment that results—can increase as our knowledge of God deepens, satisfied Christians have a reason to be *dissatisfied* with the degree to which they currently know God—whatever that degree is. They have a reason to join Paul in regarding "everything as loss because of the surpassing value of knowing Christ Jesus (their) Lord" (Phil 3:8) and to "press on toward the goal for the prize of the heavenly call of God in Christ Jesus" (Phil 3:14). And it would make sense for them to follow the Unicorn in C. S. Lewis's *The Last Battle* (the seventh book in the *Chronicles of Narnia*) when he invites his companions to "Come further up! Come further in!" toward their home with God.[13] But

---

11. Westminster Assembly, *Westminster Shorter Catechism*, question 1.

12. This is Melchert's wording. See his *Great Conversation*, 293, for a discussion of Aquinas on the topic of eternal bliss.

13. Lewis, *The Last Battle*, 196.

what about the skeptical Christian's concern that knowledge of God isn't possible? I'll address that worry in the next chapter.

> ### Soul Pilgrim Reflection Questions
>
> How satisfied are you with your knowledge of God? Is anything keeping you from making a soul pilgrimage? If so, what is it, and what can you do to eliminate it?

Practice

Journal or talk to a friend about the highlights of your life. What experiences have been most satisfying? What experiences have been least satisfying? Why? Do your most satisfying experiences include experiences of knowing God? If so, what are those experiences? Can you identify ways in which your least satisfying experiences have been connected to your being somehow alienated from God (not enjoying knowledge of God through loving fellowship with God)? Do your positive experiences include any of the benefits of knowing God discussed in this chapter? If so, which ones?

2

The Possibility
Can You Really Know God?

July 23, 2018, Santa Barbara
(from Jennifer's journal)

Fluffy white clouds drift slowly in a brilliant blue sky. A late afternoon breeze blows a strand of hair over my eyes. Brushing it away, my gaze moves to my bare toes, deliciously free of shoes and socks.

I enjoy resting on a chaise lounge after walking a trail near our neighborhood. The Jesusita loop is over three miles long with some substantial elevation gain. From our front door, I clock an hour to walk it at a comfortable stride. If I push myself, I can shave off fifteen minutes. Afterward, I enjoy relaxing with my feet up while sipping a glass of water.

Jim joins me on the back porch. He's holding the Brierly *Pilgrim's Guide*, an indication he's been reading up on the Camino. "Not sure what we're getting into. Completing the Camino could depend on the condition of our feet," he says. "I just read about a guy whose blisters caused him to call it quits. Makes me want to break in our shoes soon. How about if we plan to walk a ten-miler this weekend?"

Jim's words pull me into reality. In two short months, he and I will be walking the Camino. A tiny sliver of doubt pierces my serenity. Will we be able to do this? I feel fine after a three-mile walk. But, how will I feel after walking fifteen miles in one day? I've never walked that many miles for even two days in a row, let alone twenty-one! My pulse quickens at the thought.

I follow Jim back into the house. "Any number of things could threaten our Camino experience," I say. "But like you said, there are things we can do right now to mitigate potential problems." I realize I'm convincing myself, rather than Jim.

Jim nods. "I'm glad we talked to Jeanie. She prepared for the Camino in deliberate but simple ways. Like she said, if she can do it, so can we!"

I feel my confidence returning. Like Jim, I take heart in learning from the experience of someone who has walked the Camino before us. Coping with blisters, backaches, sore knees, and even loneliness added an important dimension to Jeanie's experience. Our friend thrived on the Camino, in spite of her difficulties. I believe we will too.

Our Camino Pilgrimage Story: Doubts about the Camino

After we decided to walk the Camino Francés, we began to wrestle with doubts. Of course, our doubts were not about the *existence* of the Camino. There are plenty of resources confirming its reality. And though our research left us with questions about the *nature* of the route, we knew we would learn more about it by experiencing it for ourselves. Moreover, we had dealt with our concerns about the *value* of walking the Camino. Our cost-benefit analysis assured us it would be a worthwhile endeavor. Instead, our worries had to do with our *ability* to make the journey. We'd rarely walked more than ten miles in one day before, and our plan was to hike an average of fifteen miles a day for many days in a row. On some days we were scheduled to walk eighteen. Could we do it? It sounded daunting!

In the midst of our doubts, it was reassuring to hear from or about other people—especially people our age or older—who had completed the Camino. Their testimonies provided us with a reason to be confident we could do it too. Nonetheless, we persisted in being somewhat unsure about our capacity to endure the long distances until we got there and actually succeeded in doing it ourselves. Though it was helpful to hear from other pilgrims about their own direct personal experience walking the Camino, our doubts weren't completely eliminated until our own experience had proven to us we were up to the task.

Doubts about God

Many people also have doubts about God. Some people doubt that God exists or are even confident that God doesn't exist. Such people either lean toward atheism or actually affirm it. Other people have doubts about *whether or not* God exists. Those with that orientation tend to fall into the agnostic camp. Agnostics suspend belief about God's existence. They don't commit themselves one way or the other. Their attitude puts them somewhere in the middle of the spectrum between atheism (belief that there's no divine reality) and theism (belief that God exists).

As I mentioned at the beginning of the previous chapter, though traditionally pilgrims chose to walk the Camino de Santiago for exclusively religious reasons, today there are many who make the trek for various "spiritual" or even merely recreational reasons. Among those in these latter categories are agnostics and atheists.[1] But clearly atheists wouldn't choose to embark on a *soul* pilgrimage, since they deny God's existence. And though some agnostics might be open to the idea of a soul pilgrimage and might even take steps in that direction, their uncertainty about God would likely hamper their progress toward knowing God.

I've never been an atheist, but I've come close to being an agnostic. During my period of serious doubt, which I described in the Introduction, my belief in God wavered. But I never concluded that we live in a Godless world. Rather, I wrestled with uncertainty about God's existence that made it difficult for me to sustain a confident conviction about his reality. Later, when my doubts were alleviated, I considered myself a believer. But as I said earlier, I didn't regard myself as *knowing* that God exists. And I didn't see the primary goal of my Christian life as knowing God more and more fully and deeply—because I thought that wasn't possible.

Christians who have doubts about whether they can know about or know God—skeptical Christians—will likely find it hard to embark on and persist in a soul pilgrimage. That was certainly my experience during my skeptical phase. During my season of *serious* doubt, I was completely unable to have a devotional life. My prayers at that time—when I prayed—consisted primarily in desperate pleas for God to give me some indication of his reality. But even when my intense uncertainty gave way to relatively confident conviction, my walk with God was hampered by my skeptical attitude about knowing God. I knew I believed, but I wasn't sure I could *know*. But what's the difference?

---

1. See for instance professed atheist Reed, "Should Only Those Following God?"

> **Soul Pilgrim Reflection Questions**
>
> Do you have any doubts about God? If so, what are they?

Believing and Knowing

It's one thing to *believe* God exists (to be a theist); it's another thing to *know* he does. Knowledge requires more than belief. Knowledge involves a sufficiently secure contact with reality. But beliefs can be either disconnected with reality (false) or connected with reality in an insufficiently secure way (true but unwarranted). Either way, the belief doesn't count as knowledge.

An example of the first way a belief can fail to be knowledge is when many people believed the planet Earth was the center of the universe. But that belief is false. So those people didn't *know* the Earth was the center of the universe—even if they had good reason for thinking it was, and even if they thought they knew it was.

Examples of the second way a belief can fail to be knowledge are harder to find. They're when someone believes something to be true, has some reason for believing it, and it turns out to be true, but his or her reason isn't good enough for their belief to be knowledge.

For instance, the first time I met my high school youth pastor, I came to believe—solely on the basis of watching him act generously—that he was a generous person. After many years of knowing him, I acquired ample evidence confirming he was indeed generous. But though my initial observation of his generous act gave me some reason to believe that to be true, it wasn't enough to have given me a basis for *knowing* it was true. Since ungenerous people sometimes uncharacteristically perform generous acts, concluding my high school youth pastor was generous on the basis of witnessing just one of his generous acts was a case of hasty generalization. And hasty generalizations don't yield grounds sufficiently strong for knowledge.

Christians who *believe* God exists but think they don't *know* he does would, of course, come to this conclusion not because they think their belief is false but because they think it isn't based on sufficiently strong reasons or adequately solid grounds. And it would be natural for these Christians to conclude as well that they don't *know* God *personally and relationally* either. It would be odd for a believer in God to say that even though he or she doesn't know whether there is a God, he or she knows God!

> **Soul Pilgrim Reflection Questions**
>
> Do you regard yourself as *knowing* God exists? Why or why not?

Reasons for Skepticism

These are the skeptical Christians I mentioned in the Introduction. As you know, I used to be one of them. You may wonder what my reasons were for thinking that, though it's reasonable to *believe* God exists, it isn't possible to *know* he does.

For one thing, I used to think belief in God involves faith *rather than* knowledge. And I also thought faith and knowledge were *mutually exclusive*. In my experience, that seems to be what a lot of people think. It's what a number of my *students* have thought. Every semester I ask my introductory philosophy students whether they know God exists. Many say "yes," but many others tell me their relationship with God is a matter of faith rather than knowledge. They think if you have faith in God or God's existence, you can't also have knowledge of God. After all, faith involves at least some degree of uncertainty, and it might seem you can know something only if you're completely certain about it.

On the other hand, some skeptical Christians think faith and knowledge are compatible, but they also believe God is nonetheless completely *beyond* knowledge. Isn't God completely unknowable? We finite and sinful humans can't comprehend God at all, can we? Doesn't our finitude alone make us incapable of knowing God or anything about God? And doesn't our sinfulness compound our incapacity to know God? Our finitude might prevent us from seeing God clearly enough to know God—or at least to know God well—and it might seem also our sinfulness completely blinds us and makes us absolutely incapable of knowing God—or anything about God—at all. And given these aspects of the human condition, wouldn't it be arrogant and presumptuous to think we can have knowledge of God of any kind?

Let's carefully examine the two reasons just given for thinking God is completely unknowable. According to the first reason, if you have faith that God exists, you can't also know that God does. But of course, Christians are people who have faith that God exists. It follows that Christians are people who can't know that God exists.

Is this a good line of reasoning? I don't think so. Though there are lots of different kinds and degrees of faith, some of which involve a relatively low amount of confidence (e.g., an attitude of mere belief, assent, trust, or hope that falls short of knowledge), there's a relatively strong kind of faith that *could* count as knowledge. This is the kind of faith the author of Hebrews has in mind: "Now faith is the assurance of things hoped for, the conviction of things not seen" (11:1). And if you have *this* kind of faith in God's existence, if you have *assurance* and *conviction* God exists, then why can't it also be the case that you *know* God exists?

It isn't true in general that if you believe a claim to be true with assurance and conviction, then you can't also know it to be true. So, if there's some special reason for thinking things are different with the claim that God exists, then skeptics need to tell us what that special reason is.

Here's another way to put the first reason to think we can't have knowledge of God: If you have *faith in God*, then you can't *know God*. Christians are people who have faith in God. So, Christians can't know God.

This way of putting the first reason is even less convincing than the first. It seems rather that you can have faith in God only if you know God well enough to know it's reasonable to place your faith in God. That is, you can trust God only if you have sufficiently good reasons for thinking God trustworthy, and you have sufficiently good reasons for thinking God trustworthy only if you know God well enough to have gotten these reasons through personal interaction with God.

So, neither of these critiques works, and since this is the case, why think faith and knowledge incompatible? Why not rather think it's possible to have *faith* God exists and also to *know* God does—at the same time? That's the position to which I've come. If I'm right, since faith involves some degree of uncertainty, it must be possible to know something is true without being absolutely certain it's true. And that makes sense. Very few of the things we know are things we're absolutely certain about.

Many of the things we know are based only on what we learn from other people. For instance, our personal knowledge of science, history, and geography (to name just a few areas of knowledge) is based mostly on what we learned in school from our teachers or read about in books. And we can rarely be *completely* sure what others say is true. That's because they might be mistaken or lying. And it's rarely possible to *prove* another person knows what she's talking about and isn't trying to deceive us. In many cases, we don't even know the people we rely on for information. Of course, we can usually be reasonably sure our sources are reliable. But that leaves some room for uncertainty. We have to *trust* them; we have to have *faith* in them when we can't see for ourselves that they're right. But that means there are some things we know to be true that we also take on faith!

Jennifer and I learned a lot of Camino-related facts by what others told us in conversation, through books, and on the internet, among other means of communication. As a result, we came to know those facts. For instance, our new friend Jeanie told us about a place to stay in the town of Estella called "B&B Zaldu." She said the proprietor would pick you up on the Camino and drive you to his guest house. She also said he would prepare a lunch for you to take with you when you resumed your hike the next day. We'd never seen this place or met this man, but we knew these things were true solely on the basis of Jeanie's say-so. We knew them because we had faith in Jeanie—we trusted her.

In the same way, soul pilgrims can have faith God exists and know God exists—at the same time. We may not be able to be absolutely certain God is real on the basis of proof, but we can trust our divinely given innate disposition to believe in God as well as our experiences of God to provide us with knowledge he's there.

It's also possible to have faith in a person and know that person—at the same time. That shouldn't be surprising at all. How could it make sense to have faith in a person if you don't know that person—or at least know enough *about* that person to know he or she is trustworthy?

We found out the hard way we shouldn't have trusted what a complete stranger told us about how to find the Camino from our *hostal* in Ponferrada. Even though the stranger was the owner of that establishment, it turns out he didn't know what he was talking about when he gave us directions. Our Brierly guidebook had given us another route, but I assumed since the proprietor was a local, he would have a better one in mind. After getting lost for over an hour, we finally reconnected with the correct path when a friendly and knowledgeable woman reoriented us. At that point, I resolved to trust our guidebook in the future, since our experience with it had shown its author to be highly reliable. The more we *knew* the author through our reliance on his instructions, the more it made sense to trust him—to have *faith* in him.

Soul Pilgrim Reflection Questions

Are you convinced faith and knowledge are compatible? Why or why not?

Reasons to Affirm We Can Know God

So, faith and knowledge are compatible. But it's still possible humans are simply incapable of knowing God or anything about God—at least for the time being in this life. After all, we're finite, and so cognitively limited. And we're sinful, and so cognitively malformed. And God is a transcendent and infinite being. That's the second reason I mentioned above for concluding knowledge of God isn't possible.

Here's a simple skeptical line of reasoning based on these human limitations: Since humans are finite and sinful and God is infinite, humans can't know God or anything about him. Of course, humans are finite and sinful and God is infinite. Therefore, humans can't know God or anything about him.

In this case, the second assumption (that humans are finite and sinful and God is infinite) is clearly true. But the first assumption (that the finitude and sinfulness of humans means we can't know anything at all about an infinite God) is questionable. In particular, Christians have a number of good reasons to deny it.

In the first place, Christians have good reasons to believe God has revealed knowable truths about himself in the Bible. These include truths about his relationship with us and his will for us. As we saw in the previous chapter, there are a number of passages of Scripture in which God reveals he loves us, wants us to know him, and wants us to be like him. These communications of God to humans are among the central teachings of the Bible. And since the Bible is God's trustworthy written word to us, we can count on its central teachings to be true. So, it's true God loves us, wants us to know him, and wants us to be like him. And if all these things are true about God, surely he would want us to know them so we could come to know him!

Sincere authors of nonfiction books write those books in order to enable their readers to know some things about the book's subject matter. John Brierly, the author of *A Pilgrim's Guide to the Camino de Santiago*, mentioned above, wrote his guides to help pilgrims know how to find their way and enjoy themselves on the Camino. He did so by providing information about routes, accommodations, cafes, and attractions, among other things. In the same way, the Divine Author of the Bible inspired its human authors to provide readers of Scripture with knowledge about God and his desires for humanity. And as I said above, among the things God clearly wants us to know is that he wants us to know him.

The Bible provides grounds for thinking God has also revealed discoverable truths about himself *in creation*. For instance, the psalmist says, "The heavens are telling the glory of God; and the firmament proclaims his handiwork" (Ps 19:1) and Paul wrote to the church at Rome about people who "by their wickedness suppress the truth" (Rom 1:18b). He wrote that these people are such that "what can be known about God is plain to them, because God has shown it to them." He goes on to say that "Ever since the creation of the world (God's) eternal power and divine nature, invisible though they are, have been understood and seen through the things he has made. So, they are without excuse; for though they knew God, they did not honor him as God or give thanks to him, but they became futile in their thinking, and their senseless minds were darkened" (Rom 1:19–21).

The combination of these two biblical passages suggests our *finitude* doesn't prevent us from having knowledge of God. Rather, our *sin* does. If this is the case, it seems reasonable to think humans can know God as long as their sin doesn't prevent them from knowing God. And the good news is God has made it possible through Jesus Christ for sinful human beings to be freed, not only from the *penalty* of sin, but also from the *power* of sin. And this aspect of salvation includes our being freed by the Holy Spirit from the power of sin to *darken our minds*.

Of course, this Holy Spirit work will not enable us to know *everything* about God. We finite creatures are simply incapable of understanding our infinite God fully. Even when the Holy Spirit enlightens our minds, we'll only be able to grasp what God reveals about himself. And his self-revelation is limited to things we're able to comprehend given the constraints of our human nature.

Our inability to know our extraordinary God thoroughly is no different from our incapacity to know even *ordinary* things completely. Jennifer and I got to know most of the Camino Francés fairly well by walking it. But there are pilgrims who know it a lot better than we do as a result of having hiked it a number of times. And even *they* don't—and can't—know *everything* about it! Similarly, even though I knew Jennifer very well before our trip, I got to know her better during our pilgrimage—primarily by means of hours of conversation each day. But there's still a lot I don't know about her. This shouldn't be surprising, since there's much I don't know about myself![2]

The Bible also provides ample reason to think the Holy Spirit will enable those seeking to know God through Jesus Christ to succeed in doing so. For instance, as I pointed out in chapter 1, 2 Peter begins with both an expression of desire and a statement of fact that presuppose the possibility of knowing God: "May grace and peace be yours in abundance in the knowledge of God and of Jesus our Lord" (1:2; the expression of desire) and "His divine power has given us everything needed for life and godliness, through the knowledge of him who called us by his own glory and goodness" (1:3; the statement of fact).

Furthermore, there are many examples throughout the centuries of people who claimed to know God—or implied by things they said and did that they knew God. And these people also lived lives best understood on the

---

2. See Clark, "Rocks, Persons, and Gods," for more thoughts along these lines.

assumption that these claims or implications of theirs were true. Included in this category are people featured in the Bible and Christians throughout the ages up to and including today.

These Christians include those I highlighted in the previous chapter as examples of famous people who placed a high value on knowing God: Augustine, Aquinas, Descartes, and Pascal. But there are others as well, including many women: Hildegard of Bingen (1098–1179), Julian of Norwich (1342–after 1416), Catherine of Siena (1347–1380), and Teresa of Ávila (1515–1582), to name just a few. And of course, there are the myriads of more ordinary people throughout history who considered themselves knowers of God, such as the two whose testimonies I quoted from Williams James's *Varieties of Religious Experience* (and many others from that same source I didn't mention).

With these witnesses from history in mind, I encourage you to consider there may be things about you and your life suggesting you either have knowledge of God already or are at least in a good position to get it. If so, then you could have introspective evidence you could use to confirm that knowledge of God is possible. The exercise at the end of this chapter will provide you with resources for reflecting on these possibilities.

Finally, though there is a widespread assumption today—perhaps especially, but not exclusively, among academics—that knowledge of God is impossible, there are no good arguments that clearly establish that to be the case. So, it seems unproblematic to assume it's possible to know God and to know things about God. If this is true, then what accounts for the widespread assumption to the contrary?

The best explanation is that, though there's no *rational* cause for skepticism about knowing God, there is a *nonrational* cause for this attitude. This nonrational cause likely consists in a number of complicated historical, social, and cultural factors. Consequently, though there's arguably no good *justification* for skepticism about knowing God, there's probably a good (but hard to formulate) *explanation* for this viewpoint. Such an explanation would appeal primarily to the gradual replacement in the Western world over the last few centuries of a Christian outlook with a secular one—in the absence of compelling reasons for thinking the latter perspective is more likely to be correct than the former one.[3]

---

3. See Taylor, *A Secular Age*, for a thorough explanation along these lines. For a more accessible treatment, see Smith, *How (Not) to Be Secular*.

> **Soul Pilgrim Reflection Questions**
>
> Do these reasons persuade you it's possible to know God? Why or why not?

Experiential Reasons for Doubt

So far, the reasons I've considered for skepticism about knowing God are *intellectual* ones. But if you're like me, you may have persistent worries about the possibility of knowing God—even if I've convinced you those intellectual objections aren't very good. And you may have ongoing doubts about whether you can know God—even if you found the biblical and testimonial considerations I offered above reassuring. You may find yourself feeling that, even though the Bible affirms we can know God and other Christians have reported knowing God, you're still not convinced *you* can.

This is how my student Paul, whom I mentioned in the Introduction, felt. His primary reason for skepticism about knowing God is that *he wasn't aware of having had any experiences of God himself*. As I said above when I described my meeting with him, I wasn't able to help him recognize any of his experiences as experiences of God. And he was disappointed about that. But I was also frustrated. And as I continued to reflect on my conversation with Paul in the weeks and months that followed, I realized part of my frustration was due to doubts about my *own* experiences of God. If God had shown up in my life in discernible ways, wouldn't I be able to help other people notice ways he was present in theirs?

But then it occurred to me that you can know something without being able to explain your knowledge adequately to others. For instance, I can know what it was like to walk the Camino without being able to articulate my experience very well to those interested in hearing about it. I can think of a number of occasions after we returned when people asked me about our trip, and I felt unable to give them an account of it that satisfied me. And that's to be expected. Our Camino journey was a rich and concrete *experience*. We weren't able to take in and process this experience fully as we were going through it. So, our own memories of it are necessarily partial. And because of the limits of language, any attempts on our part to describe our trip on the basis of these memories—either to ourselves or to others—will leave out even more content than what is contained in our memories.

In the same way, our experiences of God go well beyond what we're able to process, retain, and articulate. But that means we can have experiential knowledge of God we can't fully understand or express. So, we shouldn't think being unable to communicate well about our knowledge of God means we don't know God.

On the other hand, it can be very helpful for soul pilgrims to develop more discernment about God's presence and activity in their lives. And it can be beneficial to them as well to reflect on what they've discerned in such a way as to be able to write and speak about it articulately. If soul pilgrims can communicate with themselves and with others about their lived experiences of God, then they'll be able to grow—and help fellow soul pilgrims grow—in their knowledge of God more effectively. And such growth will help minimize their experiential doubts about knowing God if they have any.

Jennifer's daily journaling on the Camino provided a way for her to reflect on our pilgrimage experiences so as to perceive their meaning and value in retrospect. And her efforts to record her thoughts about what we did and what happened to us were rewarded by our now having a document we can continue to read over time to deepen our understanding and appreciation of our journey. We like to say to each other that the Camino gave us a gift—a gift that keeps on giving as time goes on!

In the same way, deliberate daily reflection on your walk with God (of a sort I'll discuss in chapter 8) can help you better comprehend and value how God shows up and works during your soul pilgrimage journey. And this reflection can enable you better to remember and talk about these divine visitations and operations. This is a practical way any doubts you may have about knowing God can be progressively alleviated.

The daily conversations Jennifer and I had while walking also gave us many opportunities to be more attentive to what was occurring along our path. These discussions made it more likely we would notice what was going on around us and think about the significance of those things.

Similarly, soul pilgrims who walk together on the path toward deeper knowledge of God can help each other develop an awareness of how the Holy Spirit is guiding them on and empowering them for the journey. As we'll see in chapter 9, fellowship of various kinds can contribute to your progress as a soul pilgrim—and thereby reduce the amount of uncertainty you might otherwise feel about whether you can know God or know him more deeply.

These deliberate and regular individual and communal practices of reflection and discussion provide important resources for a soul pilgrimage. Just as you can't be successful in completing a literal pilgrimage without the right kind of physical preparation, provisions, and practices, you can't hope to make progress on a soul pilgrimage apart from the appropriate spiritual readiness, resources, and routines. Also, as I pointed out in the Introduction, you can't expect a literal pilgrimage to automatically provide you with a soul pilgrimage. That's one of the main lessons I learned on the Camino Francés.

I learned this lesson gradually during our trip. Though we got our bodies to Santiago de Compostela, I didn't get my soul as close to God as I had hoped. That's because the practices that enabled us to achieve the goal of our physical pilgrimage didn't suffice by themselves to enable us to make progress on our soul pilgrimage. A soul pilgrimage requires different kinds of practices, practices I didn't engage in on the Camino as much as I had hoped I would.

Though we had set out intending to start every day by praying together and reading a daily Scripture passage contained in a Camino devotional we had found online, we didn't follow through consistently with this plan. Instead, we sometimes left our accommodation as soon as possible after waking up so we could start walking early enough to arrive at our destination before the hottest part of the day. I had also hoped to spend some time each day rehearsing the passages of Scripture I had memorized. But I wound up talking to Jennifer instead. And I rarely took advantage of time for individual prayer while walking. I could have chosen to do these things individually, and I would have had Jennifer's blessing. But it was easier to default to conversation with her—and occasionally with other pilgrims we met along the way. Finally, I had envisioned we would attend more worship services in the churches and cathedrals we passed by. But in spite of my facility with Spanish, it wasn't easy to follow the liturgy, so this goal remained largely unmet as well.

I've found what was true on the Camino is also true in everyday life. You can't deepen your friendship with God—and eliminate any experience-based doubts you might have about knowing God—if you don't take deliberate steps to walk with God every day. And just as successful ordinary physical walking requires certain kinds of resources and practices (e.g., good shoes, physical fitness), so also does spiritually walking with God (e.g., Scripture, prayer).

Soul Pilgrim Reflection Questions

Do you have any doubts about experiencing God? If so, what steps can you take to alleviate them?

Conclusion

I've argued faith and knowledge aren't opposed and it's possible to know God. I think the Bible presupposes both these claims. I also think there are better reasons to affirm than deny them. The Scriptures teach we should *both* have faith in God *and* strive to know God. God wouldn't require us to do something impossible, would he? If you believe in God and have faith in God, you should do what you can to end up knowing God too.

I also discussed experiential doubts about knowing God. You might think you don't experience God because you can't explain your experiences of God. But you can know something without being able to talk about it. And if you can become attentive enough to your experiences of God to be better able to reflect on them yourself and talk about them with others, you can facilitate your friendship with God and reduce any uncertainty you might have about knowing God.

Experiential doubts about knowing God will diminish as your friendship with God deepens. But as I said above, a soul pilgrimage doesn't happen automatically—either on a literal pilgrimage or during everyday life in ordinary circumstances. Rather, as with human relationships (as we'll see in the next chapter), a relationship with God can grow only when you do the sorts of things that enable it to grow.

In sum, the reasons considered above—both intellectual and experiential—for thinking a believer can't also be a knower are bad ones. But there's another—and better—reason a Christian might have to profess belief in God but claim not to know God. That reason is that there's more to knowing God than merely believing in God or having faith in God, and this Christian does not consider herself to have acquired this extra something yet. Unlike the reasons suggested above, this reason presupposes we can know God, and it doesn't rule out the possibility of someone's having faith in God and knowing God at the same time. Christians who have this reason for thinking they don't yet know God will find resources for coming to know God in the remainder of this book—starting in the next chapter with a closer look at what it is to know God.

Practice

At the beginning of this chapter, I mentioned doubts Jennifer and I had—before we left for Spain—about whether we'd be able to walk the long distances required to complete our pilgrimage. I said it was helpful to hear from others our age who'd finished the journey but even more satisfying to prove to ourselves we could do it—by actually doing it!

Similarly, if you find yourself with questions or even doubts about whether you have the capacity to know God, I encourage you to read about or talk to other people of God to find out whether their experiences indicate—or at least suggest—they had (or have) knowledge of God. In the process, name people in the Bible, in history, or alive today who seem to have the kind of relationship with God that involves *knowing* God. What is it about them that suggests this is the case?

Finally, make a list of things you think you *might* know about God and also a list of experiences you've had that *might* have been encounters with God. If you hesitate to put the first list into the category of "things I know" and if you aren't sure whether to put the second list under the heading, "ways I've known God," ask yourself whether you have reasons for your reluctance. If so, are they *good* reasons? If you can't think of any reasons or can but aren't sure they're good reasons, consider taking the bold step of adopting the working hypothesis that knowledge of God is possible for you. The rest of this book will provide you with ways to test that hypothesis.

3

The Profile

What Does It Mean to Know God?

May 19, 2018, Santa Barbara (from Jennifer's journal)

Jim and I sit side by side, each with an open laptop. A map, guidebooks, and a large, paper timeline take up the surface of the coffee table before us. I pencil in a beginning date on the left side of the timeline. I do the same with an ending date on the right. I write "Camino Walk" at the top center of the paper.

I pick up my printouts. My collection of travel advice from modern-day pilgrims is marked up, underlined, and highlighted. I'm ready to put my hopes, dreams, and goals for our Camino walk on the table.

Yet, Jim's preoccupation is apparent. He's not hearing the words I read from my notes. He taps the tip of his nose with his index finger. I *know* him. His gesture tells me he's formulating a plan right now, based on some information he's discovered on the internet.

Bingo. "Hey Jen, here's an idea," he says as he scrolls down a page. "Booking.com can help us put together a systematic travel plan. Between this and our guidebook, we can plot our accommodations, right down to the day."

"How important is spontaneity when choosing a place to spend the night?" I wonder out loud. Yet, as I consider our personalities, I find myself in lockstep with Jim. "Some pilgrims may resist planning ahead," I say. "But you and I work best together when we have an idea about what to expect."

"Here's how I see it," Jim responds. "Knowing our day's destination in advance will help us gauge our walk. I don't want to worry about whether accommodations will be available each night. A travel plan will free us up to enjoy whatever the Camino has to offer on any particular day."

Later, we weigh our options for specific overnight venues. We discover a number of *pensiones*, *hostales*, *casas*, and *albergues* to choose from. Neither of us is picky about beds, and both of us can spare some amenities. At sixty-two, I'm up for an adventure, but I know my limits. I anticipate being tired after walking an average of fifteen miles each day. "How about if we stay in inexpensive private rooms with easy access to restrooms?" It's a question, but I say it like a statement.

"I'm all over it." Jim tells me he's already filtered for private rooms. He grins at me. "Hey, after thirty-seven years of marriage, I get it that you like your space and some quiet in the evenings. I *know* you."

Our Camino Pilgrimage Story: Knowing What the Camino Is Like

Before Jennifer and I traveled to northern Spain to walk the Camino de Santiago, we tried to learn as much about it from a distance as we could.

We consulted the internet and talked to people who had done it. From the internet we learned that the remains of St. James the Apostle are alleged to have been buried in the cathedral in Santiago de Compostela and that for many centuries, Christians from all over Europe—and eventually from all over the world—have traveled on various pilgrimage routes, each with the label "Camino de Santiago" (or "Way of St. James") to visit the cathedral for religious and spiritual purposes. We also learned the "Camino Francés," which starts in France, has been the most popular of these routes. That's the route we chose.

Among the many questions we had about the Camino Francés during our research, we were especially interested in one: "What's it like to walk the Camino Francés?" We thought an answer to that question would help us figure out whether we were capable of doing it, whether we'd enjoy the experience, what kinds of challenges we should anticipate, and how we'd be able to keep to the right path without getting lost.

We found many answers to our question on websites, in books, from former pilgrims, and by looking at maps. But in the end, in spite of all our investigation, the knowledge we gained was lacking an important element: our direct firsthand personal experience of the Camino itself. The only way we could acquire *that* knowledge was by going to the Camino and starting to walk it!

Knowledge of God

The same is true with knowledge of God. You can learn a lot about God by thinking about God, reading about God, studying things God made, and listening to other people who've had experiences of God. But no amount of knowledge *about* God can replace knowledge *of* God. In his now classic work *Knowing God*, theologian J. I. Packer writes, "One can know a great deal about God without much knowledge of him."[1]

Like Packer, when I talk about "knowing God," what I have in mind is much more than merely knowing *that* God exists or *that* God has a certain nature—whether by means of reasoning or even through personal experience. I mean instead *being acquainted with* God—having direct, personal knowledge of God on the basis of experiences of God. And I mean an acquaintance with God that involves a *personal relationship* with God—ideally, a *friendship* with God (more on this theme shortly).

And of course, this distinction between *knowing about* and *knowing* can be applied to any person, place, or thing. Our Camino experience provides a number of examples. When we were in Pamplona, I learned that Ignatius of Loyola, the founder of the Society of Jesus (the Jesuits) was injured at the Battle of Pamplona in 1521 when a cannonball ricocheted off a wall of the fortress there, shattering his right leg. But of course, I don't know Ignatius himself, since he's been dead since 1556. And before our visit, we'd heard Pamplona is the place where the "running of the bulls" occurs every year during the Festival of San Fermin from July 6 to 14. But it wasn't until we were there that we could get to know the city itself—including the bullring (*plaza de toros*) at the end of the bulls' route. Just as you can know facts about Ignatius, Pamplona, and the Pamplona Plaza de Toros without knowing this person, place, or thing personally, you can also know God exists and has certain characteristics without knowing God.

Also, knowledge about God's existence (and other facts about God) doesn't come in degrees; you either know God exists or you don't, and you either know God is loving or you don't.[2] But as I emphasized in chapter 1, you can know God—just as you can know another human being—to a

---

1. Packer, *Knowing God*, 26.

2. Of course, you can know a few facts about God or a lot of facts about God. So, your factual knowledge about God can grow over time even if your knowledge of an individual fact about God can't.

lesser or greater extent. You can *grow* in direct personal knowledge of God. And this growth is not merely a matter of continuing to learn new facts about God.

> **Soul Pilgrim Reflection Question**
>
> How would you compare your relationship with God to a relationship you have with a close friend?

Knowing a Person

When we know God, we know a person.[3] In my soul pilgrim quest to grow in my knowledge of God, it's been helpful to think about how I know fellow *human* persons. It's easier to learn something new when you start with something familiar. I know more about knowing people than I do about knowing God. I assume it's the same with you. Let's see what knowing people can teach us about knowing God.

Knowing a person—as opposed to merely knowing *about* a person—requires actual *contact* with that person. I know a number of things about Pope Francis, but I don't *know* Pope Francis. I haven't actually *met* him. But I do know the new pastor of my church. I introduced myself to him the first Sunday he joined our congregation. At the present time, I don't know him well—yet. I could get to know him better. Getting to know a person *better* requires spending *time* with that person.

But just spending time in the presence of a person won't suffice for getting to know that person *well*. I've attended a number of worship services at our church in which our new pastor has presided and preached. As a result, I've learned some things about him. But I haven't really *gotten to know him*.

To get to know somebody, you have to *do things* together—you have to *interact*. When you do things with other people, you can not only learn things about them by *observing* them; you can also learn things *from* them by attending to what they *reveal* about themselves to you. And the more they reveal about themselves—especially when their self-disclosure is significant—the more deeply you'll know them.

Jennifer and I experienced this dynamic on the Camino. Even after thirty-seven years of marriage, we found being together almost constantly for a month resulted in enhanced mutual knowledge. This increase in

---

3. More accurately, when we know God, we know a being who is *three* persons. But I'll often refer to God as if he were a single person.

knowledge was the result of watching each other react to novel situations and of talking together for many hours a day about what we did and saw. For instance, I found out that though she likes the security of knowing where she is, where she's going, and how to get there, she also relishes being surprised along the way by the unexpected. And I discovered this aspect of her personality, in part, not only by hearing her affirm it, but also—and especially—by watching her live it out.

What's true of persons in general is also true of God. Knowing God personally requires direct *contact* with God, and growing in your personal knowledge of God requires *spending time interacting* with God (especially in specific ways I'll discuss in chapters 8 and 9). In the process, you come to know more and more things *about* God and you come to grow in your knowledge *of* God—you get to know God better and better. Your relationship with God develops. Your friendship with God deepens. Your intimacy with God increases.

> **Soul Pilgrim Reflection Questions**
>
> Do you interact with God? If so, in what specific ways and how frequently?

Knowing Humans and Knowing God

So, our relationship with God is like our relationship with other humans—at least in certain respects. But our relationship with God is also *unlike* our relationship with other humans in a number of important ways. And these differences have consequences for our personal knowledge of God.

First, and most obviously, though God became a human being in Jesus Christ, God doesn't currently typically relate to humans as someone with a body we can experience with our five senses. As Jesus tells the Samaritan woman, "God is spirit" (John 4:24). In addition, in his first letter to Timothy, Paul refers to God as "invisible" (1:17). Paul also says to the Corinthians that in our current relationship with the Lord "we walk by faith, not by sight (2 Cor 5:7). Since God is an invisible spirit, we can't see God, but we can have access to God "by faith."

Here's another difference. Though we human beings grow in our knowledge of each other as we relate to each other, God already knows everything about us even before we begin to relate consciously to him. So, he doesn't grow in his knowledge of us as we grow in our knowledge of him. As the psalmist says, "O Lord, you have searched me and known me"

(139:1). Of course, God's complete knowledge of us soul pilgrims is to our advantage. As Jesus says to his audience in the Sermon on the Mount, "your Father knows what you need before you ask him" (Matt 6:8). And among the things our Father knows is what soul pilgrims need in order to grow in their knowledge of God.

Also, though sometimes we initiate a relationship with another human being and sometimes other human beings initiate a relationship with us, God is always the one who takes the first step in reaching out to us. Of course, God created us in the first place. And his creating us in his image is what provides us with the ability to have a relationship with him. As divine image-bearers, humans have an innate general knowledge of God (or at least an innate capacity to acquire such knowledge—Rom 1:19–20), an inborn general sense of his will (Rom 2:14–15), and a deep-seated desire to be loved that only God can satisfy completely and permanently (Ps 16:2, 11). And we learn from the first epistle of John that "We love because he first loved us" (4:19). So, our ability to love God and others depends on his having loved us in the first place. In all these ways, God has taken the initiative in our relationship with him, and our ability to reciprocate and to grow in friendship with him depends entirely on his making the first moves and helping us respond to him.

Finally, though human beings sometimes interact to benefit each other and sometimes to harm each other, God always acts toward us to benefit us (even though how he treats us may not always *seem* beneficial to us). Also, there's nothing we can do to God that will either benefit or harm him, though we can do things that will either honor and glorify him or dishonor and disrespect him. We can also do things that either please or displease him.

We'll need to keep in mind both the similarities and differences between human-human and divine-human relational knowledge as we seek to understand the character of the latter and grow in our relational knowledge of God.

Because of the similarities, we can get to know God by *encountering* God, *listening to* God, *talking to* God, *trusting* God, *cooperating* with God, *collaborating* with God, and *communing* with God.

Because of the differences, we'll need to learn to do all these things with God even though God is unlike us in being *disembodied, all-knowing, always at least one step ahead of us in the relationship,* and *perfectly benevolent, self-contained, and invulnerable to harm.*

As I think about these differences, I struggle most with not being able to see and hear God with my physical eyes and ears. Jennifer and I got to know each other better on the Camino because we could look at each other and hear each other while we walked and talked together. But I can't do that with God—at least not physically. So how can I get to know God better? You probably ask yourself that question too. It's one of the main things I'm trying to figure out by writing this book. I want to know God and grow in my knowledge of God, but I can't see God. So how does it work? How can God and I be friends and grow in friendship when we can't take a walk together or share a meal?

Also, are these differences between relationships with people and relationships with God even *consistent* with characterizing our ideal relationship with God as a *friendship*? Normally, we think of friendship as a *reciprocal* relationship in which there's an equal give-and-take between the friends. And this sameness of contribution presupposes mutual dependence and vulnerability between them. But God doesn't need or depend on us as we need and depend on him. And God isn't vulnerable to harm as we are.

Yet James says Abraham was "called a friend of God" (2:23) and Jesus called his disciples "friends" (John 15:15). So, the Bible clearly implies the possibility and preferability of human friendship with God. Consequently, though we might hesitate to apply our ordinary concept of friendship to our relationship with God, God himself has revealed that there's a type of friendship he desires to have with us—a relationship of intimate loving union and communion.

The main way God showed this desire was by the incarnation of God the Son as a human being. In taking on human nature to be Immanuel ("God with us"), the independent and invulnerable God voluntarily put himself in a position of dependency and vulnerability. So even though God in his divine nature has no needs and can't be harmed, he chose to experience deprivation and even death as a human being. As a result, though God still doesn't need us and can't ultimately be harmed by us, he has intimate firsthand knowledge of what it's like to be a hungry and hurt human. And he brings this knowledge to his relationships with you and me so as to make a genuine friendship with him possible—in spite of the differences between us.

I find that really encouraging. By becoming human, God brought himself down to our level to make it easier for us to be his friend. He meets us "halfway," so to speak. Rather than staying aloof in heaven, he came down to earth to be with us. And because Jesus was tested and tempted in all the ways we are, he's able to sympathize with our weaknesses (Heb 4:15). The differences remain, but they've been minimized to some extent—because of Jesus.

> **Soul Pilgrim Reflection Questions**
>
> Are these differences an obstacle in your friendship with God? If so, in what specific ways do they affect your relationship with him?

Relationship Growth

Obviously, relationships between two persons grow when factors that facilitate growth are present and factors that hinder growth are absent.

One thing that facilitates a relationship between two persons—including a personal relationship between a human being and God—is when both parties *make themselves directly available to each other in ways that are conducive to the development, growth, maturation, and perfection of the relationship*. Availability to another person comes in both degrees (more or less available) and kinds (e.g., direct vs. indirect, communicative vs. silent, loving vs. unloving, etc.). Some combinations of degree and kind of availability to another person are more conducive to the growth of the relationship with that person than other combinations are.

For instance, clearly, a practice of two people making themselves frequently available to each other in direct, communicative, and loving ways is a practice generally more conducive to growth in that relationship—and growth in mutual knowledge between the two persons involved—than a practice of two people making themselves available to each other only occasionally and in ways that are relatively indirect, uncommunicative, and unloving. And unsurprisingly, the most important of these three dimensions of availability is whether the interaction is loving or unloving (though frequent and direct communication is an important way love can be effectively expressed and nurtured).

In his best-selling book *The Seven Principles for Making Marriage Work*, psychologist John M. Gottman argues, on the basis of his careful and extensive observation of married couples over time in his Seattle "Love Lab," that what often passes for the best marriage advice is inadequate. He's found that though active listening and successful conflict resolution skills can contribute to marital success, they don't suffice as a means to cultivate and maintain a healthy marriage—and they aren't always necessary to achieve that goal either! He says, rather, that "at the heart of my program is the simple truth that happy marriages are based on a deep friendship. By this I mean mutual respect for and enjoyment of each other's company. These couples tend to know each other intimately."[4]

---

4. Gottman and Silver, *The Seven Principles*, 19–20.

But what does this important observation about human marriages have to do with our relationship to God? For one thing, it shows that for personal relationship growth and health, *rules* are not as important as *respect*, *effort* is not as beneficial as *enjoyment*, and *information* is not as valuable as *intimacy*. In other words, learning the right techniques and working hard to employ them can't replace valuing, appreciating, and loving the other person—in relationships with humans and with God. In short, loving someone is the key to knowing them and growing in friendship with them. This is certainly true of a friendship with God. According to 1 John, "love is from God; everyone who loves is born of God and knows God. Whoever does not love does not know God, for God is love" (4:7b–8). If you want to know God, you have to be born of God and love God with the love that God gives you. That's the key to growing in deep friendship with God.

But does God really make himself fully available to us in direct, communicative, and loving ways? Since God's mind and will are not fully comprehensible to us, it might seem that the answer to this question is "no." However, God has revealed himself to us in the Bible, in Jesus Christ, and through the Holy Spirit. And this multifaceted divine revelation is a *direct and loving communication* to us, since the Word of God inspired, incarnate, and indwelling is a loving Word spoken directly to each of us. And though God's Word to us is *partial*, in the sense that God remains a mystery to us in many ways, it's nonetheless *sufficient* for the purpose of our intimate loving union and communion with him. God makes himself fully available to us *for the sake of our friendship with him*.

What an amazing privilege it is to be invited by the sovereign Creator and Lord of the universe into an intimate loving friendship! Why is it then that I have such a hard time making myself available *to him*? Perhaps it's because I can't just sit down with him the way I can with Jennifer and other friends. But honestly, I think my struggle usually has more to do with my reluctance than with God's distance—though there are certainly times when God seems distant too. What can I do as a soul pilgrim to decrease my reluctance to grow in friendship with God? And is there anything I can do to make God seem less distant?

Soul Pilgrim Reflection Questions

Is your friendship with God growing? Why or why not?

Personal Availability

When it comes to availability or unavailability to another person, it's clear we can have complete control only over *our* availability and not over the other person's. And there are things we can do to increase the degree of our availability to another and to vary the kind of our availability. But though we can do what we can to *persuade* or even try to *force* another person to be available to us, that person can always exercise their power to remain relatively unavailable to us. We may be able to force someone to be with us physically, but we can't force a person to be open to us personally.

An example of our inability to control another's personal availability to us can be found in Gottman's discussion of the signs of troubled marriages. As an illustration of the sign he labels "stonewalling," he recounts an interchange between Rita and Mack. After Rita complains that Mack doesn't control his drinking at parties, Mack stonewalls. He "looks down, avoids eye contact, says nothing." When Rita laughingly responds by saying, "I think for the most part, we get along pretty well," Mack "remains silent, makes no eye contact, head nods, facial movements, or vocalizations" and when Rita says, "Don't you think?" Mack remains unresponsive—as impassive as a stone wall.[5]

What do these observations mean for our growth in friendship with God? For one thing, God will never coerce us. He gave us the gift of free will. This freedom gives us the power to choose whether or not to accept God's love for us and whether or not to love God and others. Our ability to choose to love or to refrain from loving is an essential element in our capacity for genuine loving relationships. Such relationships can't be coerced, but must be entered into freely by both parties. One can be forced to *act as if* one loves another, but one can't be compelled genuinely *to love* another. Consequently, since God wants to be in a loving relationship with each of us, he won't coerce, force, or compel any of us to love him. Such an abusive treatment of us, which would fail to wait for our *consent*, would be contrary to the nature of divine love—and it would be entirely ineffective. Rather, God will always resort to *persuasion* by attempting to woo us or draw us.

Also, we can't coerce God. God is the absolutely free and sovereign Lord of the universe. This may be obvious. But keeping it in mind can help us avoid relating to God as if he were a vending machine into which we insert our prayers expecting automatically to receive what we've requested. God isn't a tool for us to use as a means to further our personal agendas. God isn't under our control. Rather, we're completely at his mercy, and

---

5. Gottman and Silver, *The Seven Principles*, 33–34.

ideally, we would be disposed to make ourselves fully available to him in the service of his kingdom agenda.

In addition to our inability to control how another person *relates* to us, we are unable to control how much we can *know* another person. This lack of control is one thing that makes knowing a person different from knowing a place or thing. We can exercise a relatively high degree of control over an impersonal object to come to know it and grow in our knowledge of it. This is the kind of thing natural scientists do when they study nature and natural objects (and it's one important reason why natural science is a more rigorous route to knowledge than the social sciences are). Since rocks don't have a hidden interior life they can choose whether or not to reveal, geologists have more control over their subject matter than psychologists and theologians do over theirs.

Our getting to know another person depends entirely on their willingness to relate to us in ways that will reveal aspects of their inner life to us—ways that will disclose to us what they're thinking, feeling, and wanting. Stonewalling will prevent this kind of disclosure, as will aloofness. Clearly, God doesn't stonewall, like Mack does, as a result of hurt feelings or anger. But God can sometimes seem aloof, silent, or hidden. Nonetheless, as I said above in connection with our inability to understand God fully, these experiences of divine absence or apparent unavailability shouldn't be interpreted as indications God is generally unwilling to be available to us.

Knowing God personally and relationally requires making ourselves available to God (and God making himself available to us) through ongoing mutual interactions. In general, if we want to know God and grow in our knowledge of God, our attitude toward him needs to be one of trusting and humble openness and receptivity. And our behavioral response to God needs to be one of prompt and faithful obedience to his callings, commands, and cautions. We need to be willing to allow God to transform us, and we also need to be willing to take risks in order to do things God wants us to do when those things are outside our comfort zone.

Having just written that paragraph, I realize that my own hesitation and lack of progress as a soul pilgrim has more to do with my being fearful and risk-averse than it does with my being prideful and rebellious. Soul pilgrims need to be both humble and courageous, but as individuals, we have different strengths and weaknesses.

> **Soul Pilgrim Reflection Question**
>
> How willing are you to humbly trust and obey God, to allow God to transform you, and to take risks in your relationship with God?

Obstacles to Relationship Quality and Growth

Relationships between persons can grow only if all the persons involved are both willing and able to do and allow what's necessary for that growth to occur. God is both willing and able for our friendship with him to develop—and to help us to be willing and able to grow in intimacy with him. God's *willingness* to be our friend is made clear throughout the Bible in the way he interacts with people such as Abraham—but especially in the way Jesus Christ, God the Son incarnate, identified his disciples as his friends (John 15:15). And God's *ability* to befriend us is also demonstrated by how Jesus was able to develop friendships with his followers, such as Lazarus, Martha, and Mary (John 11). Finally, *God's desire and ability to assist us* in drawing closer to him are manifested in his gift to us of the Holy Spirit, whom Jesus called the *Paraclete*. This word, which has been translated as "Advocate," "Helper," "Counselor," and "Comforter," comes from two Greek words: *para* meaning "alongside of" and *clete* meaning "come." Clearly, a divine person who comes alongside us to advocate for us and to comfort, counsel, and help us is both willing and able to be our friend.

But humans tend to be deficient in one or both of these areas (openness and aptitude). In order for a soul pilgrim's relationship with God to grow, willingness is more important than ability. That's because if people are able but not willing to know God (or grow in knowledge of God), he will not override their free choice. But if people are willing but unable, then God will do what he can to help them acquire the capacity for deepening their friendship with him over time.[6] So, we will focus here on impediments to relationship growth due to human *unwillingness*.

One way to think about the role of our wills in our relationships with others is to focus on the *kind* of relationship we want to have with them. It will be helpful to categorize types of relationships along a spectrum, from desiring to be as uninvolved with a person as possible on one end of the continuum to desiring complete intimacy with a person on the other end. And the part of the scale that includes relationships one desires to have contains

---

6. I say, "do what he can" and "over time" since some people who are willing to grow in friendship with God may be unable, at least for a time, to do so as a result of trauma and abuse—perhaps of a religious sort. But it seems reasonable to appeal in such cases to Jesus's assurance that "for God all things are possible" (Matt 19:26).

those that differ in the degree and kind of involvement and closeness one prefers.

We all know the difference between a mere acquaintance and a friend. And we're also able to distinguish between a casual friend and a close friend. Many people can identify a "best" friend (though others may resist singling out one friend for this role and may instead prefer to talk about their "closest friends"). One thing that varies across this spectrum of relationships is degree of willingness to be with the person in a transparent and vulnerable way. Clearly, we generally want to spend more time in such a condition with closer friends than we do with others.

As I said above, Jennifer and I truly enjoyed and benefited from hours spent walking together and talking with each other every day of our Camino pilgrimage. And we met and chatted with a number of other pilgrims along the way. But though we often found these other connections pleasurable and profitable, our desire to sustain them was limited by our relative unfamiliarity with these people. The same is true of our relationship with God. Earlier, I said that the more we love God, the more we will know him. Our love for God will motivate us to know him more deeply. We can now add that the more we know God, the more we will love him and love to be with him. These principles are crucial for soul pilgrims to keep in mind as they journey on their soul pilgrimage toward closer union and communion with God.

In addition to degrees of friendships there are also kinds of friends. The ancient Greek philosopher Aristotle (384–322 BC) identified three types of friendships: (1) friendships of utility, (2) friendships of pleasure, and (3) friendships of goodness.[7] What makes each of these sorts of relationship a *friendship* is that the people involved regard each other with good will (rather than indifference or ill will).

Each of these three types of friendship is characterized by the main thing the friends want to get out of the relationship. In the case of friendships of utility, the friends want to *benefit from* the relationship. Examples of this type of relationship include business partners and professional colleagues. In friendships of pleasure, the people interact primarily for the sake of *enjoyment*. Friends in these relationships are drawn to qualities in the other person they find pleasant, such as physical attractiveness, sense of humor, or genial personality. Finally, friendships of goodness are characterized by a mutual admiration of each other's character and an effort to help each other grow in virtue.

---

7. Aristotle, *Nicomachean Ethics*, 163–87.

Aristotle pointed out that the first two kinds of friendship are relatively insecure. The first can end when one or both friends get what they want and the second can cease when at least one friend gets bored. In either case, desire to stay in the relationship can quickly and easily fade.

But since friendships of goodness are based on the mutual possession and recognition of virtue—which tends to last and which motivates one to be loyal—they're relatively secure. But they're also relatively rare, since few people are genuinely good. Aristotle believed if one is able to develop such a friendship, one has the best kind of friendship possible, and is truly blessed. Since friendships of goodness can be both useful and pleasurable, they combine the benefits of the other two types. And since friends in such relationships want each other to be good more than they want each other to be happy, they'll tell each other things they need to hear even if they're not things they *want* to hear.

It's important to emphasize that friendships of goodness, as I understand them, unlike friendships of utility and pleasure, aren't based on something *other than* the relationship that the friends strive to get out of the relationship for *themselves* (e.g., money, influence, pleasure, etc.). Instead, they're based on something *inside* the relationship—*helping each other* acquire the very virtues that make genuinely loving friendships possible (e.g., sympathy, loyalty, generosity, etc.). The best of friends want the best for each other. And what's best for each friend and for the friendship itself is for each friend to become a genuinely good person—or better, a genuinely *loving* person. Genuinely loving persons, from a Christian standpoint, are Christlike in virtue of being self-sacrificially loving. They're the sorts of friends Jesus had in mind when he told his disciples that "No one has greater love than this, to lay down one's life for one's friends" (John 15:13).

This summary of how relationships vary in degree of closeness and kind of outcome desired can help us think about obstacles to relationship quality and growth. The ideal friendship would consist in two friends who want to grow in both how close they are to each other and how much they want to help each other become good people. It seems clear from Paul's epistles that he had many friendships that approached this ideal. For instance, in his letter to the Philippians he refers to both Timothy and Epaphroditus with affection and esteem (2:19–30). But such friendships are rare. As fallen, sinful people we tend to be self-protective and self-centered and thus to resist intimacy out of fear of being hurt and to resist growing in virtue because of pride. As I said above, my own tendency is to be fearful rather than prideful. What about you?

So, both fear and pride can be hindrances that make us unwilling to grow in friendship beyond a certain point. And when we're unwilling to grow in friendship with someone, we'll tend to settle for inferior degrees and types of friendship, such as casual friendships of utility or pleasure—both of which can tend to be friendships of convenience in which the friends focus on what they can get from each other rather than on what they can give to each other.

Again, when fear and/or pride make us unwilling to grow in friendship with someone, we can prefer to fall back on conditional friendships of utility and pleasure rather than to strive to build unconditional friendships of goodness and virtue. But the latter type of relationship is the only kind that will ultimately satisfy our need for a loving relationship that is complete and lasting. For one thing, intimacy requires mutual trust, but mutual trust is possible only between genuinely trustworthy friends. And people can be genuinely trustworthy only if they're people of real virtue and good character.

Ideally, soul pilgrims will want to have a deeply intimate friendship of Christlike goodness with God. That is, after all, the ultimate goal of a soul pilgrimage, as I've been saying. Of course, since God is perfectly good and loving, our friendship with him will not be a shared project of *mutual* development in virtue. That's one of the ways the ideal friendship with God differs from the ideal friendship between humans. But it will be aimed at mutual intimacy and also at *our* divinely enabled moral and spiritual growth in Christlikeness. Also, the language of obedience doesn't fit well in the context of friendships between ordinary humans. But Jesus told his disciples, "you are my friends if you do what I command you" (John 15:14). So, this is another way our friendship with God differs from our friendships with each other. God's perfect wisdom includes knowledge about what's best for us and his sovereignty gives him the right to require that we strive for perfection ("Be perfect as your heavenly father is perfect"—Matt 5:48). But his perfect (self-sacrificial) love for us shows that this wisdom-based authority is that of a true friend who wants to equip us for genuine loving communion with him (and each other).

Unfortunately, self-centeredness, fear, and pride can diminish a pilgrim's desire to be related to God in that way. Pilgrims may prefer to do things their way rather than God's. They may be unwilling to trust that a deeper friendship with God will be in their best interest. And they may be too proud to admit they need deep personal transformation to be able to endure and enjoy intimacy with God.

As a result, they may wind up treating their friendship with God primarily as a means for their own personal benefit or their own selfish pleasure. And they may be unwilling to engage in the practices needed to allow God to move them beyond a self-serving relationship with God to a

God-glorifying one. If so, they risk at best stagnation (failing to make progress in their pilgrimage) and at worst, idolatry (moving away from God and toward a God-substitute, such as their own personal comfort, security, and convenience). My own soul pilgrimage has been slowed by stagnation on some occasions and aborted by idolatry on others. I've realized the antidote is willingness to allow God to help me go deeper with him (true intimacy) and to become more like him (real virtue). And I'm aware that this willingness can lead me to take risks—to experiment.

> ## Soul Pilgrim Reflection Question
>
> Is fear or pride keeping you from putting yourself in a position to allow God to draw you to him and restore his image in you?

Experimental Theology

One way our personal and relational knowledge of God can grow over time is through experimentation. Here's how it works. As we attempt to make ourselves available to God by adopting a prayerful attitude of submissive, humble, and open trust and willingness to obey God, we may sense God's Spirit is prompting us to do something (or refrain from doing something). This prompting may come in a variety of strengths and forms. We may experience it as a suggestion, a request, or even a command.

Let's suppose it's a directive to do something we've been reluctant to do as a result of self-absorbed indifference, laziness, worry, anxiety, or fear. Whatever the reason, it's something we've been disinclined to do. It could be to have a difficult but important conversation with a family member or friend, to give more generously to God's kingdom work in some specific way, to talk to a neighbor about one's faith in Christ, or to get involved in a local effort to help a disadvantaged group of people.

Whatever it is we sense God's Spirit inviting, calling, or compelling us to do, we hesitate to do it, because doing it would be outside our comfort zone. Doing it would require both a kind and degree of motivation we've not tended to have (sufficient diligence or courage) and a willingness to risk the possibility of discomfort, inconvenience, embarrassment, awkwardness, loss of time and/or money, etc. That is, obeying the Spirit would require a willingness on our part to sacrifice something we value.

In such circumstances, we're unlikely to obey the prompting of God's Spirit unless we believe God will enable us to do it in spite of our discomfort and prevent any negative consequences we may experience from diminishing our ultimate well-being. That is, doing what God wants us to do will require us to trust God—to have faith in him that he "has our back."

If our response to an apparent prompting by God's Spirit is to fail to respond affirmatively and to refrain from trusting obedience, then we'll miss an opportunity for growth. The growth we'll be unable to experience by means of our inaction will be growth in our ability to trust and obey God and growth in our knowledge of God.

These kinds of growth are dependent on each other. Our ability to obey God depends on our ability to trust God, and our ability to trust God depends on our knowing that God is trustworthy. When we trustingly obey God on the basis of what we perceive to be an invitation on God's part to do something (such as to talk to a neighbor about our faith in Christ), then we put ourselves in a position to grow in our knowledge of God—including our knowledge of God's trustworthiness. And our growth will involve the development of our abilities or skills into settled habits—spiritual virtues. The more we know God, the more we'll know how to trust and obey God. And as we get better at this "know-how," we'll grow in spiritual discernment.

Doing what we think God wants us to do will enable us to find out whether God will empower us to do something we know we couldn't do without God's assistance. And our ability to confirm that God provides for us in this way will also give us a way to assure ourselves that God was really present in our lives through the Spirit and that God was really speaking to us (calling us, commanding us, reassuring us) through the prompting of the Spirit.

Moreover, these confirmations add to our store of personal relational knowledge of God so as to give us a firmer basis for confident obedience to God in the future. Given our experience of God's response to our obedience, we'll be better able going forward to recognize God's presence, voice, provision, and protection. And that increased recognitional knowledge of God will enable us to be increasingly trusting and obedient. Ideally, this cycle will continue to make us more and more trusting of God, obedient to God, and knowledgeable of God as time goes on.

What I've just described is an example of the process of experimental theology. As a soul pilgrim who's an experimental theologian, you adopt a hypothesis about an apparent directive of God. Then you test that hypothesis to see whether doing what God seems to have directed will result in what you believed God would do with and for you. Engaging in this experimental process in relationship to God will put you in a position to either confirm what you already believed about God's presence, communication, and support or to learn something new about God if something unexpected should occur. Of course, both of these things might happen, since God could relate to us in a way that combines both what we would expect of God and something we wouldn't.

At this point in my soul pilgrimage, the sort of experimentation I've described is more a plan I've begun to implement than a practice I've perfected. I still have a lot to learn. Though I came up with the basic idea some years ago during a morning devotional time, I didn't begin to act on it until I read *If You Want to Walk on Water, You've Got to Get Out of the Boat,* by John Ortberg. The book is about growing in faith by taking risks in response to God's call. Ortberg illustrates this idea by discussing aspects of Peter's daring experiment with sea-stepping in response to Jesus's invitation (Matt 14:25–32). Even before finishing the book, I realized that the trial-and-error approach to life with God modeled by Peter and explained by Ortberg should be a key component of every soul pilgrimage.

But soul pilgrims are not likely to engage in such experimental theology unless they think God is communicating with them through the Holy Spirit. And they're unlikely to pick up such communications unless they're sufficiently attentive and discerning to be able to notice and recognize the "voice" of God. So, a pilgrim's availability to God in relationship with God will require not only a willingness to trust and obey God, but also a more fundamental ongoing attitude of discerning attentiveness and mindfulness toward God. In chapters 5 and 6, I'll talk about recognizing signs of the Spirit's presence and guidance, and in chapters 8 and 9, I'll discuss individual and communal practices that can help pilgrims grow in their disposition to discern the Spirit's indwelling and direction.

> ## Soul Pilgrim Reflection Question
>
> Are you willing to be attentive to the Holy Spirit for opportunities to experiment in faith and obedience with what the Spirit seems to be prompting you to do?

Practice

First, think of someone you know well—a close friend or family member. Now think of things you know *about* that person—many of which you learned by personally being with that person and directly talking to that person. Make a list of some of these things. List some of their physical characteristics, some of their personality traits, and some of their virtues and vices. Write down some of the things they've done and some of the things that have happened to them. Imagine continuing to add items to this list until you have a thorough sketch of him or her and of his or her life.

Now imagine writing a biography of that person on the basis of this list. If you can, imagine that you're omniscient about this person—you know everything about him or her that God knows about him or her. If that were the case, you could write an absolutely complete and perfectly accurate biography of them. Now ask yourself, "Would reading this biography enable someone who's never met my friend or family member to know him or her as I do?"

One reason to say "no" is that even a complete description of a person won't tell you what that person looks like or sounds like. So, imagine putting lots of photographs of them in the book. Better yet, imagine supplementing the book with a *video* of them—and make the video as long and varied as you like so it includes shots of them in various kinds of circumstances doing and saying various kinds of things. Suppose you could even include a video of their entire life! Would all these resources suffice to enable someone who's never met your loved one to *know* that person (as opposed to merely knowing *about* that person)?

I hope you agree with me that the answer to that question is "no." What's missing that's needed for personal, relational knowledge of your friend or family member is *knowing what it's like to be in relationship with him or her*. And the only way to get that kind of knowledge of a person is to have a history of personal interactions with him or her that collectively make up your relationship with that person.

Once you've completed this initial exercise, do it again, but this time with God in mind. That is, list things you know about God, etc. Of course, you won't be imagining including pictures of God or videos of God (except in the case of pictures and videos of the *incarnate* God, Jesus Christ). But you'll be imagining you've exhausted every means you have available to provide a complete and thorough list or account of what can be known *about* God. I hope this exercise will enable you to see that there's more to knowing God than knowing about God. Seeing this truth, and seeing it clearly, will help you understand why personal relational knowledge of God must supplement knowledge about God. It's one thing to know *about* a soul pilgrimage toward God; it's another thing altogether to *engage* in that pilgrimage!

11

My Own Know Me

"I am the good shepherd. I know my own and my own know me, just as the Father knows me and I know the Father."

—John 10:14–15

4

God's Person

What Can You Know About God's Nature?

October 3, 2018, Foncebadón to the Iron Cross (from Jennifer's journal)

"Blisters!" Yesterday a weary pilgrim we passed pointed to his feet. He shook his head and muttered as he hobbled toward a bus station. "Don't let the damn things ruin your Camino."

Just before dawn, I put tape underneath my toes where the beginnings of blisters appeared last night. Jim double-checks his knapsack to make sure he's put in two changes of socks.

We've prepared well. We followed the advice of seasoned pilgrims to make sure our shoes were carefully fitted with extra room. We broke them in by walking many miles before leaving home. Now on the Camino, we remember to expose our feet to air on a regular basis. And we keep several pair of woolen socks at the ready so our feet will remain dry.

"I've got my rock in my pocket. Is yours in your knapsack?" Jim anticipates the plans we've made for our arrival at *La Cruz de Ferro*, the highest elevation of our Camino. He points to the map in our Michelin guide, indicating an eighteen-mile trek today, most of it a steep descent. His focus however, is on the first hour. "Are you ready for an arduous climb before all the descending?" he asks me.

I'm not hungry, but we each eat a complimentary *tostada española* and drink a *café con leche* before leaving our *albergue*. A hearty breakfast should sustain us for the immediate climb.

When we step into the dark predawn, my body exhilarates in the cold air. What will this day bring? My work today is to walk the Camino. I take delight in my simple yet challenging schedule. My responsibilities from back home feel a million miles away. I relish the change of pace.

In the darkness we can barely see the yellow arrow. Painted on the side of a dilapidated shack, it points to a trail at the edge of town. Our layers protect us from the cold as we walk. Today's forecast for unseasonably hot weather seems ludicrous in the chilly morning air.

We begin climbing right away. No time to ease into today's path. In a matter of minutes, we are both panting, pausing often to catch our breath. Each pause is an excuse to look out on a forested wonderland. The first day's light filters through tree branches. I'm reminded of scenes from *The Lord of the Rings*.

The sun is in full view when we crest onto a plateau. We join a few other pilgrims silently gathered in front of *La Cruz de Ferro* at this early hour. The research we did in advance didn't prepare me for what I see. The rustic wood pole holding up the iron cross is startlingly humble. Though *La Cruz de Ferro* marks the highest point on the Camino, there's nothing flashy about it.

We walk toward the massive mound of stones piled up at its base. I'm dumbfounded by the number of them. Pilgrims can't reach the pole unless they wade through what look like thousands. "Not what I expected," I whisper to Jim. Yet as I think about how many pilgrims have laid stones down since the eleventh century, not surprising at all.

The Camino tradition of leaving a stone at the foot of the cross represents the letting go of something. In this case, we knew what to expect. By learning about this tradition ahead of time, we're prepared to participate in it.

Jim removes a fossilized rock from his pocket. Taken from our cherished Jesusita trail in Santa Barbara, the ancient rock symbolizes a long-standing anxiety that he would like to leave behind. He places his stone at the base of the cross.

I pull a stone from my knapsack. My stone survived a fire that burned our house down some years ago. It was part of a larger rock that protected an iceberg rosebush in our garden. That rosebush blossomed weeks later, when everything around it remained charred. My stone, then, is a symbol of safekeeping. In spite of the loss of precious treasures from my childhood and our children's, my family is alive and well. I can let those material things go. I lay my stone down. I feel lighter. I'm ready to move on.

Our Camino Pilgrimage Story: Knowing about the Camino

As I said at the beginning of chapter 3, we didn't really find out what the Camino de Santiago was like until we walked it. But I also said we came to know a number of things *about* the Camino before heading to Spain. We realized the more we knew about the Camino Francés before our trip, the more we would know what to look for when we got there and started knowing it directly and experientially by walking it. We figured knowing about the Camino in advance would help us recognize significant aspects of it and know how best to interpret, understand, and appreciate those aspects. We also assumed our knowledge of the nature of the Camino would help us bring appropriate resources with us (e.g., the right kind of shoes to prevent blisters, rain gear, trekking poles, maps, guidebooks, a rock to leave at the Cruz de Ferro, etc.). Having these things facilitated our growth in firsthand knowledge of the Camino as we walked it.

Three important types of knowledge about the Camino were especially helpful in this regard: historical, geographical, and cultural. The first helped us understand the Camino through time, the second enabled us to learn about the Camino in space, and the third assisted us in coming to know about the nature and variations of human life in communities along the Camino across time and space. The historical knowledge provided us with information about how and why the Camino was created, developed, and maintained. The geographical knowledge consisted in facts about the nature and variations in terrain, agriculture, climate, and population density. And the cultural knowledge covered similarities and differences in customs, language, cuisine, and art. All this knowledge about the Camino put us in a better position to know what to look for and how to understand what we would see and experience. Among other things, this knowledge made it easier to recognize and interpret various kinds of signs (linguistic, cultural, geographical, and directional) we encountered when we got there.

Knowing about God

In order to learn to recognize the signs of God's presence and activity (see chapters 5 and 6), you have to start with some assumptions about God. These assumptions are open to correction to a greater or lesser extent based on your subsequent experiences and the degree to which they were confirmed by your previous experiences.

Serious soul pilgrims will naturally assume the reality of God. And they'll supplement this fundamental assumption with assumptions about God's nature—assumptions about what God is like.

In retrospect, I can see that my ideas about God during different periods of my life played an important role in how I related to God at those times.

As a child, I thought of God primarily as an authority figure I needed to obey and please. My sole purpose in connection with God was to behave myself. If I did something wrong, I felt guilty and sensed God's disapproval. If I did the right thing, I was satisfied with myself and with God. My conception of God determined what I expected out of my interactions with him. Since my understanding of God's nature was limited, so was my relationship with God.

After my public profession of faith in Christ as a teenager, my thoughts about God matured. I started listening more carefully to sermons and reading the Bible and Christian books more frequently. I still wanted to please God, but came to think that what God wanted from me was to become more faithful in Christian practices such as Bible reading, prayer, worship, fellowship, evangelism, and service. God was like a coach to me—helping me to become a better Christian. That way of thinking about God was a step in the right direction. But my focus was more on self-improvement than on knowing and loving God more deeply. Once again, my assumptions about God shaped what I looked for in my lived experiences with God.

During my skeptical Christian phase as a young adult, God seemed more distant—aloof and even absent. As a result, God's authority in my life diminished and my dependence on him for growth weakened. Though I believed in God and continued to engage in various Christian activities, my relationship with him was like one you have with an uncle you don't see very often and communicate with infrequently. As my skepticism became less serious, my involvements with God became more meaningful and more central to my life. But my thinking of God as largely unknowable prevented me from seeing him as a friend who wants to share his life with me.

Now that I'm a soul pilgrim Christian, I'm eager to use what I know about God to help me grow to know and love him more deeply. In particular, as I said at the beginning of this section, I want my assumptions about what God is like to assist me in recognizing signs of God's presence and activity in my life. And I invite you, my fellow soul pilgrim, to do the same.

But here we face a problem and a danger.

> **Soul Pilgrim Reflection Question**
>
> What's something important you know about God that could help you get to know God better?

A Problem and a Danger

The problem is we're incapable of comprehending what God is like in himself apart from his self-disclosure to us—and we aren't capable of knowing God completely in *any* circumstances. So, we should think of what we can know about God as knowledge of *what God has revealed about himself in a way we limited humans can understand* rather than as knowledge of *what God is like in himself apart from his revelation to us*. In thinking this way, soul pilgrims can honor both the Christian tradition that God is mysterious (incomprehensible as he is in himself) and yet knowable (understandable through his self-revelation to us). With respect to their knowledge of God, soul pilgrims should think of themselves as being like children who can understand the adult world only through the simple analogies adults use to characterize it to them.[1]

For instance, when Jennifer and I returned to the States after our Camino, we spent a month living near our daughter, son-in-law, and grandsons. At that time, our three-year-old grandson Jack wanted to know what we'd been doing on our trip. We tried our best to give him an account of our pilgrimage that was both faithful to our experience and understandable to him. After some trial and error, we told him we went on a big hike that took many days in a faraway place where the people spoke a different language. We showed him our backpacks and trekking poles. We said we walked all the way to a big church in an important city where people went to be with God together. And we mentioned that there were a lot of other people—people we didn't know—walking with us. Jack's resulting knowledge of our Camino was like a soul pilgrim's knowledge of God: generally accurate but limited to familiar ways of thinking.

Even when we base our beliefs about God's nature on what God has disclosed, we need to be careful not to assume God is exactly like the model of God we construct out of the concepts God gives us as tools to think about him. The Bible tells us God is strong, wise, good, and loving. We can understand what that means only because we've experienced created persons that are strong, wise, good, and loving. But God is the Creator, and God is uncreated. So, God doesn't possess these attributes in the same way creatures do.

---

1. My colleague Sameer Yadav suggested this idea to me.

The danger is we'll end up thinking of God as being like a created thing. And to the extent such an inferior conception of God informs our worship, we'll be guilty of idolatry—worshipping a creature rather than the Creator.

Similarly, no matter how much people learn about the Camino de Santiago, their knowledge will never be complete and may not be entirely accurate. Even the most experienced pilgrims, who've taken multiple pilgrimages, must humbly admit there will always be more for them to learn—that they'll never know everything about the Camino. And every pilgrim's way of thinking about the Camino is influenced by their particular experiences of it. Just as Camino pilgrims must acknowledge the Camino to be more and perhaps different in some respects from what they think about it, so also soul pilgrims must admit that God is greater than how they think of him and possibly not quite the same as their idea of him in some ways.

So, the problem is that what we can know about God is limited to what he reveals to us as he relates to us, and the danger is that we'll take an incomplete and possibly distorted view of God to be the whole accurate story about him. In order to solve this problem and avoid this danger, we soul pilgrims need to do at least two things.

First, we must always approach our thinking about God with humility, caution, and an openness to ongoing learning and correction—at least about the more controversial elements in our concept of God. Of course, these attitudes must be balanced with adequate confidence—at least about the less controversial aspects of our theological perspective—so we can make progress in our pilgrimage toward deeper knowledge of God. And this confidence is warranted, because we can count on what God clearly reveals to us about himself to be true.

Second, we must rely in our thinking about God entirely on what God reveals to us about himself in various kinds of ways (see below). And we must also consider our resulting concept of God as *our construction of what God is like on the basis of materials God has provided us.* Then we'll not automatically assume we know what God is like in himself apart from his revelation to us, and we'll also be reminded of our need for openness to correction.

Soul Pilgrim Reflection Questions

Is your conception of God both based on God's revelation and open to correction? If not, what changes do you need to make in your thinking about God?

A Perfect God

Given these important considerations, we can begin to reflect on what God is like. A strong theological tradition suggests God's nature is to be perfect—that God has all the "perfections" and is therefore a perfect being.

We often use the word *perfect* to talk about different kinds of things in their ideal state. For instance, a perfect apple would be crunchy, sweet, and juicy, rather than mealy, bland, and dry. And it wouldn't have any bruises or worms. And a perfect Camino would be blister-free (as ours was, thank the Lord!). But limited parts of God's creation like apples and Caminos aren't *perfect in every respect*. Even perfect apples won't satisfy your hunger forever. And perfect Caminos will come to an end at some point. But God is a perfect *being*, and so God's perfection is *unlimited*. He has *all* the perfections.

We can figure out what at least some of these perfections are by reflecting on characteristics we value—characteristics we consider worth having and better to have than not to have. Among these is being a conscious personal being with all the features that go along with that. These additional features include being capable of knowing, willing, and acting. We also value personal beings capable of being loving and morally good on the basis of their capacities for knowing, willing, and acting. Once we have these valuable properties in mind, we can reflect on what would be required to make a personal being *perfect*. That is, we can think about what would make such a being perfect in knowing, willing, acting, loving, and being morally good. This is a basis on which we can arrive at the conclusion that God is *maximally* knowledgeable, powerful, loving, and good.

And God is *everywhere*. That means God is present at every point of space-time in the universe—including where we are at any given time. But God isn't present at every point of space-time as a *physical* being. Aside from the incarnation, God doesn't "take up space" anywhere. So, God doesn't take up space *everywhere*. If God did, God would fill up *every* space, and there wouldn't be any spaces left for created physical things to occupy! Rather, God is present everywhere and "everywhen"—at least in virtue of having complete knowledge of what is happening there and then and in virtue of having the ability to exercise complete control over every point of space-time. That means God is *sovereignly* present at every space-time location.

Sometimes people refer to these attributes of God by saying he's omniscient (all-knowing), omnipotent (all-powerful), omnibenevolent (all-good), and omnipresent (present everywhere). And these abstract terms may sound rather removed from a soul pilgrim's lived experience. But even if the words seem impersonal, the ideas expressed by them are deeply significant for a soul pilgrimage. Soul pilgrimages, like physical ones, are a mix of the known and the unknown. You may know where you've been and where you are, but you don't know the specifics about where you're going, what you'll do when you get there, and what will happen to you. But if you know that your pilgrimage guide is perfect in power, wisdom, and love, you can rest trustfully in your uncertainty—knowing you are safe and secure under his leadership.

My knowledge that God is perfect has benefited me greatly on my soul pilgrimage. It's sometimes seemed too good to be true that there's a perfect personal being who wants to have a relationship of intimate loving communion with me. But it's been immensely reassuring to know that my eternal destiny is in the hands of someone who has the ability and desire to transform me into a person who can enjoy loving God and others in the eternal community God has in store for us.

> **Soul Pilgrim Reflection Question**
>
> What does God's perfection enable you to *count on* in your soul pilgrimage?

God's Revelation

By itself, God's complete sovereign presence everywhere in the universe doesn't mean God is present *to us*. In order for God to be present to us, two additional things have to happen. First, God must *reveal* himself *directly and personally* to us, and second, we must *perceive, notice,* and *properly interpret* God's direct and personal self-revelation to us. Moreover, to grow in our ability to recognize God's presence in our lives, we must *trustingly and appropriately respond* to God's manifestations of his presence to us on an ongoing basis.

Christians believe God has revealed himself to human beings. When God reveals something to us, he discloses either himself or things about himself and/or about his relation to the creation and to us. And he conveys these things to us through either word or deed or both. That is, he makes it possible for us to know these things by speaking to us and/or by acting in some other way discernible by us.

Christians also believe God has revealed himself to us both generally and specially. God's *general* revelation involves God's making things knowable to us through the medium of creation. God's general revelation is *available* to all properly functioning and sufficiently mature human beings through our sensory observation of nature and through the rational and moral dimensions of the human nature God created us to have—a nature God created in his image. As a result, we can learn things about God and God's will by means of our perception of creation, our reflection on God's nature (illustrated by our reflection above on God's perfection), and our intuitions about morality (God's will for us). This revelation is *general* in at least two ways: it's accessible by all normal and sufficiently mature human beings, and its content consists in general truths about God and God's relation to creation.

Our Camino experience was greatly enriched by our recognition that the diverse natural beauty we witnessed throughout each day on the trail pointed beyond itself to its almighty, wise, and generous maker. And the enjoyment of a soul pilgrim can be similarly enhanced by looking to the magnificence of creation for signs of God's benevolent handiwork. The perfect God we know intuitively is also the extravagant divine artist we meet in the natural world.

The American theologian Jonathan Edwards (1703–1758) wrote that after his conversion to Christ, his experience of nature was augmented:

> My sense of divine things gradually increased, and became more and more lively, and had more of that inward sweetness. The appearance of everything was altered; there seemed to be, as it were, a calm, sweet cast, or appearance of divine glory, in almost everything. God's excellency, his wisdom, his purity and love, seemed to appear in everything; in the sun, moon, and stars; in the clouds and blue sky; in the grass, flowers, and trees; in the water and all nature; which used greatly to affix my mind.[2]

Edwards's soul pilgrimage was clearly enhanced by his divinely given ability to perceive God's glory generally revealed in creation.

God's *special* revelation consists in things God shows and tells us that aren't automatically available to all humans and that contain more specific content than God's general revelation does. Christians consider the incarnation of God the Son (the second person of the holy Trinity) to be the most important way God has revealed himself specially to humans. The incarnation of God the Son involved a particular human being at a particular historical time and place (Jesus of Nazareth in the first century). Therefore, only those human beings who have learned about the birth, life, ministry, death, resurrection, and ascension of Jesus—and the *meaning and implications* of these events provided in the Bible—are in a position to benefit from God's special revelation in and through Christ.

---

2. Quoted in James, *Varieties*, 243.

Just as a literal pilgrimage requires certain kinds of equipment to be successful, such as a Camino guidebook, a soul pilgrimage does as well—and a Bible is among a soul pilgrim's most important resources. General revelation functions like a map of Spain. It can provide helpful general information about one's pilgrimage. But special revelation works more like a Camino guidebook. Both are needed for more specific orientation and guidance—the latter for a literal pilgrimage and the former for a soul pilgrimage. As soul pilgrims, the better we know our guide and goal, the better able we'll be to follow him and commune with him.

We also learn from the Bible (and from Christian history after the Bible) that God has revealed himself specially to individuals and groups by other means as well. These other means include visions, dreams, angelic visitations, and divine apparitions of various kinds ("theophanies"). The latter category includes God's use of created things in unusual supernatural (miraculous) ways—such as God's appearing to Moses in a burning bush or Jesus's appearing to Saul (Paul) in a flash of light on the road to Damascus. These revelations of God are both relatively *private* (since they're accessible to only an individual or small group of individuals) and relatively *extraordinary* (since they don't occur normally in the course of everyday life).

But the testimony of countless Christians over the years confirms that God also reveals his presence personally, privately, and directly to individual human beings in relatively *ordinary* ways as well. Consider for instance what an elderly French man wrote about his experience of God:

> Jesus has come to take up his abode in my heart. It is not so much a habitation, an association, as a sort of fusion. Oh, new and blessed life! Life which becomes each day more luminous . . . there is a royal song of triumph on my heart because the Lord is there . . . Formerly, the day was dulled by the absence of the Lord. I used to wake invaded by all sorts of sad impressions, and I did not find him on my path. Today he is with me; and the light cloudiness which covers things is not an obstacle to my communion with him. I feel the pressure of his hand, I feel something else which fills me with a serene joy; shall I dare to speak it out? Yes, for it is the true expression of what I experience. The Holy Spirit is not merely making me a visit; it is no mere dazzling apparition which may from one moment to another spread its wings and leave me in my night, it is a permanent habitation.[3]

---

3. Quoted in James, *Varieties*, 409–10. See also the section above entitled "Testimonies of Ordinary People" in chapter 1 for another good example of an individual who experienced God's presence in ordinary ways (the forty-nine-year-old man who wrote about his ordinary life with God).

I'll be focusing on God's ordinary ways of revealing himself to individuals in the following two chapters. These divine methods are both easier and more difficult to study than the extraordinary ones are. The respect in which they're easier to examine is that they occur more frequently. The way they're harder to investigate is that they're subtler. So, we'll have potentially more information to work with but it will be harder to detect and to classify.

One reason I'm highlighting ordinary Christian experiences of God's presence rather than extraordinary ones is that most Christians have very few—if any—experiences of the latter sort. As a result, most Christians' personal knowledge of God will be based primarily on their ordinary experiences of God's presence in their lives. Another reason I'm featuring typical and more mundane experiences of God is that the practices we'll be considering in Part III are meant primarily to facilitate openness to God's usual modes of presence in our lives and only secondarily to put us in a position to be receptive to God's unusual ones.

> **Soul Pilgrim Reflection Questions:**
>
> Have you had any extraordinary experiences of God? If so, how do they compare with your ordinary experiences of God?

An Apparent Obstacle

When we begin to think about how to recognize God's presence in our lives, it's important to start by acknowledging an apparent obstacle, mentioned in the previous chapter, that would seem to prevent our being successful in this endeavor: God's being a spirit. Though we can know that fellow human beings are present with us by means of perceiving their bodies in physical proximity to us, we can't use the same method to tell that God's with us. Since God doesn't ordinarily show up in our lives today in physical form, for the most part we can't experience God with our senses to confirm he's here with us at any given time. We can't see, touch, smell, or taste God—in the literal senses of these words that involve consciousness of sensible properties of physical objects. And though many people have reported hearing God by means of an audible voice of some kind (e.g., Paul hearing the Lord Jesus speak to him on the road to Damascus), that kind of experience falls into the category of "extraordinary" experiences of God's presence. But, again, our primary concern here is ordinary ones.

I admit I haven't had a strong and unmistakable sense of God's presence. I do have memories of occasions when I experienced an unusual sensation in connection with a God-related activity. In each of these circumstances, I felt momentarily as if I were enveloped and indwelt by a kind of weightiness charged with deep significance. And this meaningful heaviness had the effect of softening and humbling me—sometimes producing a feeling of warmth or a tingling sensation in my body. It's hard to describe.

Specific examples of these incidents include praying as an adolescent with an older church member before making an evangelistic call on people who had visited our church; worshipping with my high school church youth group team before we conducted a vacation Bible school at a neighboring church; listening to a sermon that seemed directed especially at me; watching a video—in a college chapel service—of a U2 concert featuring their performance before a vast crowd of the song "Where the Streets Have No Name"; reading the chapter in *The Wind in the Willows* entitled, "The Piper at the Gates of Dawn"; and sitting on an airplane in midflight when another passenger nearby had a medical emergency and I felt a strong sense that I should pray for him.

In spite of God's spiritual nature, these experiences of mine may have been encounters with God. And many other people (such as the elderly French man I quoted above) have reported being able to sense God's presence with them at various times. One of our tasks in the next chapter will be to try to figure out what the typical nonphysical indicators are on which people have relied to enable them to discern that God is with them. We'll also attempt to determine what it is about these signs that have put these people in a position to tell they are signs of *God's presence* (rather than signs of something else or not signs of any objective reality—reality outside their own subjective consciousness—at all).

Soul Pilgrim Reflection Questions

Have you ever had a sense of God's presence with you? If so, what was it like?

What God Has Revealed about Himself

One promising way to approach these questions is to start by thinking about everything we already know about God's nature, character, and characteristic ways of interacting with human beings. We can draw this knowledge initially from what God has revealed to us both generally (in nature and human nature) and specially (in Jesus Christ and in the Bible). This knowledge about God will provide us with a basis on which it can be reasonable to *expect* God to manifest his presence to us in relatively ordinary ways. And we can supplement this body of knowledge with reports of God's people throughout the history of the Christian church and around the world today—reports about how these people believe God has made his presence known to them. Once we have these resources available, we can use them to guide us in our search.

Based on what I've come to know about Jennifer's personality and character, I've come to expect her to say and do certain kinds of things in different circumstances. When we were on the Camino, I could anticipate she would want a *café con leche* with her (meatless) breakfast. And I knew she would want to get started walking early in order to arrive at our destination before the hottest part of the day. I was also convinced she would hang in there enthusiastically without complaint when she was tired, hungry, or hot. And I expected that at least once during the day, she would say something about our beloved grandchildren! The more I know about her, the more I know how she'll characteristically act and react in different contexts. In the same way, the more we know about God, the more we'll know how God will typically show up in our lives.

But as we employ our knowledge about God, we should be open to the possibility that God may, at least occasionally, make his presence known to a person in unexpected ways, be present to different individuals in different ways, and manifest himself to the same individual in different ways at different times. It seems reasonable to think God tailors his mode of presentation to people in such a way as to meet their individual needs at a particular time. Given these possibilities, soul pilgrims should adopt an *experimental* approach (of the sort I described in the previous chapter) to their search for signs of God's presence in their life. This approach will combine the formation of hypotheses (about how you might recognize God's presence) based on your existing knowledge about God—with an openness to the rejection or revision of these hypotheses on the basis of your ongoing experiences of God.

In the same way, Jennifer sometimes surprised me by acting or reacting in ways I hadn't expected. Though I knew she was an adventurous eater, I wasn't prepared for how delighted she was with a plate of tender and juicy *pulpo gallego* (Galician-style octopus). And though I knew she enjoyed keeping a record of our trip in her journal, I didn't anticipate how artfully she would end up describing our pilgrimage experiences. Furthermore, in spite of my awareness of her love of history, I wouldn't have predicted how fascinated she was with the centuries-old stone buildings we encountered as we wandered through the Spanish countryside.

So, God, like our fellow humans, can sometimes defy our expectations of him. But in spite of this possibility, for simplicity I'll be assuming here that, for the most part, God makes his presence known to us in ways both relatively expected and relatively uniform from one person to the next and from one time to the next.[4] And in that case, direct experiences of God's presence (and his guidance, provision, protection, and empowerment) provide confirmations of things we can know about God more indirectly—through reading the Bible, hearing from other Christians, or reasoning about the existence, nature, and providence of God. It's one thing to *infer* that God is there, that God speaks, and that God acts (or to take another person's word for it that these things are true); it's another thing to *sense* God's presence, to *hear* God's voice, and to *witness* the effects of God's work in our own lives.

> **Soul Pilgrim Reflection Question**
>
> Based on what you already know about God, how would you expect God to show up in your life?

The Incarnate God

We can supplement our assumed knowledge of God's perfect nature (summarized above) with our knowledge of the incarnation of God the Son (probably God's most surprising act in history!). Since the Bible teaches that God has revealed himself most fully in Jesus Christ (John 1:14 and Heb 1:3), soul pilgrim experimentation should be guided primarily by this assumption. That will mean soul pilgrims should study the Gospels carefully to learn about Jesus's character, intentions, and characteristic ways of interacting with people.

Knowing about God through his incarnation as Jesus of Nazareth enables soul pilgrims to step closer on their soul pilgrimage to knowing God more directly and fully. As a human being, God became accessible to us in a way that is "up close and personal." Jesus's original disciples were privileged to see God-in-the-flesh *physically*, though they couldn't adequately understand and appreciate that fact before Jesus was raised from the dead. After the resurrection, they could correctly echo Job's response to God's appearing to him in a whirlwind: "I had heard of you by the hearing of the ear, but now my eye sees you" (Job 42:5). Thomas's exclamation upon seeing the

---

4. Though it may be that, given the highly secular nature of our contemporary culture, God has adopted different strategies to reach us than he employed with our forebears who lived in more religious cultures.

risen Christ implies a realization of this sort: "My Lord and my God!" (John 20:28).

Though we soul pilgrims today aren't able to see God physically the way his first disciples could, we can be reassured by Jesus's response to Thomas's sight-based confession of faith: "Have you believed because you have seen me? Blessed are those who have not seen and yet have come to believe" (John 20:29). And we have advantages not available to the first believers. We have the New Testament record of the life, teachings, death, and resurrection of Jesus along with the apostles' explanation of the meaning of these things. And we can picture these events in our imagination on the basis of our reading of the four Gospels in light of these interpretations (as Ignatius of Loyola, the founder of the Society of Jesus, or Jesuits, encourages us to do in *The Spiritual Exercises*).

From the Gospels, we learn Jesus's primary concern was to announce to his hearers that his presence among them meant the kingdom of God had drawn near. And he told them they needed to change their mindsets and dispositions to be fit to enter that kingdom. That announcement and advice shaped how Jesus interacted with people. In his parables, he provided various ways for the receptive members of his audience to understand the nature of God's kingdom and the differences between those suited for that kingdom and those not. And in his more direct teaching (such as in the Sermon on the Mount), Jesus combined a verbal portrait of those to whom the kingdom belongs with specific exhortations and admonitions aimed at urging his hearers to become people with characters appropriate for kingdom membership.

Close attention to what Jesus told his initial audience will help soul pilgrims see they are on a kingdom journey and they should expect the king to show up as their teacher and guide along the way. They will appreciate the importance of being open to his invitations, instructions, exhortations, and corrections as they strive to realize their goal of deeper intimate union with him. The more you know about your divine teacher and guide, the more you'll be able to recognize his presence with you. And the more you're able to recognize his presence with you, the more opportunities you'll have to listen to him, obey him, and become the kind of person capable of deep companionship with him.

In addition to recording what Jesus taught and preached, the Gospels also describe what he did and allowed to happen. In the former category, the most significant of his actions involved the exercise of his supernatural power to perform miracles of provision (e.g., feeding the four thousand and five thousand), protection (e.g., calming the storm), power (e.g., causing the fig tree to wither), and restoration (various healings and resuscitations), and to demonstrate his sovereign power over the satanic forces of evil by means of the exorcism of demons. These actions represent what Jesus envisioned the kingdom of God would be like in its fullness. What they have in common is God's provision of what humans need for physical, emotional, spiritual, and relational health, wholeness, and well-being.

Soul pilgrims who know what Jesus's kingdom agenda is will be more likely to make that agenda their own as they follow him on the path. And they'll be more likely to partner with other soul pilgrims to do the king's work on their way down the trail together. They'll realize the soul goal of getting closer to God automatically includes becoming people who share God's character, concerns, and causes. And when soul pilgrims join together in Christian service, they facilitate their growth in godliness and their intimacy with God—as we'll see in chapter 9.

Among the things Jesus permitted to happen (that he had the power to prevent), the most significant are the things he allowed to happen *to himself*. These things include his baptism by John, his temptation by Satan, his transfiguration by the Father, his arrest, trial, and crucifixion by the Jewish and Roman authorities, and his resurrection and ascension—again, by God the Father. For our purposes, these permissions are significant because they're specific examples of his willingness to obey his Father and suffer in various ways for our sake. And those examples provide soul pilgrims with a model to emulate in their own relationship with God the Father.

I've personally benefited from a deepening familiarity with the Gospels' portrayals of Jesus. The more I've learned about how Jesus related to God the Father and to other people, the more I've come to see how to love God and fellow human beings in the ways Jesus did. And in line with the theme of this chapter, I've also gained a more concrete idea about the ways I can expect Jesus to show up in my life as he continues to invite and enable me to abide in his love.

> ## Soul Pilgrim Reflection Question
>
> Given what you know about Jesus's interactions with people from the Gospels of Matthew, Mark, Luke, and John, how do you think he wants to interact with you?

God the Holy Spirit

Since the Scriptures indicate that the resurrected and ascended Christ makes his presence known to members of his body (the Christian church) by means of the Holy Spirit, soul pilgrims should also pay attention to what Jesus says about the Spirit and what other parts of the New Testament teach about the Spirit's ministry in the lives of believers.

The New Testament makes it clear Jesus intended to continue proclaiming his kingdom message and engaging in his kingdom ministries after his resurrection and ascension. How? Through his followers. And it's also clear Jesus has chosen to do these things in his followers by means of the Holy Spirit, who indwells each individual believer and enables the community of believers to be the body of Christ in the world. Accordingly, soul pilgrims should look in their lives and their churches for evidences of the Spirit's continuation of the kinds of things the Gospels portray Jesus as having said and done as he invited people into his kingdom and equipped them for kingdom membership.

We're focusing in this chapter on what we need to know about God to learn how to recognize God's presence in our lives. I've indicated we'll be looking for regular and ordinary ways God manifests himself to us personally and directly. Now we're in a position to see these regular and ordinary methods are implemented by the Holy Spirit who indwells Christians. God the Son became incarnate in Jesus Christ to become human and to be with us humans. Then the resurrected and ascended Jesus Christ (in partnership with God the Father) sent God the Holy Spirit to Christians both individually and collectively to continue his work with human beings. As a result, God is with followers of Christ (and potentially with all human beings) even more intimately than God was with humans before Christ and even after Christ before Pentecost. And the ongoing and intimate presence and action of the Holy Spirit in our lives is the presence and action of God in our lives.

What this means is that soul pilgrims who wish to learn how to recognize the signs of God's presence in their lives should find out whatever they can about what the Holy Spirit does in individual believers. A good place to start is with what the New Testament writers say about the manifold roles of the Spirit. I'll provide a brief overview of those roles in the next chapter as a basis for formulating some general principles we can use to search our own minds and hearts for traces of the Spirit's efforts to encourage and equip us to do the work of Christ in the world both on our own and together—as the body of Christ.

For the most part, our goal will be to find ways to confirm the *presence* of the Holy Spirit by means of recognizing the *actions* of the Spirit. Though there may well be times when we can discern or perceive the Spirit is simply with us—apart from our awareness of something the Spirit is *doing* in us—more often than not, our access to God's presence through the Spirit will be via what the Spirit *does*. And that's because God sent us the Spirit to indwell us for a variety of purposes over and above just accompanying us in our life's journey—as important as that is in itself.

My own understanding and appreciation of the person and work of the Holy Spirit has grown significantly over the years. As a child attending a traditional church, I was introduced in the liturgy to the "Holy Ghost." As a result, I had a sense of a mysterious and shadowy individual who had something to do with God but might also show up in a cartoon. During my teenage years, I tended to think of the Holy Spirit primarily in connection with the charismatic movement, which in my mind was characterized mostly by the gift of speaking in tongues and such special supernatural events as being "slain in the Spirit" (both of which I hoped—unsuccessfully—would happen to me when I attended an all-night prayer meeting at a local Pentecostal church in high school). But over the years since that time, I have come to realize that the role of the Holy Spirit in the life of a Christian is both more central and more comprehensive.

When we look to the Bible to learn how God the Spirit is with us and acts in us and through us, we should keep in mind what we're assuming about God's nature and Jesus's earthly teaching and ministry. That is, we should remember God is perfect and triune and God the Son became incarnate as Jesus of Nazareth to invite people into God's kingdom and to prepare them for kingdom living by means of instruction, exhortation, admonition, demonstration, self-sacrificial submission (culminating in his death on the cross), resurrection, ascension, and contribution (of the Holy Spirit). The role of God the Holy Spirit is to continue the work of Jesus in his body, the church (see John 16:12–15). So, we should expect the ministries of the Spirit to correspond to the nature of God and the teaching and ministry of Jesus Christ. In the next chapter, we'll focus on how knowledge of the Spirit's different ministries in our lives can provide us with a means to recognize God's presence and activity in them.

Soul Pilgrim Reflection Question

When was the last time you made an effort to be attentive to the work of the Holy Spirit in your life?

Practice

Think about a time in your life when you learned about a person, place, or thing before you actually met that person, visited that place, or experienced that thing. To what extent did your prior knowledge enable you to get to know that person, place, or thing once you encountered him, her, or it? How did that initial knowledge help you grow in your firsthand experiential knowledge? Now compare that experience with one in which you happened upon a person, place, or thing that was entirely unknown to you up to that point. Did your lack of prior knowledge hamper your ability to get to know him, her, or it (and to get to know him, her, or it better)?

5

God's Presence

What Are Signs of God's Presence in Your Life?

October 3, 2018, Camino de Santiago (from Jennifer's journal)

"Look, Jen!"

Ever alert, Jim is quick to notice a bird or sign or unusual feature of the landscape. He's inclined to share his finding with another human being immediately. My tendency, on the other hand, is to take in a discovery slowly and wordlessly. I often reflect before sharing my thoughts with someone else. The difference between us may stand out in other contexts but somehow the Camino provides a comfortable backdrop for both proclivities.

Now Jim looks at the breathtaking view from our vantage point on Mount Irago. I take my eyes off the stones surrounding the iron cross and prepare to switch gears. I walk over to Jim and follow his gaze.

"Ahhh." I share Jim's sense of wonder at the vast plateau and the brushstroke of fall colors on the mountains around us. He pulls binoculars out of his knapsack and hands them to me. The range of topography gives me a new insight.

Each day we cover so much territory that the morning before seems like a long time ago. Looking to the east is looking at the past. Our elevated vista provides us with a different perspective of where we have been. We take turns pointing out the landmarks we most enjoyed on the trail yesterday.

"Do you see the old stone buildings we viewed yesterday from the street?" I point to a remote spot on the plain below.

Jim squints. "Yes!" Then he sweeps his arm to the right. "And look at the vineyards where we plucked those tasty grapes."

When we turn to the west, we see novel territory. We're headed there today, into the future. Jim points to a speck of a city off in the distance. "I believe that's Ponferrada," he says, identifying today's ultimate destination. It seems far away and at a considerably lower elevation than we are right now. I shake my head to think of the distance we still must cover by foot before nightfall.

"Crazy to think we're about to traverse the land between here and there," Jim says, as if to read my mind.

"Can we possibly make it there by evening?" I wonder.

But I know we will. A tingle rises from somewhere inside of me. The terrain varies so much. I like the *not* knowing what is around the bend. I like the surprises that emerge as we walk—almost like getting lost.

Yet, we're not in the wilderness. We've come to trust the Camino signs—the scallop shells and yellow arrows that keep us on track and point us in the right direction. The signs provide us with reassurance as we navigate unfamiliar terrain.

Our Camino Pilgrimage Story: Signs of the Camino

Once we got to the Camino and started walking, we noticed there were signs of various kinds along the way to help pilgrims know which direction to go. Over time, we learned to recognize these indicators. They included a yellow arrow pointing to the right path in the correct direction of travel, a scallop shell, and a pilgrim carrying a walking stick with a drinking gourd hanging from it. Sometimes just one of these symbols would appear on the trail and sometimes more than one. And each of these markers came in different variations. For instance, sometimes the arrow and scallop shell showed up together as figures painted yellow on a field of blue. And sometimes the shell was bronze and embedded in a concrete or stone walkway. But regardless of which symbol, symbol combination, or symbol variation we saw, we were grateful for the reassurance it (or they) provided us we were on the Camino heading in the right direction rather than on the wrong route.

But the mere presence of these signs didn't suffice to keep us on the Camino. We also had to *see* them, *notice* them, *understand* them, *trust* them, and *follow* them.

Since we usually got an early start—before dawn—it was often dark when we set out for the day. In those circumstances, we couldn't see markers right in front of us unless we had adequate light from the moon or our iPhone flashlights. And even in broad daylight, a yellow arrow might be within our visual field, but we would miss it if we weren't attending to it (which is what happened to us on a few occasions!). Interpreting the signs correctly was usually not a problem, though sometimes it was hard to tell—at least initially—to which of multiple paths an arrow was pointing. And at first, we thought the scallop shells were always oriented so that their converging lines pointed to Santiago. But after encountering some with the reverse orientation—when we knew we were heading in the right direction—we discarded that assumption. At times we wondered whether any pranksters had deliberately set up a sign pointing in the wrong direction to throw off unwitting pilgrims. But over time, our experience confirmed all the signs we followed were reliable indicators of the true path. And this result gave us good reason to believe those who made the signs and those who maintained them did so to help us and other pilgrims find our way to Santiago. Coming to believe this about them put us in a position to trust these people by relying on the signs they created or sustained—even though we didn't know who they were and had never seen them. Over time, we got more and more adept at following the signs (on the basis of seeing, noticing, understanding, and trusting them).

Learning to Recognize Signs of God's Presence

Soul pilgrims also need signs to assist them on their pilgrimage toward deeper and deeper intimate knowledge of God. As I said above, knowing God (as opposed to knowing about God) requires being with God and interacting with God. And *growing* in one's personal knowledge of *any* person—including the personal being who is the Triune God—requires an *awareness* of that person's presence with you and interaction with you. So soul pilgrims will need to learn how to be aware of God's presence with them, communications to them, empowerment of them, and interactions of other sorts with them. And learning to be aware of these things involves learning how to recognize them on the basis of their typical characteristics—or signs.

As an aspiring soul pilgrim, I've felt both hesitant and frustrated as I look for signs of God's presence and activity in my life. I've felt hesitant because Jesus said, "An evil and adulterous generation asks for a sign" (Matt 16:4). At first, this verse made me wonder if it would be wrong to ask God for signs that he's with me. But then I thought about the verse's context. Jesus was responding to "the Pharisees and Sadducees" who had "asked him to show them a sign from heaven" to test him (Matt 16:1). And these religious leaders were *critics* of Jesus. Their request for a sign wasn't sincere, but rather an attempt to discredit him. And their demand for a "sign from heaven" was an indication of their insistence on setting the terms and their stubborn refusal to be satisfied with a more reasonable indication of Jesus's authority.

Also, Jesus implied they already had signs available to them. They just didn't know how to (or were unwilling to) *interpret* them properly: "You know how to interpret the appearance of the sky, but you cannot interpret the signs of the times" (Matt 16:3). Jesus's miracles and teaching pointed to his divine origin. They just didn't have the eyes to see and ears to hear: "'seeing they do not perceive, and hearing they do not listen, nor do they understand'" (Matt 13:13).

In addition, Jesus told them that an evil and adulterous generation *would* be given a sign: "the sign of Jonah" (Matt 16:4). What does that mean? Since "Jonah was in the belly of the fish three days and three nights" (Jonah 1:17) before "the Lord spoke to the fish, and it spewed Jonah out upon the dry land" (Jonah 2:10), it's clear the sign of Jonah is the death and resurrection of Jesus. That's the decisive sign of his divinity—for all who have the faith and humility to discern and accept it.

And the Gospel of John calls seven of Jesus's miracles "signs" because when they're rightly understood, they call our attention to his divinity. And they culminate in Jesus's raising of Lazarus from the dead, a sign Jesus is "the resurrection and the life" (John 11:25)—the sign Jesus mentioned would be given even to an evil and adulterous generation.

After thinking this through, I concluded it's okay for humble, sincere, and faithful soul pilgrims to ask God for the ability to discern signs of his presence and activity in their lives. Such people are motivated by a desire for deeper intimacy with God. What's inappropriate is to refuse to believe in or trust God in the absence of clear and convincing signs.

But I've also been *frustrated* as I've looked for signs of God in my life. They're not like the physical signs on the Camino that are easy to see and understand. The Camino signs are visible to the public; signs of God are usually private and accessible to only one person at a time. They're also typically subtle and often subject to more than one interpretation. How do I know that something that *seems* like a communication from God to me really *is* a divine message sent my way?

For instance, in May of 2002, Jennifer and I were scheduled to take our first flight after the airplanes had crashed into the World Trade Center in New York City on September 11, 2001. After we parked our car in the Santa

Barbara airport long-term lot, I realized I was afraid of getting on the plane. But just as I was wondering what would happen to our kids if our plane got hijacked by terrorists, I saw a bumper sticker on a parked car that said "Fear Not." I was immediately reassured, because it seemed to me that God had brought that sticker to my attention in order to comfort me. But later, when I reflected on the episode, I wondered whether it was just a coincidence. Just as my soul pilgrim self had begun to emerge, my skeptical Christian self reared its ugly head.

And yet it seems good to be reasonably cautious about interpreting an event as involving a message from God. Many foolish and harmful deeds have been done in the name of the Lord by people who were too hasty to be sufficiently careful when they thought God had spoken to them. Even great Christian saints, who progressed far down the soul pilgrim path, were hesitant about construing their experiences—even relatively dramatic and extraordinary ones—as orchestrated by God. Teresa of Ávila, for instance, was often wary of the possibility that what seemed to be a God-given experience might instead be merely a product of her own mind or even caused by Satan. She relied on other Christians to help her make good judgments about the origin of these experiences.[1] And she matured in her discernment skills—her ability to "test the spirits" (1 John 4:1–6)—over time.

After reflecting on the example of Teresa and other saints, I came to see that soul pilgrims shouldn't hesitate to look for signs of God's presence and activity in their lives, but they *should* hesitate before deciding they've found some. I became convinced soul pilgrims need to ask God to help them develop the eyes of faith to detect God and the ears of faith to hear him—but they should also ask God to give them the ability to distinguish God's "shape" and "voice" from other objects of inner vision and audition.[2]

I'm currently in the process of learning how to look for God more attentively and find God more discerningly in my life. As I grow in the exercise of both of these skills, I've become more aware of possible divine encounters, encouragements, and exhortations. Hopefully, I'm also becoming savvier about distinguishing reality from illusion in these matters. Among the candidate experiences of God I've considered lately are apparent reminders to pray for a particular person, purported appeals to avoid giving in to a specific temptation, seeming suggestions to read a certain book, and ostensible invitations to spend solo time with God. Since each prompt seemed to come from outside me, was consistent with God's overall will, and appeared

---

1. Teresa, *Interior Castle*, 177.
2. For more on learning to hear God's voice, see Willard, *Hearing God*.

in retrospect to serve God's purposes in my life, I've tentatively come to think of them as genuine divine nudges.

> ## Soul Pilgrim Reflection Questions
>
> Have you ever sensed God was with you and/or thought God might be speaking to you? If so, what was it about these experiences that led you to believe you were in touch with God rather than something (or someone) else?

The Fourfold Ministry of Jesus Continued by the Holy Spirit

I've come to think my efforts to be more attentive and attuned to what God is doing in my life can be facilitated by my knowing more about what God is up to in the world more generally. In the previous chapter, I said God is present with us today through the Holy Spirit, whom Jesus sent us to continue his work in the world in and through us. For ease of exposition, I'll divide the main aspects of Jesus's work—and the Spirit's continuation of it—into four main categories:

1. Proclamation/Invitation;

2. Exhortation/Admonition;

3. Instruction/Demonstration; and

4. Reconciliation/Communion.

Jesus invited people into God's kingdom, urged them to trust and obey him, taught and showed them what the kingdom is like, and promised to be with them and unite them with God.

These categories correspond roughly to the classic stages or dimensions of Christian mystical experience: conversion, purgation, illumination, and union.[3] Here's how. Jesus's proclamation of the kingdom and invitation into it involves repentance and *conversion*—a change of mind and a turning away from self toward God. When Jesus exhorts and admonishes his followers, he does so in order for them to be cleansed, refined, purified, or *purged* of their selfishness and transformed into people who can obey the two great commandments to love God with all they've got and their neighbor as themselves. And Jesus's instructions and demonstrations (his telling

---

3. See Underhill, *Mysticism*.

and showing) are meant to enlighten or *illumine* his followers to know the truth about God and themselves in relation to God. Finally, all these aspects of the Lord's work in our lives are aimed at reconciling us to God (and each other) for the sake of eternal loving communion or *union* with God (and each other). And once again, the Spirit continues these ministries of the Lord today.

In Part III, we'll look more carefully at these elements of Christian mystical experience from the standpoint of the soul pilgrim by focusing on practices that can facilitate maturation in each dimension. Here we'll emphasize the characteristic ways in which the Holy Spirit acts in the lives of pilgrims to enable them to make progress in each area. And we'll also discuss potential ways pilgrims can discern the Holy Spirit is at work in these respects.

Initially, I had concerns about using Christian mystical categories to characterize the soul pilgrim's path. For one thing, I was worried it would be unrealistic to aspire to the kind of relationship with God many Christian mystics have enjoyed. As unmarried members of religious communities, many of the well-known mystics were able to devote the bulk of their time to the sorts of religious practices that make close communion with God possible. But I'm married with kids and grandkids, and I have a mortgage, a full-time job, and all of the responsibilities that go along with those things. Can an ordinary person reasonably hope to have an extraordinary relationship with God?

I was also worried about what some have identified as dangers of the mystical life: heresy and individualism. Some mystics got so caught up in their individual experiences of God they diverged from the teaching of the church based on the Bible and/or neglected the needs of the Christian community and the world that the body of Christ is called to serve. I certainly don't want to be a heretic or a hermit.

But in spite of these concerns, I've come to see much value in the Christian mystical tradition. I've become convinced God calls all Christians to a life with him of the sort Christian mystics desired. And I've been persuaded ordinary Christians can engage in the practices that facilitate this kind of life in the midst of their daily routines. I've also come to the conclusion that mystical practices and experiences can be based on solid biblical teaching. And I've realized that these activities can be engaged in and the resulting experiences can be enjoyed by a mission-minded community of Christians who desire to know, love, and serve God together as they participate in Jesus's ongoing ministries through the guidance and power of the Holy Spirit.

Once I was reassured that I could benefit from the mystics' examples without going off the rails of orthodoxy and community, I was excited to see how Jesus's fourfold ministry could be characterized in such a way as to correspond to the fourfold mystical path of conversion, purgation, illumination, and union.

> ### Soul Pilgrim Reflection Questions
>
> What are your thoughts and feelings about Christian mystics? Are you open to learning from them and following their lead as you walk the soul pilgrim's path to deeper union and communion with God?

Conversion

Jesus started his ministry by proclaiming the kingdom of God had come near, and he invited the members of his audience to repent, believe the good news, and follow him—so he could enable them to "fish for people" by proclaiming the kingdom and inviting people into it (Mark 1:15, 17). And after Jesus was resurrected, he told his disciples to wait in Jerusalem for the baptism of the Holy Spirit, when the Spirit would "come upon them" to empower them to "be his witnesses" to the entire world (Acts 1:5, 8).

As I mentioned in the Introduction, my own conversion to Christ involved a combination of childhood participation in my church's ministries (Sunday school, worship services, vacation Bible school, and youth group) and the influence of a visiting evangelist (who shared the gospel and gave an "altar call"). As I reflect back on this time, I can see now that God had prepared me through those ministries by the Holy Spirit to be primed for and receptive to the visitor's message and invitation. Given the formation I'd experienced at church, I was ready to "repent, believe the good news, and follow Jesus." And I also began to think about sharing my new faith with others.

One of my first evangelistic efforts involved inviting an unchurched ninth-grade classmate to junior high youth group. I figured he would become a Christian just by listening to the youth leader's talks, being with Christian kids, and singing Christian songs. After attending the meetings for a few weeks, he decided he wasn't interested any more. So, he stopped coming to the group. As a result, I stopped spending time with him at school—since I had befriended him solely for the purpose of bringing him to Christ. He was understandably angry when he discovered my "friendship" was conditional in this way. Though I had benefitted from the work of the Holy Spirit in my own conversion, I hadn't been sensitive to the Spirit's leading by sticking with my classmate as a genuine friend—whether he accepted the gospel or not. I was willing to "fish for people," but I hadn't "waited for the Spirit." I had a lot to learn about the role of the Spirit in evangelism.

I eventually realized more fully that the Holy Spirit is operative in both bringing people to Christ and equipping Christ followers to share the good news of Christ. The Spirit convicts people of sin (John 16:8–11), testifies on behalf of Jesus (John 15:26), and powerfully assists those who preach the gospel (as in the case of Paul's proclamation to the church at Corinth—1 Cor 2:45). Jesus says, "no one can come to (him) unless drawn by the Father who sent (him)" (John 6:44) and "no one knows the Father except the Son and anyone to whom the Son chooses to reveal him" (Matt 11:27). It seems clear the Father draws people to the Son by means of the Holy Spirit and the Son reveals the Father to people—also by means of the Holy Spirit. So, the Spirit plays a vital role in bringing people into the kingdom to share life with the Triune God and in equipping members of the kingdom to be instrumental in this effort as well.

As a young adult, I learned the Holy Spirit had used me during my teenage years to help bring my nephew Jonathan into the kingdom. During the summer following my senior year in high school, Jonathan lived with my parents and me after my sister and his father got divorced. Years later, he told me I was influential at that time in introducing him to the Christian faith. He reminded me I gave him a Bible (which he still has today). He sees that time as the beginning of his journey of Christian faith.

What's the difference between my junior high evangelistic failure and my senior high success? Looking back, it seems to me now my dependence on the Holy Spirit in the latter case made all the difference. In my first attempt, I was motivated by a desire to do my Christian duty, and I acted unilaterally out of a sense of obligation. In the second case, I was motivated by my growing enthusiasm for following Christ, and I relied more heavily on the Spirit out of a sense of personal inadequacy. As a result, I was less "in the way," and the Spirit was able to use me more effectively to reach my nephew as a result. I see this now more in retrospect than I did at the time—in part because Jonathan didn't fill me in on my role in his conversion until some years later.

Soul pilgrims who are following Christ are indwelt by the Holy Spirit, whom the Father and the Son have given us for the purpose of continuing the kingdom work of Jesus (God the Son incarnate) in us and through us. Consequently, we soul pilgrims should be attentive for signs the Holy Spirit is present in us at a given time in such a way as to prompt and empower us to share our testimony as witnesses to the presence and activity of God in our lives. And the more we're aware of God's presence and activity in our lives, the more effective we can be as witnesses whose testimony can help confirm the truth of the gospel's claim that Jesus has opened the door to abundant life with God in God's kingdom. The more we share what God is doing in our lives, the more attractive that kind of life will be to others.

Our decision to go on the Camino was due primarily to the testimony of a friend who had walked the Camino Francés himself. Though we had been inspired by watching *The Way*, a movie about a father walking the Camino after his son died attempting the trek, we weren't motivated to walk the Camino ourselves until we heard Bart's personal stories about his own experience. His delight was contagious, because it was evident his pilgrimage had been genuinely life-changing. And he drew on his personal memories to make the Camino come alive in our imaginations—just as soul pilgrims can rely on signs of God's presence in their lives to share with others what life with God is like.

What are signs of God's presence through the Spirit of Christ for this purpose? According to Lewis Smedes, "In a sense, we are not aware of Christ within at all. We do not feel, or intuit or sense His presence as something distinct from ourselves... the test is in the effects of the Spirit and the power in our moral lives."[4] Though I don't share Smedes's skepticism about sensing the presence of Christ within, it does seem to me that the signs of the Spirit's presence and activity in our lives will be discernible at least in part through positive moral changes in our psychological states and our behaviors—especially states and behaviors we wouldn't have expected to have possessed and engaged in on our own apart from God's influence and enablement. Examples of such psychological states are a conviction another person is in need of Christ and open to the gospel, a desire to share Christ with that person, and a subsequent attempt to do so that seems to be accompanied by more wisdom and courage than we ordinarily feel able to muster.

I recently had an experience of this sort with a family friend who isn't a Christian. While the two of us were chatting at a summer gathering—as we had on a number of previous occasions—our conversation suddenly went deep. We began to talk about what it is that makes life worth living. In the midst of our interchange, I sensed in him a hunger for purpose and meaning as well as a genuine interest in my vision of the good life. In response, I found myself sharing my personal experience of Christ with a degree of confidence and clarity that was unusual for me. Our discussion went on for some time, and when it ended, the expression on his face indicated that what I had said touched something deep in his soul. And I had a strong feeling I had been empowered by the Holy Spirit to speak with uncharacteristic

---

4. Smedes, *Union with Christ*, 156.

boldness and eloquence. It seemed to me that the very words I had spoken were given to me as gifts while I was speaking them.

> ### Soul Pilgrim Reflection Questions
>
> As you look back on your conversion—or your earliest memories of being a Christian—do you remember experiencing anything that could be taken as a sign of the Holy Spirit's work in your life? If so, what sign or signs do you recall? And if you have ever shared your faith with someone, were you aware of signs the Spirit was guiding and empowering you as you did so? If so, what were they?

Purgation

Jesus lays out his blueprint for kingdom living in the Sermon on the Mount (Matt 5–7). In doing so, he makes it clear that mere external behavioral conformity to the requirements of God's law won't suffice to make a person fit for life in God's kingdom. Suitability for life with God in God's community requires something more radical: a righteous *character*. As Jesus said to his listeners, "unless your righteousness exceeds that of the scribes and Pharisees, you will never enter the kingdom of heaven" (5:20). The righteousness of the scribes and Pharisees consisted solely in their *behaving* according to the requirements of the law (and in some cases, according to their overly lenient interpretation of the law)—regardless of their inner attitudes and motivations. But true righteousness is rooted in the latter.

My appreciation of the importance of character in the Christian life has grown stronger the more I've taken the soul pilgrim approach to my faith seriously. When I was a satisfied Christian in my early years, I tended to make right belief my top priority. Then when I transitioned to a skeptical Christian orientation in my young adult years, my emphasis was on right behavior. But now, though I continue to think both orthodoxy and orthopraxy are essential aspects of Christian living, I see the possession of a Christlike *character* as more fundamental. It seems to me now how we think and act is a product of the kind of person we are. And the kind of person we are is a matter of our character. As a soul pilgrim, I believe the more we allow God to transform us into the likeness of Jesus Christ, the more we'll see the world and relate to people as Jesus did. Again, Jesus taught that genuine righteousness is grounded in the fixed dispositions of our hearts.

In the Sermon on the Mount, he hammers this point home in a series of contrasts between the moral traditions his Jewish audience had received ("you have heard that it was said to those of ancient times") and his own interpretation of what God requires of us ("but I say to you"). In each case (see 5:17–48), only avoiding a prohibited behavior (murder, adultery, divorcing one's wife without a certificate, swearing falsely, being excessively vengeful, being unloving toward one's enemies) isn't enough; life in the kingdom also requires avoiding the inner attitude and disposition that causes the wrong action or prevents the right action (anger and contempt, lust, disrespect for the sanctity of marriage, insincerity, vengefulness, hatred of one's enemies). And consistently avoiding those bad attitudes and dispositions requires a fundamental transformation of character. When Jesus says, "Be perfect, therefore, as your heavenly Father is perfect" (5:48), he makes it clear that the character required of kingdom people is nothing less than the character of God.

During my early satisfied Christian phase, I assumed Jesus's call to godly perfection was an impossible ideal meant only to convince us we can't be saved apart from God's mercy and forgiveness. I didn't think Jesus wanted us actually to strive to become morally mature. It seemed to me such efforts would be fruitless. And I considered them attempts to earn God's favor on the basis of works—rather than attempts to become more Christlike by faith in God's grace. But I now believe Jesus sincerely meant for us to become like God in character. And I see growth in godliness as an essential part of a soul pilgrimage. Godliness is required for full intimate loving communion with God—and genuinely loving fellowship with others.

But aren't people who make an effort to be godly just trying to earn their salvation through works rather than by grace? Not necessarily. You can aim to become Christlike not in order to merit God's favor but to cooperate with God's gracious plan to transform you into the likeness of Christ. As Dallas Willard was fond of saying, "Grace is not opposed to effort, it is opposed to earning. Earning is an attitude. Effort is an action. Grace, you know, does not just have to do with forgiveness of sins alone."[5] Grace has also to do with *empowering* soul pilgrims to mature morally and spiritually. And our efforts should involve putting ourselves in a position to allow God to transform us in this way. But how does this process work?

Soul pilgrims can acquire a godly character by relying on the Holy Spirit rather than on their own efforts unaided by God. According to Paul, "the just requirement of the law" can be fulfilled in those "who walk . . . according to the Spirit" (Rom 8:4). And Paul says, "those who live according to the Spirit set their minds on the things of the Spirit" (8:5) which is "life and peace" (8:6). He implies that those whose mind is set on the Spirit

---

5. Willard, *The Great Omission*, 61.

are not hostile to God but submit to God's law and (therefore) please God (8:7–8). It seems none of these good results is automatic, but each requires people to cooperate with the Holy Spirit by *walking with* or *living according to* the Spirit and by *setting their minds* on the things of the Spirit. Moreover, Paul says, "if by the Spirit you put to death the deeds of the body, you will live" (8:13). So, we must eliminate—or *purge*—behavior that is at odds with God's will. But from the context it appears doing so requires a dependence on the Holy Spirit to help one change one's fundamental inner orientation.

As an aspiring soul pilgrim, I struggle to consistently surrender my life to God and rely on the power of the Spirit. I start each day resolving to abide in Christ, walk in the Spirit, and practice the presence of God, hoping and praying I'll resist temptations to sin and respond to the guidance of the Spirit with trust and obedience. But by the end of the day, I'm acutely aware of all the ways I've fallen short of this goal. Instead of being persistently willing to deny myself and act with self-sacrificial love, I too frequently give in to unwholesome self-indulgent behaviors and fail to go beyond my comfort zone to love and serve others unselfishly to the glory of God.

But I'm encouraged that St. Paul and other saints had the same sort of experience. In Romans, Paul describes his inner conflict by saying, "I do not understand my own actions. For I do not do what I want, but I do the very thing I hate" (7:15) and "For I do not do the good I want, but the evil I do not want is what I do" (7:19).[6] He characterizes this interior war as a battle between his "delight in the law of God in his inmost self" (7:22) and the "law of sin that dwells in (his) members" (7:23). I think he's making a distinction between his God-given desire to be righteous and his deeply engrained sinful habits. Fortunately, he ends by thanking God he will be delivered from these habits through the Spirit of Christ.

Even so, it can be easy to be discouraged by this inner conflict—especially during early stages of one's soul pilgrimage. In the same way, Jennifer and I faced challenges on the first few days of our Camino walk that diminished over the course of our literal pilgrimage. We needed to get used to walking long distances in hot weather. And we had to fight the temptation to stop and rest too frequently. But because of our hope of reaching our destination each day (and our final destination in Santiago de Compostela), we endured the physical discomfort, and our perseverance finally paid off in increased strength, confidence, enthusiasm, and ability. Soul pilgrims can hope and pray for the same outcome in their journey toward the development of a Christlike character that will enable them to live a godly life.

---

6. Some biblical scholars think Paul is describing his pre-conversion experience in this passage and others believe he is characterizing his post-conversion experience. I side with the latter.

Ultimately, we pilgrims must *live* by the Spirit to manifest the *fruit* of the Spirit (Gal 5:22–23). And this fruit consists in godly character traits—love, joy, peace, patience, kindness, generosity, faithfulness, gentleness, and self-control—which are the inner source of godly behaviors. But once again, we must not only depend on the Spirit to produce these positive results, we must also enlist the Spirit's aid to eliminate the inner causes of negative behaviors. As Paul puts it, "those who belong to Christ Jesus have crucified the flesh with its passions and desires" (5:24). But Paul implies that the ongoing effectiveness of this process requires both *living* by the Spirit and *being guided* by the Spirit: "If we live by the Spirit, let us also be guided by the Spirit. Let us not become conceited, competing against one another, envying one another" (5:25–26).

What are the signs of God's presence through the Spirit when it comes to the purging or cleansing of our characters to rid us of attitudes and behaviors contrary to God's will? In this case, we should expect the Holy Spirit to convince us of the legitimacy of biblical exhortations and admonitions intended to encourage righteous attitudes and behaviors and to discourage unrighteous ones. And we should also expect the Spirit to plant in us a desire to be Christlike in our characters and way of life. We should also look for signs the Spirit is empowering us to become godlier on the basis of these beliefs and desires—especially as we consciously, deliberately, prayerfully, and trustingly rely on the Spirit to help us in these ways.

My current soul pilgrimage experience suggests this process of purgation and transformation involves relatively specific ongoing "prompts" or "nudges" that I take to be signs of the Holy Spirit's work in my life. For instance, for some time now, I've had a recurring conviction that I need to contact an estranged friend with whom I had an angry encounter some years ago. When this thought occurs to me, I have a strong sense I need to ask my friend to forgive me for some hurtful things I said during that conversation. Unfortunately, though these apparently Spirit-produced directives have emerged persistently off and on for some years now, I've neglected to follow through by writing to my friend. I think what's holding me back is my fear that the ensuing conversation would be uncomfortable. And unfortunately, I love being comfortable more than I love my friend and more than I love my Lord who wants me to become more like Christ in my character.

I'm also experiencing something similar with a strong sense I should be contributing more money to a Christian ministry dear to my family that is in serious financial trouble due to the COVID-19 pandemic. But so far, I've been procrastinating. As in the former case, it's become clear to me, as St. Augustine would put it, that my loves (affections, values, priorities) are disordered.[7] I love my own financial security too much, and I love God and the people involved in the ministry too little.

The Spirit is calling me to obey in both of these cases not only to mend a relationship and help a ministry but also to purge me of my undue love of self. I need to live by and for myself less and live for and by the Spirit more.

> **Soul Pilgrim Reflection Questions**
>
> Do you have thoughts about things it would be good for you to do or things it would be good for you not to do—thoughts that could plausibly be interpreted as invitations or admonitions from the Holy Spirit? If so, do you respond to them with trust and obedience or instead with hesitation and procrastination?

Illumination

As I mentioned above, Jesus said that, as the Son, he knows the Father and enables others to know the Father also when he chooses to reveal the Father to them (Matt 11:27). He also tells his disciples, "If you know me, you will know my Father also. From now on you do know him and have seen him." And in response to his disciple Philip, who asked Jesus to show him (and the other disciples) the Father, Jesus said, "Have I been with you all this time, Philip, and you still do not know me? Whoever has seen me has seen the Father" (John 14:7–9).

Jesus is in a uniquely privileged position to provide people with knowledge of God in these ways because of his special relationship with the Father. In a conversation with the Jewish authorities, Jesus says, "The Father and I are one" (John 10:30) and "the Father is in me and I am in the Father" (10:38). The prologue to the Gospel of John begins by referring to Jesus as "the Word" who was "in the beginning with God" and also "was God" (1:1–2). It goes on to affirm that "the Word became flesh and lived among us" (1:14) and ends by stating that, "No one has ever seen God. It is God the only Son, who is close to the Father's heart, who has made him known" (1:18). The author of Hebrews puts it this way: "(The Son) is the reflection of God's glory and the exact imprint of God's very being" (1:3). So soul pilgrims should look to Jesus in their quest to be illumined by knowledge of God and to grow in knowledge of God.

---

7. See Augustine, *On Christian Doctrine*, 23.

As a soul pilgrim journeying toward deeper knowledge of a mysterious God, I'm heartened to know that my guide is a human being just like me—a human being who not only reveals God in virtue of being God-in-the-flesh, but also a human being whose birth, life, ministry, teaching, death, resurrection, and ascension are recorded in the four New Testament Gospels. So, the God I'm striving to know has become less mysterious—more knowable—through the incarnate Word and the words written about him. Now as I read about him, I can learn what kind of person he was—and is—and my imagination is trained better to look for him in my life as his Spirit reaches out to me.

Jesus also told his disciples he would ask the Father to give them "the Spirit of truth" (John 14:17) "to be with (them) forever" (v. 16). About this Spirit Jesus said to them, "You know him, because he abides with you, and he will be in you" (v. 17b). And this Holy Spirit would also illumine them: "But the Advocate, the Holy Spirit, whom the Father will send in my name, will teach you everything, and remind you of all that I have said to you" (v. 26). According to Paul, God has revealed his wisdom—centered on Christ and his crucifixion—"through the Spirit." He goes on to explain:

> For the Spirit searches everything, even the depths of God. For what human being knows what is truly human except the human spirit that is within? So also no one comprehends what is truly God's except the Spirit of God. Now we have received not the spirit of the world, but the Spirit that is from God, so that we may understand the gifts bestowed on us by God. And we speak of these things in words not taught by human wisdom but taught by the Spirit, interpreting spiritual things to those who are spiritual. (1 Cor 2:10–13)

I'm assuming that among the "gifts bestowed on us by God" the Spirit helps us understand are the specific ways we individual soul pilgrims need to grow in Christlikeness. So, though it's easy for me to be discouraged about my failure to follow through with the apology and contribution I shared about at the end of the previous section, I'm encouraged to think I'm making progress on my soul pilgrimage insofar as I'm becoming more and more aware of my guide's directions and my need to learn to follow them. When the Spirit illumines soul pilgrims, they can learn more about God and more about themselves. And they can learn how better to follow the path toward more likeness to and intimacy with God. In this way, the enlightening and purifying ministries of the Spirit work together, as we come to know what true godliness requires, the specific ways in which we fall short of it, and the moral and spiritual benefits of heeding the Spirit's calls to trust him and obey his instructions. These ministries of the Spirit are among the advantages of being in Christ.

Paul certainly wanted the members of the churches he founded to acquire an appreciative understanding of the benefits of being in Christ. In his letter to the church at Ephesus, he tells his readers that he prays

> that the God of our Lord Jesus Christ, the Father of glory, may give you a spirit of wisdom and revelation as you come to know him, so that, with the eyes of your heart enlightened, you may know what is the hope to which he has called you, what are the riches of his glorious inheritance among the saints, and what is the immeasurable greatness of his power for us who believe, according to the working of his great power. (Eph 1:17–19)

Though it's not clear whether Paul's use of the word *spirit* here refers to the Holy Spirit as the agent of wisdom and revelation, what he says in other places about the ministry of the Holy Spirit in the lives of believers makes it natural to suppose he has the Spirit in mind for this role.

So, the Holy Spirit provides willing and attentive soul pilgrims illumination about the teaching of Jesus and about the wisdom and gifts of God. The Son reveals the Father and the Spirit continues the work of the Son by revealing the Father and the Son. Once again, pilgrims would do well not only to study the Word of God but also to listen to the Spirit of God. Both are sources of illumination and enlightenment about God and also means of growing in personal knowledge of God. Furthermore, the Holy Spirit enables us to know we are children and so heirs of God (Rom 8:16–17) and that Jesus Christ abides in us (1 John 3:24). In the incarnation, God the Son came to dwell with us. And as I've been saying, after his crucifixion, resurrection, and ascension, Jesus sent the Holy Spirit so God could abide with us even more intimately and permanently.

When Jennifer and I were walking the Camino, we needed frequent guidance for various purposes. In addition to the various Camino signs along the way, we relied heavily on a couple of guidebooks.[8] We consulted these guidebooks many times each day to get our bearings, figure out where various resources were located, and learn how far we were from our day's destination. Other pilgrims were using the same guides—some on their smart phones. In the same way, soul pilgrims should consult the Holy Spirit frequently throughout each day to reflect on their day's journey so far, get their spiritual bearings, draw on the Spirit's provisions, and see where the Spirit is leading next. Such dependence on our guide is necessary for

---

8. Brierley, *A Pilgrim's Guide,* and Michelin, *Michelin Guide.*

growing in godliness, learning about ourselves and about God, and deepening our friendship with God.

The signs of God's presence through the illuminating work of the Holy Spirit include our being enlightened to understand the teaching of Jesus and the meaning of the gospel and also to affirm the truth of what Jesus taught and of what the gospel claims. These signs also include our ability to be confident that we are God's children and heirs and that God loves us, is with us, and will always be with us. Furthermore, as Paul's prayer for the Ephesians suggests, the signs of God the Spirit in us are both cognitive and affective. That is, they involve both the mind and the heart. Our grasp of the truths God wants to communicate to us will be accompanied by a heartfelt recognition of the great value of his gifts to us and the assurance of our present and future possession of them made possible by God's faithfulness and power.

Soul Pilgrim Reflection Questions

What is the Holy Spirit teaching you about God and about yourself? How are these lessons contributing to your growth in Christlikeness? How are they serving to help you to deepen your intimate loving union with God?

Union

As I pointed out above, the Gospel of John portrays Jesus as praying not only that those who believe in him may be one, but also that the relationships between the Father and Son on the one hand and believers on the other hand be characterized by intimate communion and union. Jesus describes these relationships as involving mutual "containment." He prays, "As you, Father, are in me and I am in you, may they also be in us" (17:21). So, Jesus is asking that his followers be "in" the Triune Godhead. But Jesus also says to the Father, "I in them and you in me" (17:23), so Jesus is also asking that the Godhead be "in" his followers. Jesus is asking the Father for a relationship of mutual containment between the Triune God and Christians. And from the larger context, this relationship seems to be one of intimate loving communion—the goal of a soul pilgrimage. We can also call it a "union" as long as we're clear in our minds that it's a union of mind, heart, and will that maintains the distinctions between the different personal beings involved.

Perhaps our Camino experience can provide a rough analogy. Once we embarked on the trail after leaving home, we gradually adjusted our behaviors to the rhythms of pilgrimage life. We established a routine of getting up early, securing our hiking equipment, and walking many miles as we followed the signs—with occasional stops to rest and refuel before reaching our day's destination. And this routine to which we adjusted ourselves enabled us gradually to get to know the Camino better and better. Over time, we became more observant of and attentive to specific aspects of the region of northern Spain through which we were walking. We witnessed vast vineyards (some yet to be harvested), long flat plains stretching for miles under the hot sun, quaint farming villages with ancient stone walls and buildings, and eventually mountains covered with evergreens and morning mist.

Our growing awareness of the natural context of our trek made us feel increasingly that we were not just walking the Camino—but living in the world of the Camino. The more we felt this way, the more we enjoyed the Camino—the more affection we had for it. We were in it and it was in us—in our minds and hearts! And this sense of communion and deepening union with the Camino grew more acute over time. Even now, though we're miles away, when we imagine ourselves in that world, our affection for it swells within us. We have an ongoing relation of mutual containment (of sorts) with the Camino de Santiago.

And this is like the relationship with God the Holy Spirit facilitates for soul pilgrims as they walk the soul pilgrimage path. What are signs of the Holy Spirit's work in our lives to create and maintain this communion and union? We've already seen that Jesus said this to his disciples about the Spirit: "You know him, because he abides with you, and he will be in you" (John 14:16–17). So, the Spirit is always with and in us soul pilgrims. And what Jesus says implies we can *know* the Spirit simply in virtue of the Spirit's abiding with and in us.

But how can we know *that* the Spirit is in us and abiding with us? I think the best answer to this question is that we know that the Spirit is present with us because we can experience what the Spirit is *doing* to, in, and through us. And the previous three categories (conversion, purgation, and illumination) concern activities of the Spirit—activities that are discernible, as I have suggested above, by means of some of our psychological states (convictions, desires, and decisions) and behaviors (especially ones we think we would be unlikely to have or engage in without the influence of the Spirit in our lives).

As I reflect back on my day today, I'm aware of moments when, in retrospect, it seems to me now that the Spirit was active in my mind and heart. After getting out of bed, getting dressed, and turning the coffee maker on, I sensed the Spirit inviting me to turn to God by engaging in my daily devotional exercises (a "conversion" from self-absorption to God-directness).

And as I was reading a passage of Scripture (Matt 6:25–33), I experienced the Spirit's reminder not to worry about my life but instead to "strive first for the kingdom of God and his righteousness" (v. 33)—an invitation to be purged of my selfish anxieties. And as I listened to our pastor's sermon, the Spirit spoke to me through my pastor's remark that we needn't worry about loved ones who've strayed from Jesus—because Jesus won't ever stray from them (illumination about the steadfast love of God). Finally, as I reflect on these loving and gracious ministries of God in my life today, I'm moved to turn directly to him in loving communion—grateful for our deepening friendship and union.

My experience shows soul pilgrims can both know the Spirit abiding in them, and—if they're sufficiently reflective—know *that* the Spirit is abiding in them. But the first kind of knowledge seems possible without the second. There were times on the Camino when, though Jennifer and I were directly aware of the trail we were walking on and observant of the scenery we were passing, we weren't thinking much about either. Perhaps our minds were on our tired feet or our empty stomachs. Perhaps we were engrossed in conversation about an unrelated topic. Still, we were experiencing the Camino.

In the same way, knowing the Spirit is one thing and knowing that you know the Spirit is another. If a soul pilgrim is simply a person who knows God and wants to know God more and better, then soul pilgrims are not necessarily also people who know that they know God. That means that skeptical Christians—Christians who aren't sure whether they know God (or even think they don't know God)—could be genuine soul pilgrims. But it will help such skeptical Christians make progress in their pilgrimages if they can learn to recognize the ways God is present and active in their lives—by means of learning to recognize the signs of the Spirit's presence and activity in their lives. The more a soul pilgrim is able to recognize these signs, the more the pilgrim will be in a good position to grow in the knowledge of God by responding to these signs of God's presence and activity with trust and obedience. That's because responding to these signs trustingly and obediently will enable soul pilgrims to engage in the kind of experimental practical theology I'm recommending in this book as the primary way they can make progress in their pilgrimages toward deeper and deeper knowledge of God.

> ### Soul Pilgrim Reflection Questions
>
> Would you say the Holy Spirit lives in you? Do you *know* the indwelling Spirit? If so, how *well* do you know the Spirit? And if you do know the Spirit, would you also say that you *know* that you know the Spirit? If so, how would you explain to someone *how* you know that the Spirit is with you and in you?

Practice

Reflect on your life and try to think of experiences you've had that might seem to involve knowing God directly through awareness of God's presence with you. What do these experiences seem to have in common, if anything? It may be helpful to revisit the places in each of the four sections of this chapter ("Conversion," "Purgation," "Illumination," and "Union") where I discuss signs of God's presence through the work of the Holy Spirit.

6

God's Provision

How Can You Tell When God Guides and Empowers You?

**October 3, 2018, Camino de Santiago
—Descending Mt. Irago (from Jennifer's journal)**

Jim beckons to me with a sweeping movement of his hand. He's inviting me to take the first step of our seventeen-mile descent. "I'm thinking the most challenging part is right here at the top," he says. We gaze over a downward mile of treacherous loose rock. We plan to take this stretch slowly, a departure from our natural tendency to move briskly. We adjust the lengths of our trekking poles so they're long enough to plant firmly on a lower piece of mountain. I've mentally prepared for this challenge, yet I feel unnerved by the steep decline of this mountainside. I recognize the unsettled feeling in my stomach. Fear.

I flash back to my teens when I spent a lot of time springboard diving. I never really conquered my fear of heights. Learning a new dive worked best when I didn't overthink it, especially from the three-meter board. Many years later, I know this much. Water is more forgiving than rock when tumbling to its surface.

I remember Ricky, a fellow diver, who had no fear. I envied his ability to execute any dive off the higher platforms with little forethought and much finesse. Unfortunately, Ricky's cocky attitude put off his teammates. His boastful pride prevented him from forming the thing he wanted most—friendships.

Jim pulls me into the moment. "Shall we get started?"

"No time like the present," I say, believing that if I don't start now, I'll lose my nerve. Once I step forward, I keep my eyes on the rocky ground. Beautiful scenery surrounds us, but I need to concentrate on each step, so I won't slip. I stick my trekking poles into the mountain. Step. Step. Repeat. Without a word, the two of us work out a pattern. After minutes of negotiating our way down and around rocks of varying sizes, we stop and take stock of where the other person is. The one farthest down waits for the other to catch up.

"Let's veer to the right here, and then cross to that patch of slate." Jim thinks out loud as much for my benefit as for his own. I trust his judgment but choose a wider path to avoid the steeper slope.

When we come together again, I raise my eyes to the sky, and experience a sense of vertigo. I crouch, dip my head, and wait for the momentary dizziness to leave. The sun beats down. Heat envelops my body. No shade on this side of the mountain. Such a contrast to the morning chill!

In order to take some layers off, I need the security of some footholds. Better yet, I need a solid rock to lean on. Keep moving. Trekking poles first. Step. Step. Repeat. Just as I get my momentum going, my feet find footholds—even better, they show up next to a giant rock.

Such a small provision feels like a godsend! I lean my poles against the rock and set my backpack on top of it. I tie my sweatshirt around my waist and put my jacket vest in my knapsack. I replace my beanie with a visor. I look back to see Jim, twenty feet behind, doing his own adjusting. I drink the water that remains in my bottle while I wait for him to catch up. I use the moment to gauge our progress. We're halfway down this mass of rock. There's no going back. But I'm fortified knowing we've come this far.

Once Jim joins me, we refit our pole straps securely and continue downward. My legs feel wobbly, but they still hold me up. Although I slip a few times, my trekking poles keep me from falling. Jim loses his balance but rights himself with his poles. Now he moves ahead of me, looking back to see where I am and how I'm doing.

After thirty minutes of descending this way, we reach the base. We look up at the rocky terrain we just hiked down. I feel giddy. I high-five Jim.

"How are you doing?' he asks.

"Feeling proud! But also weak. You?"

"Relieved. Thirsty!"

"How much water do you have?" I ask him.

"More than you." Jim eyes my empty bottle. He offers me what he has left.

We need to replenish our water, so we don't linger. It doesn't take long to spot the familiar yellow arrow painted on a rock. As we step forward on flat ground, another sign indicates the village of Manjarin a short distance away. Someone has carved the word *"agua"* on the sign with an arrow pointing straight ahead. We're encouraged by the promise of water.

Our Camino Pilgrimage Story: The Camino Guides and Provides

In addition to the signs on the Camino that tell you where it is and which way to walk to stay on it heading in the right direction, there are also signs of other kinds along the way that indicate places pilgrims can stop, things pilgrims can see as they continue to walk, and things pilgrims can do. Among the places pilgrims can stop are places to rest, places to eat and drink, places to purchase supplies, places to pray and worship, and places to spend the night. The signs leading to or fixed upon these places play the role of invitations to pilgrims to choose opportunities for different kinds of activities and experiences. And among these opportunities are ones that offer pilgrims resources or provisions for the journey. So, the Camino contains both guidance and provision. It provides you with guidance and guides you to provisions. Some Camino pilgrims of an especially mystical bent like to say, "The Camino provides!"

We didn't take advantage of all these opportunities. There were too many of them! And not all of them "had our names on them"; not all of them "called out to us." But some of them seemed appropriate means to accomplish our purposes, fulfill our felt needs, and/or satisfy our desires. And our having these purposes, needs, and/or desires made us especially attuned to these particular signs and to the places they pointed to. When we humans experience a deficiency of some kind (an unmet goal, unfulfilled need, or unsatisfied desire), we tend to be more attentive to things in our environment that seem potentially likely to remove it. But there were also signs that made us aware of purposes we hadn't considered pursuing, needs we didn't realize we had, desires we weren't in possession of, and—importantly—obligations and opportunities for doing good about which we were ignorant or insufficiently appreciative. Hence, the Camino guides and provides in such a way as to comfort and to challenge the pilgrims who walk it.

Recognizing God's Guidance and Provision

In this section of the book, we're focusing on the nature of personal intimate knowledge of God by paying attention to what we can know about what God is like, how we can recognize when God is present to us, and what some signs are of God's activity in our lives. The present chapter has to do with our ability to discern God's activity—especially his guidance and provision. In the last chapter we looked at four different areas in which God is potentially present in our lives through the work or ministries of the Holy Spirit. And I emphasized we can become aware of the presence of the Holy Spirit with us primarily by looking for how the Spirit's various activities in these four areas are manifested in the form of states of mind we wouldn't be likely to have apart from God's influence and empowerment—states that include convictions, desires, and attempts to act on the basis of these convictions and desires characterized by an amount of wisdom, courage, and good will it would be unlikely for us to experience apart from God's guidance and provision.

In my own soul pilgrimage, I've had to work at becoming more self-aware and self-reflective than I've usually been to notice thoughts, feelings, aspirations, and hesitations that are possible signs of God's guidance and provision. In the same way, Jennifer and I sometimes had to make an effort to attend to signs on the Camino. We sometimes got so lost in conversation or caught up in looking at the scenery we missed signs that pointed us in the right direction on the trail or indicated the location of a place we wanted to stop. One time we walked for over a mile before we realized we'd taken a wrong turn. We had to backtrack and remain especially vigilant until we discovered where we'd gone astray.

But even though we occasionally neglected to watch for the signs on the Camino, we were generally motivated to keep an eye out for them. Why? Because we didn't want to get lost in an unfamiliar place, and we wanted to get to our desired destinations (ultimately, to the cathedral in Santiago de Compostela). I wish I could honestly say the same is always true for me on my soul pilgrimage. Even though I know intimate loving union and communion with God is vastly more important than arrival in Santiago, I struggle more with being regularly attentive to signs of God's presence and activity than I did watching out for signs on the Camino. Later in this chapter, I'll discuss some reasons I think this is true of me—and why it might be true of you as well.

> **Soul Pilgrim Reflection Questions**
>
> Do you regularly strive to be attentive to possible signs of God's presence and activity in your life? Why or why not?

The Holy Spirit's Activity

Let's briefly review the four categories of the Holy Spirit's activity in preparation for investigating the signs of God's guidance and provision more specifically and carefully. First, the Spirit is active in the conversion of people's minds, hearts, and entire selves to God by means of the Spirit's guiding and equipping Christians to proclaim the good news that God's kingdom has been made available to human beings through the life, ministry, teaching, death, and resurrection of Jesus Christ—and by inviting humans into the kingdom by means of that proclamation.

Second, the Spirit is operative in the cleansing of Christian soul pilgrims from sin (purgation) through enabling soul pilgrims to understand, accept, appreciate, and act on biblical exhortations (encouragements) to behave in godly ways and to heed admonitions (warnings) to avoid behaving in ungodly ways—and not just to behave in some ways and refrain from behaving in others, but more importantly and fundamentally, to become a person with a more Christlike character.

Third, the Spirit works to educate, enlighten, or illumine us by means of helping us understand the meaning of biblical doctrines and by enabling us to accept the truth of biblical teaching—teaching that takes the form of both instruction and demonstration.

And finally, the Spirit facilitates union with the Triune God by means of helping soul pilgrims who've been converted to Christ, are being purged from sin and equipped for righteousness, and are being illumined to understand and accept the teachings of Scripture. And the Spirit does this through the ministry of reconciliation and the creation and maintenance of divine-human communion.

Given this summary, we can begin to drill down into more specific accounts of how attentiveness to our psychological (cognitive, volitional, and emotional) states and our behaviors could yield a basis for recognizing the work of God the Holy Spirit in these four areas of ministry in and through our lives. Generally speaking, the Spirit is involved in both our intellect (mind) and will (heart) in all four of these ministry domains. The Spirit provides us with wisdom (intellect) and with motivation (will). The wisdom consists in knowledge and understanding and the motivation consists in emotion, desire, and intention. The Spirit guides us by giving us wisdom and enables us to act on the basis of that wisdom by providing us with the motivation we need for that purpose.

I'll illustrate this work of the Spirit by means of a recent experience I had in my own soul pilgrimage. I'm in the process of rememorizing Jesus's Sermon on the Mount (why didn't it stick the first time?). When I was going over Matthew 5:23–24 ("So when you are offering your gift at the altar, if you remember that your brother or sister has something against you, leave your gift there before the altar and go. First be reconciled to your brother or sister, and then come and offer your gift."), I had the following thoughts. I remembered the previously mentioned brother in Christ who probably had something against me (I still hadn't asked him to forgive me for how I conducted myself during an angry encounter with him some years ago). Then it occurred to me that the verses imply my soul pilgrimage efforts to deepen my union with God were being impeded because of this broken human relationship. And this thought made me want to take steps to do what I could to repair it (to temporarily leave what I was offering to God in order to go and try to be reconciled to my estranged friend).

As I reflect on this mental episode triggered by my rehearsal of Matthew 5:23–24, it seems to me now that it was brought about by the Spirit. The Spirit enabled me to see how this passage applied to my circumstances (illumination), encouraged me to turn from my selfish neglect of a troubled relationship toward selfless love (conversion), offered to empower me to contact my friend by purifying my motives (purgation), and promised to reward me with deeper intimacy with God as a result (union).

Sometimes the Spirit gives us this guidance and provision in response to our request for it and other times the Spirit guides and provides by initiating wisdom and motivation that we haven't asked for but are willing to receive. Often when the Spirit guides us and provides for us in response to our prayers, we experience those ministries of the Spirit as comforting, consoling, and encouraging. But frequently when the Spirit offers guidance and provision that is unrequested by us, we experience these movements of the Spirit as challenging, difficult, and even disconcerting. And finally, whether in response to us or not and whether comforting or challenging, the Spirit's directives will take the form of either encouragements to do, be, or allow something or warnings to refrain from doing, being, or allowing something.

I experienced the Spirit's admonition to me to reach out to my friend to be reconciled as both unrequested and challenging. And I've experienced the Spirit's response to my recent repeated requests for an alleviation of anxiety as a welcome and comforting response to my prayers. But the Spirit has also provided me with unbidden favors—such as the unexpected discovery of some devotional works that offered just the insights I needed at a particular time. And the Spirit has also responded to my all-too-rare requests for opportunities to grow in patience and perseverance by allowing me to experience trials that required me to exercise those virtues. So, the Spirit works in our lives whether we request it or not and in ways that are both consoling and disconcerting.

In general, God works through the Spirit to (1) turn our mind and heart toward him, (2) transform our heart to be submissive to his will, (3) renew our mind to be enlightened by his teaching, and (4) unite our mind and heart to his so we come to share his perspectives and concerns and act on the basis of them. In doing so, the Spirit makes us progressively more Christlike or godly.

> ## Soul Pilgrim Reflection Questions
>
> Have you experienced both comforting and challenging activities of the Holy Spirit in any of the four categories listed above either in response to your prayers or unrequested? If so, what were these specific acts of the Spirit's guidance and provision?

Fear and Pride

God engages in the fourfold work of the Spirit mentioned above in such a way as to honor the free will he gave us. Because God is perfectly loving, he will not force or coerce a person to change. But this divine restraint means we can resist these divine ministries in various ways. And if we're unwilling to allow God to do these things in our mind and heart, then he won't be present to us and active in us in these ways, and we'll miss opportunities for knowing God and growing in the knowledge of God.

But why would we be unwilling to allow God to convert, purify, and illumine us in such a way as to enable us to become more intimately united to him in love? After all, as we saw in chapter 1, there's nothing more valuable or worthwhile for a human than to know God in this way. The two main obstacles to our full cooperation with God for this purpose seem to be our *fear* and our *pride*. We may fear what God will do to us or what God will allow to happen to us. We may not be fully convinced God wants the best for us. So, fear is a deficiency of will based on unbelief or a lack of trust. It involves a fundamental lack of confidence in God. We may also be too proud to acknowledge our dependence on God and God's sovereign authority over us as our Creator and Lord. We may have an overinflated view of our ability and/or value. So, pride is a deficiency of will based on a false belief and refusal to submit. It involves a fundamental overconfidence in ourselves based on ignorance of our true condition.

Both fear and pride can be obstacles on the Camino de Santiago as well. Fear can prevent a would-be pilgrim from embarking on the pilgrimage in the first place. I'm grateful the initial worries Jennifer and I experienced about being able to walk up to twenty miles a day for days in a row didn't prevent us from following through with our quest. But fear can be paralyzing for pilgrims in the midst of their journeys as well.

The young couple I mentioned in chapter 1—Beth and Travis—left the Camino early because of unexpected and unwelcome discomforts and disappointments they experienced at the outset of their journey. They decided hanging in there until Santiago wasn't worth taking the risk of facing more inconveniences along the way. They were more afraid of possible injuries than they were of missing out on the satisfaction of daily adventures and the reward of a *Compostela*. Instead of mastering their fears, they let their fears master them.

But pride on the Camino can be a problem as well. Some people start their pilgrimage with excessive confidence in their ability and equipment, and end up suffering a setback as a result. A common example of such hiker hubris is the novice pilgrim who shows up on the trail with inadequate footwear and an unreasonable goal for daily mileage. After just a day or so, many of these foolish neophytes find themselves significantly slowed by the blisters they've accumulated on their feet. Their pride may not have led to a literal *fall*, but it did cause them to falter!

So, fear and pride can be impediments on a literal physical pilgrimage as well as on a metaphorical soul pilgrimage. Since these vices are the main things that prevent God from being present and active in our minds and hearts in redemptive ways, they'll need to be diminished and eventually eradicated for the Spirit to be able to transform us spiritually, intellectually, emotionally, morally, and behaviorally so we'll be able to know God and grow in relational knowledge of God. Consequently, we should expect that as we become even minimally open to God in spite of our fear and pride, the Spirit will begin to work to bring our fear and pride to our attention so we can be in a position to acknowledge these attitudes and to realize our need to eliminate them. This is the stage in the Spirit's work often called "convicting of sin" (where sin is whatever is separating us from loving communion with God).

As I think back on my life in Christ, I'm aware of seasons I was prideful and seasons I was fearful. As a *satisfied* Christian, I was complacent about my relationship with God and critical of people I thought didn't have one.

I realize now I was more like the self-congratulatory Pharisee than the self-deprecating tax collector in Jesus's parable (Luke 18:9–14). As a *skeptical* Christian, I was critical of my former self and other people I believed to be similarly deluded who thought knowledge of God possible. Both my satisfied and skeptical Christian stages were characterized by the sin of pride.

In my current soul pilgrimage experience, fear has become the main obstacle preventing me from making better progress toward full and deep union with God. As a result of the chastening of my pride through the setbacks and difficulties of life, I'm no longer overly confident—for the most part. But I've swung to the other end of the spectrum. Now I tend to be beset by worries, anxieties, and fears. My ability to trust God fully and obey him completely is hampered by my concerns about health, money, work, and relationships, among other things. Though I've committed Matthew 6:33 to memory ("But strive first for the kingdom of God and his righteousness, and all these things will be given to you as well."), I haven't committed my life fully to living faithfully on the basis of it. So, fear has replaced pride as my main besetting sin.

As we begin to cooperate with the Spirit by acknowledging these sinful attitudinal impediments and desiring their removal, we'll become more likely to pray that our fear will be replaced by courage and that our pride will be supplanted by humility. As we persist in praying for these attitudinal changes, we'll be practicing an openness to God that will enable the Spirit to respond. And if we pray expectantly, we'll be in a position to discern the Spirit's responses in the form of providing us with increasing amounts of courage and humility in circumstances in which we'd been characteristically fearful and prideful. Witnessing these changes will not only provide us with confidence God has heard and answered our prayers; observing them will also give us evidence the Spirit is active in our minds and hearts and therefore present to us in our lives. And this evidence is strengthened to the extent we have good reason to think these improvements in our characters couldn't be explained apart from the supernatural work of the Spirit to bring them about and sustain them.

My recent experience provides an example. As I write this paragraph, the world is in the eighth month of the COVID-19 pandemic. During this time, the citizens of the United States have experienced a health crisis, an economic downturn, racial unrest, and deep social and political division—among other serious challenges. And tomorrow is election day—the day that will determine who will be president of our nation and which party will have more control of our government. People on both ends of the political spectrum are afraid of the outcome—afraid the other party will take power and lead the country to utter ruin.

To my shame, I've allowed these external circumstances to rule my inner life. Instead of maintaining complete trust in the almighty and ever-loving God with my future and the future of my loved ones, I've given in all too often to worry, anxiety, and fear. But I've also adopted the practice of praying regularly for courage and peace. And over the last few months, I've noticed a gradual improvement in my mental life—in spite of setbacks along the way.

I believe this betterment to be a direct result of my deliberate application of Paul's advice to the Philippians not to "worry about anything, but in everything by prayer and supplication with thanksgiving (to) let your requests be made known to God" (4:6). As a result of my experimentation along these lines, I've experienced more and more of what Paul said would occur when we turn our worries into prayers: "And the peace of God, which surpasses all understanding, will guard your hearts and your minds in Christ Jesus" (4:7). It's been helpful to have these verses memorized so I can rehearse them to myself in the midst of a bout of anxiety. I've also benefited from having memorized the following prayer:

> Beloved source of security: I wish for total freedom from all forms of destructive fear. In its place, lead me into the freedom of surrender. You hold me while I grow, and in this confidence I release anxieties about my life—its survival and success—and trust you with my unfolding story. Amen.[1]

Of course, cowardice and pride are not the only sins that block our receptivity to the Spirit and/or prevent the Spirit from working in our lives. There are also envy, gluttony, lust, unrighteous anger, and greed. But each of these additional sins (and others I haven't listed) are arguably rooted in cowardice and/or pride, which are themselves rooted in a fundamental idolatrous desire for absolute lordship over one's life and the complete autonomy of freedom from submission to any higher authority. Both cowardice and pride are due to an unwillingness on our part to cede control over our lives to God—either because we don't trust God enough (fear), or we trust ourselves too much (pride), or both.

The problem is we aren't capable of experiencing the fullness of abundant life, well-being, and flourishing on our own apart from depending on the life only the Triune God can give to humans. And as a result, our persistence in resisting God will ultimately result not merely in a failure to live well, but also in our complete and utter destruction. Just as our bodies

---

1. Hass, *Centering Prayer*, prayer for June 12.

cannot survive without food and water, our souls cannot survive without divine nourishment. But God won't force feed us.

> ### Soul Pilgrim Reflection Questions
>
> Does either pride or fear—or both—prevent you from making progress on your soul pilgrimage? If so, what steps have you taken, if any, to allow the Holy Spirit to humble you or give you courage?

Divine Hiding and Human Suffering

Since God loves us perfectly and consequently wants the best for us, he wants us to learn to be open to his life-giving love and power. But as long as we're unrepentantly fearful, prideful, or both, we'll not be sufficiently open to God. And if we aren't open to God, God won't reveal himself to us through the presence and activity of the Holy Spirit (even if God is working "behind the scenes" to draw us to him). It may seem to people whose fear or pride has created a barrier between them and God that God is "hiding" from them. Some people think a perfectly loving God wouldn't hide himself in this way. But since God's ultimate aim is for people to humbly submit to him and courageously depend on him, God may well act elusively with fearful people to enable them to realize their need for God to strengthen them. And God may well act elusively with prideful people to refrain from reinforcing their excessive opinion of themselves.[2]

One potentially effective way out of this impasse is for God to allow such people to suffer so as either to become more fearful—and potentially more likely to call out to God for help—or more humble—and potentially more likely to recognize their dependence on God. As C. S. Lewis said in *The Problem of Pain*, "God whispers to us in our pleasures, speaks in our conscience, but shouts in our pains: it is his megaphone to rouse a deaf world."[3] Such suffering is potentially redemptive, because, though there's no guarantee suffering will cause a person to turn to God, suffering puts people in a position to realize they aren't in complete control of their lives. And people in this position will have an opportunity to become more open to

---

2. I don't mean to imply here that everyone who experiences God as absent is culpably fearful or prideful. There are many possible reasons for God to seem hidden to a person that don't involve that person being responsible for their being in that condition. See Rea, *The Hiddenness of God* for an explanation of the experience of God's hiddenness in terms of the nature of God as transcendent.

3. Lewis, *The Problem of Pain*, 91.

God—an opportunity they wouldn't be as likely to have in more pleasant circumstances.

It shouldn't be surprising that we tend to turn to God more frequently when we need God. And times of suffering are times of need. The more serious our suffering, the more we *realize* our need. If our suffering is serious enough, we realize our need for *God*. Though the old adage that there are no atheists in foxholes may not always be true, it expresses an important general truth.

Jennifer and I certainly consulted our guidebooks and other people on the Camino when we were lost and needed direction or hungry and thirsty and lacked food and drink. And the more urgent our need, the more serious we were about relying on others.

The same is true for soul pilgrims in their relationship with God. When my worries, anxieties, and fears become acute and I can't just get rid of them at will, I'm more likely to turn to the Lord. Reflecting back on the last few years, I can see that many of the times I've been most active in my prayer life have been times I've been especially anxious or fearful. Whether it was anticipating a surgical procedure, wondering what was happening to a family member I hadn't been able to reach for a while, trying to figure out how to manage a significant financial loss, or dealing with the destruction of our house after it burned down, I "let (my) requests be made known to God" more frequently than usual. And sometimes in those circumstances, it seemed to me, at least initially, that God wasn't responding. But that apparent divine silence just motivated me to persist in my petitions (like the woman in the parable of the widow and the unjust judge, which Luke says is "about (our) need to pray always and not to lose heart" (18:1).

What all this shows is that a perfectly loving God can deliberately withdraw from being present to a person and can legitimately permit a person to suffer. Both an experience of God's absence and an experience of suffering's presence can contribute to a person's being more open to the work of the Holy Spirit. While suffering, fearful and prideful people may be motivated to seek God. Initially, they'll seek him to alleviate their suffering. But ultimately, they may also ask him to make them both courageous and humble. Ideally, they'll end up asking God to direct and equip them in their efforts to love and serve others and steward God's creation—all to the glory of God.

> **Soul Pilgrim Reflection Questions**
>
> Do you tend to turn to God more frequently when you're worried, anxious, fearful, or suffering? Are you willing to turn your worries into prayers and your times of suffering into opportunities for getting closer to God?

Laodicean Indifference

So far, we've been thinking about how people can experience difficulties in their soul pilgrimages toward deeper knowledge of God as a result of their being unwilling or unable—through fear and/or pride—to follow the path that will lead them in the right direction. That's the path of genuine courage and true humility. But soul pilgrims can also fail to make progress on their journeys even though they aren't actively resistant in these ways. Another obstacle to progress in a pilgrimage is *indifference* due to presumed lack of need. When I was a satisfied Christian, I often fell into this category.

Consider the members of the church of Laodicea, to whom John wrote a letter dictated by the Lord Jesus Christ, whom John saw in a revelation on the island of Patmos. Through John's letter, Jesus says the following to the Laodicean Christians:

> I know your works; you are neither cold nor hot. I wish that you were either cold or hot. So, because you are lukewarm, and neither cold nor hot, I am about to spit you out of my mouth. For you say, "I am rich, I have prospered, and I need nothing." You do not realize that you are wretched, pitiable, poor, blind, and naked. Therefore, I counsel you to buy from me gold refined by fire so that you may be rich; and white robes to clothe you and to keep the shame of your nakedness from being seen; and salve to anoint your eyes so that you may see. I reprove and discipline those whom I love. Be earnest, therefore, and repent. Listen! I am standing at the door, knocking; if you hear my voice and open the door, I will come in to you and eat with you, and you with me. To the one who conquers I will give a place with me on my throne, just as I myself conquered and sat down with my Father on his throne. Let anyone who has an ear listen to what the Spirit is saying to the churches. (Rev 3:15–22)

The Laodiceans were neither actively and fervently pursuing nor deliberately and passionately avoiding life with God. Instead, they were passively, apathetically—and prematurely—pleased with their current condition.

Why? Because they thought they had everything of value they needed to live blessed lives. They thought they'd prospered and become rich as a result. But they were wrong; they were under an illusion. Rather than being prosperous, they were wretched. And instead of being in an admirable condition, they were deserving of pity. That's because, in contrast to what they thought about themselves, they were really poor, blind, and naked. What they needed more than anything was to acknowledge their deficiencies and turn to the only one with the resources required to make them truly wealthy.

These resources included refined gold (the riches of Christlike characters perfected by suffering to bring them out of spiritual poverty), white robes to cover their shameful nakedness (the clothing of the righteousness of Christ to cover their sinfulness), and salve to anoint their eyes (spiritual vision to replace their blindness with insight into their true condition and their need for deeper intimate loving communion with God). Jesus advised them to "buy" these things from him. That's not, of course, because he thought they had anything of sufficient value to offer in an equal exchange for these invaluable spiritual treasures. Rather, he was implying they could receive these things from him only if they were willing to pay the price required to make them willing and able to receive them. The cost to them was the self-sacrifice involved in humbly recognizing their utter dependence on God for their well-being and in prayerfully requesting that God graciously supply them with what they needed in spite of their being undeserving of these gifts.

How could these Laodicean soul pilgrims have been so deluded about their actual spiritual condition? There are at least two possible reasons. One is that their temporary worldly material prosperity tricked them into thinking all their needs were satisfied. The other is that, partially as a result of their complacency, they failed to engage in a regular habit of rigorous and radical reflection and self-examination. Radical reflection would have enabled them to see the fickleness of worldly fortune and radical self-examination would have put them in a better position to see their tendency to be taken in by mere appearances of wealth and to be far too easily pleased with things that wouldn't fully and ultimately satisfy them.

Believe it or not, some people who walk the Camino are relatively indifferent about reaching the Santiago Cathedral. They care more about the social scene and recreational opportunities along the way. As a result, though they might have fun, they miss out on an opportunity for a more meaningful experience. Fortunately, there's something about being on the Camino and among religiously serious pilgrims that makes it harder to be indifferent to its spiritual significance. Jennifer and I experienced the power of the Camino and its community to captivate and shape our imaginations.

The more we walked, the more we saw ourselves as participating in the drama of journeying to a holy place with others whose hearts were pulled in the same direction.

And thankfully, Jesus loves deceived and indifferent soul pilgrims so much that he's willing to confront them and scold them for their failures. He does this not to *punish* them but instead to *discipline* them. That is, he does it not to inflict deserved pain on them but rather to teach them a lesson that will provide them with an opportunity for learning and growth. He also admonishes self-satisfied and stalled pilgrims to get serious about their soul journeys by forsaking their rest stops of complacency and by attending to the sound of his voice and of his knocking at the door of their hearts. It will be up to them to open the door. But if they do, Jesus promises to enter the most intimate part of their lives in order to enjoy fellowship with them—feasting together on their mutual love.

In order for soul pilgrims to reach this prized destination of their soul pilgrimage, they'll need to conquer their sinful resistance and indifference. But if and when they do—with the guidance and provision of the Holy Spirit—the Lord Jesus will enable them to rule with him on his royal throne. So, the goal of a soul pilgrimage will not only involve the privilege of intimate loving communion with God; it will also entail the responsibility of the shared stewardship of God's loving community.

Jesus's letter to the Laodiceans may include a reference to the fourfold ministry of the Holy Spirit described above. The white robes could represent *conversion*: repentant sinners clothing themselves with the righteousness of Christ. The refined gold could symbolize *purgation*: the process of acquiring a Christlike character through suffering and dying to oneself. The eye salve could stand for *illumination*: learning to see yourself as you really are and to recognize God as God reveals himself and his will as he enables you to understand it. Finally, the shared meal and throne could point to *union* with God: sharing in God's life and in God's rule—to be where God is and to share in God's work.

> ### Soul Pilgrim Reflection Questions
>
> Are you ever indifferent about your relationship with God? Do you sometimes allow positive circumstances to lull you into complacency so you don't care whether you're growing in friendship with God and Christlikeness? If so, what does Jesus's counsel to the Laodiceans suggest you should do?

Walking with Perseverance

Soul pilgrims who contend with fear, pride, and/or indifference know a soul pilgrimage isn't a walk in the park. Rather, it's a challenging journey requiring a "long obedience in the same direction."[4] Successful soul pilgrimages entail endurance, persistence, determination, and "grit."

That's why soul pilgrims need a guide who will not only show them the way but also challenge and encourage them to stay the course and rid themselves of anything that would slow them down or prevent them from arriving at their destination. And that's why we need the Holy Spirit to help us eliminate any fear, pride, or indifference that would keep us from growing in our Christlikeness and knowledge of God. As we've seen, those negative attitudes can also hinder us from being attuned to the Spirit's direction and empowerment in the first place. And they can make it more difficult for us to trust and obey the Spirit when we do pay attention to him.

The author of Hebrews likens the Christian life to a race Christians are running while the faithful people of God who've already finished their marathon watch. And this Spirit-inspired writer urges us to hang in there and to discard anything that might slow us down:

> Therefore, since we are surrounded by so great a cloud of witnesses, let us also lay aside every weight and the sin that clings so closely, and let us run with perseverance the race that is set before us, looking to Jesus the pioneer and perfecter of our faith, who for the sake of the joy that was set before him endured the cross, disregarding its shame, and has taken his seat at the right hand of the throne of God. (12:1–2)

Though the soul pilgrimage metaphor involves walking rather than running, this advice is applicable to soul pilgrims nonetheless. We need to lighten our load so we can stick with our journey. And we need to look to the Spirit of Jesus—who knows the way and enables us to walk it—as we go.

Before our Camino, Jennifer and I found a lot of advice to future pilgrims on the internet. Among the more important recommendations were suggestions about what to take with you. What these counsels had in common, in spite of their diversity, was the warning to *pack light*. And that makes a lot of sense. It's hard enough to walk an average of fifteen miles a day *without* a pack. The degree of difficulty increases with each extra pound.

---

4. This is the title of a now classic devotional work by Eugene H. Peterson. Ironically, Peterson got the title from the nineteenth-century atheist philosopher Friedrich Nietzsche, who recognized the need for disciplined perseverance in order to attain any worthwhile goal (see Nietzsche, *Beyond Good and Evil*, 95).

That's why pilgrims who carry too much on their backs eventually downsize by getting rid of unnecessary items or giving them to someone else to carry for them. Jennifer and I used a luggage transport service for that purpose; our daypacks contained only what was absolutely essential for the hike. As a result, our journey was easier and more enjoyable than it would otherwise have been.

Soul pilgrims who realize their fear, pride, and/or indifference are obstacles can trade them for Jesus's yoke. Our soul pilgrim guide and goal has invited us to do that: "Come to me, all you that are weary and are carrying heavy burdens, and I will give you rest. Take my yoke upon you, and learn from me; for I am gentle and humble in heart, and you will find rest for your souls. For my yoke is easy, and my burden is light" (Matt 11:28–30).

And his servant Paul has also urged us to "bear one another's burdens, and in this way you will fulfill the law of Christ" (Gal 6:2). Soul pilgrims who walk with Jesus and with each other will find it easier to persevere on their soul pilgrimage than they would if they tried to go it alone.

But they'll need to be willing to persist in partnering with the Holy Spirit for this purpose, and they'll need to continue engaging in the practices that make this partnership possible. These are things I don't always do—or at least don't always do well. I've already mentioned the pride I carried in my spiritual "pack" as a young satisfied and then skeptical Christian and the fears I continue to take with me as a soul pilgrim Christian. But I've experienced some reluctance to open myself to the Holy Spirit recently that doesn't seem due to either pride or fear. Am I indifferent? I don't think so. I really want to deepen my personal knowledge of God. So, what's going on? As I reflect on my state of mind during these periods, it seems to me I'm just naturally self-centered. Sometimes I just want to be left alone to do my own thing—especially when I'm tired. And when that's my frame of mind, my preference for autonomy overpowers my desire for God.

This is the power of our sinful nature—a power all soul pilgrims need to deal with, to a greater or lesser extent. It can create a condition of spiritual inertia, and it can feel like swimming upstream when you try to act against it. It's what Paul calls the "flesh." Here's his advice about how we should handle it: "Live by the Spirit, I say, and do not gratify the desires of the flesh. For what the flesh desires is opposed to the Spirit, and what the Spirit desires is opposed to the flesh; for these are opposed to each other, to prevent you from doing what you want" (Gal 5:16–17).

This flesh-Spirit battle is what makes a soul pilgrimage challenging and demanding. It would be easier in some ways not to embark on a soul pilgrimage at all. And one reliable sign that you are on such a spiritual journey is that you become more acutely aware of your shortcomings as you go.

That can be discouraging. But it's important to press on. Remember (from chapter 1) that knowing God in intimate loving union and communion is the only thing that will ever truly fulfill us.

In his Sermon on the Mount, Jesus highlights the importance of choosing the pilgrim's path: "Enter through the narrow gate; for the gate is wide and the road is easy that leads to destruction, and there are many who take it. For the gate is narrow and the road is hard that leads to life, and there are few who find it" (Matt 7:13–14). But we can't find and enter the narrow gate without the Spirit's guidance. And we can't keep walking the hard road to life without the Spirit's enablement. We need the Holy Spirit's fourfold ministry to help us continually turn to God, grow in Christlikeness, deepen our knowledge of God, and enjoy union with him.

> ### Soul Pilgrim Reflection Questions
>
> Do you find life with God relatively easy or relatively difficult? Or would you say that it is sometimes smooth and other times rough? To what extent do you feel you need to *persevere* in your soul pilgrimage? And how much are you relying on the Holy Spirit to help you do that?

General and Specific Signs of the Spirit's Guidance and Provision

We can look for signs of the Spirit's guidance and provision in each of the four areas of the Spirit's ministry to us. Of course, the most obvious and accessible source of divine guidance is in the Bible—the written Word of God, which provides us with authoritative teaching about what's true (about God, God's will, human nature, and the human condition) and what God calls us to do (to turn to God, be transformed by God, be taught by God, and find out how to "taste and see that the Lord is good" so we can be among those who are happy in virtue of taking refuge in him—Ps 34:8). And among the things we learn from the Bible are what we can expect God to provide us when we ask him properly (e.g., God's presence, God's love, the Spirit, mercy, forgiveness, grace, power, wisdom, etc.). In short,

> His divine power has given us everything needed for life and godliness, through the knowledge of him who called us by his own glory and goodness. Thus, he has given us, through these things, his precious and very great promises, so that through them you may escape from the corruption that is in the world

because of lust, and may become participants of the divine nature (2 Pet 1:3–4).

But we can also expect the Spirit to guide us and provide for us more personally, directly, and specifically in our minds and hearts (and also through the counsel and support of fellow soul pilgrims). And we can use what God reveals in the Bible about the Spirit's general guidance and provision to learn what to look for in these sources and how to recognize these activities of the Spirit when they occur. Like any skill, this skill of discerning the Spirit's presence and activity is one that develops and grows over time as we hone it through regular practice. Over time, we can hope to learn how to identify the communications of the Spirit to us—whether those communications are verbal or nonverbal (e.g., a directional prompting, nudge, or pull). And we can also hope to distinguish the Spirit's supernatural empowerment of us from reliance on our purely natural capacities.

> ### Soul Pilgrim Reflection Questions
>
> What recent experiences have you had that seem to you to have included the Spirit's guidance and provision? What specifically is it about those experiences that suggest divine involvement?

Summary

In sum, God may refrain from revealing himself—his presence to and activity with a person (including a soul pilgrim)—due to that person's willful resistance to God or unconcerned indifference to God. But God may use experiences of suffering and of his absence to draw actively resistant people to him—such as the prodigal son of Jesus's Luke 15 parable, who "came to himself" when he was away from his father's house and also penniless and starving. And God may also actively confront and admonish apathetic and indifferent people (such as the members of the Laodicean church) to wake up, change their ways, and listen for Jesus's voice and knocking at the door of their hearts. God's promise is that those soul pilgrims who open that door and let God in will be rewarded with knowledge of God through direct encounter with the Spirit of Jesus in the form of intimate loving communion. And soul pilgrims can count on the Spirit's guidance and empowerment to provide them with signs to direct them on their soul pilgrimage toward this goal and to enable them to continue journeying to this destination. But these pilgrims will need to learn what they can do to grow in their recognition of these signs and in their ability to keep walking in the direction they indicate—especially when the road becomes difficult to walk.

> ### Soul Pilgrim Reflection Questions
>
> Do you *want* to look for signs of God's guidance and provision in your life? If not, are you struggling with fear, pride, or indifference? Or are you like me in finding yourself lapsing periodically or even frequently into a pattern of general self-centeredness—whatever the cause?

Practice

Make a list of things you think God may have been (or may be) trying to communicate to you *specifically* through the Holy Spirit. What do these communications have in common, if anything, in terms of their form and content? Identify an important area of your life in which you think you need to be stronger than you feel you are capable of being on your own (e.g., because of worry, anxiety, or fear). Then pray God will provide you with the strength (e.g., courage) required to make progress in this area. Also, think of any personal moral or spiritual growth you may have experienced that seems not to be explicable apart from God's grace at work in your life.

III

Growing in Grace and Knowledge

"But grow in the grace and knowledge
of our Lord and Savior Jesus Christ."

—2 Peter 3:18a

7

The Path

How in General Does Knowledge of God Grow?

October 6, O Cebreiro to Alto do Poio (from Jennifer's journal)

My legs ache. I'm ready for a midday meal. "We must be close to the café in Alto do Poio," I tell Jim.

Just two hours ago we congratulated each other. "Only midmorning, and we've already reached the highest point of today's hike," I crowed.

"Great start to what could be our longest day," Jim added. We both assumed we'd have a leisurely descent for the remainder of our eighteen-mile trek. Boy, were we mistaken.

We departed O Cebreiro in high spirits. We kept a good pace through several villages and hamlets. At first, the chilly air invigorated us on a path that continued to bend and climb. "The trees and scents remind me of the Pacific Northwest," I told Jim.

My comment prompted him to talk about a childhood camping memory at Kalaloch Beach on the Pacific Coast of the Olympic Peninsula when he dug for razor clams. "It rained a lot of the time, even in the summer. But you already know that," he said.

Yes, I knew exactly what he meant. After growing up within three miles of his Bellevue neighborhood, I was familiar with many of the places he talked about. What were the chances we'd meet at the same California high school after our families had moved south within a year of each other?

Back on the path, we grew silent when the Camino's inclines became more demanding than our Michelin guide indicated. My gnawing hunger started to overtake me. I should have eaten a bigger breakfast. I should have packed more food. My own needs consumed my thoughts so that I could no longer appreciate the beauty of the lush green and purple mountains surrounding us.

Now, consulting our Michelin map, Jim determines we should be in the vicinity of a café in the tiny town of Alto do Poio. "It must be around the bend," he says several times to me. But after more minutes pass, my hopes plummet. No café in sight. I note the path ahead looks like an abrupt and *steep* climb upward, disappearing under a canopy of trees. Did we somehow miss the café? But, a sign with the yellow Camino arrow confirms we're on track.

I sit down on a fallen piece of log. I eat the last of the peanuts from my knapsack. "I'm done," I groan. "I can't do any more uphill." In reality, I know I have no choice but to keep walking. But I'm wondering whether I can even stand up.

Jim ignores my comment. His expression matches his resolve. "Let's keep going," he says quietly. "The café can't be far from here."

I'm furious with Jim for his unfailingly positive attitude. I want food. I want water. I want this unrelenting stage of the Camino to be behind me. The worst part is my pride. I'm disappointed in my lack of resolve. I'm disappointed in my weakness.

We start the ascent. I lag behind Jim. It's a slow climb, for about a third of a mile. The muscles in my legs protest. I feel a toe blister forming on my left foot. Finally, we break out of the forest.

A wall of rock obscures my view of a structure ahead, nearly straight above us and to the right. Voices waft down to confirm a gathering of people. Undoubtedly the café we've been looking for.

I take stock of what's required to get there. The five hundred feet immediately ahead reveal the steepest part of our climb yet, much like a ladder. This is an exercise of the will. Every step is a choice to stay with it. We must move forward if we want to complete this stage of our journey. And so, we climb.

At last, cresting the steep ridge, we step onto flat terrain, and behold the café on our right. I almost expect the patrons to cheer wildly from their outdoor tables. But no one takes notice of us. They're deep into their meals and conversations. I wonder if these patrons struggled to get to this point as we did, only to forget their immense effort once they sated themselves with food, drink, and rest?

Funny how one's perspective can change within minutes. Relief and gratitude replace my self-doubt and shame, now that the most difficult stage of today's climb is behind us. The Camino has delivered once again—in spite of my shortcomings.

The slightest sprinkle of rain feels refreshing on our faces as we take time out to rest and refuel. "Hey, Jen, look at the sky," Jim points to dark clouds that have formed in the distance ahead. "The last stage of today's Camino promises to be a wet one."

Our Camino Pilgrimage Story: The Stages of the Camino Francés

The Camino Francés is 764 kilometers (nearly 475 miles) long and is divided into thirty-three traditional stages. So, each stage is an average of just over twenty-three kilometers (a little more than fourteen miles). The shortest stage is 18.4 kilometers (11.5 miles) and the longest is 28.5 kilometers (17.7 miles). These are the *traditional* stages, and each stage starts in one village, town, or city and ends in another. But pilgrims are free to divide up their journeys differently. There are plenty of places to stay along the way in other communities in between these traditional stopping (and starting) places. And pilgrims can either shorten or extend the overall amount of time they spend on their journey by walking a longer or a lesser average distance each day. We met one family consisting of a father, mother, and three young sons who told us they'd set aside sixty days for their walk. So, they divided their trip into shorter stages. Since we had a limited time for our pilgrimage, we traversed a few of the traditional stages by bus or train.

But the one thing that remains constant in spite of all these pilgrimage variations is that, one way or another, pilgrims who plan to finish their trip in Santiago need to pass through each stage (from wherever they chose to start) sequentially. For instance, we started our walk in Pamplona. Thus, during our first day we walked the stage from Pamplona to Puente la Reina. And after spending the night there, our second day we walked the stage from Puente la Reina to Estella. The only way to get from Pamplona to Estella on the Camino Francés, when you're following the traditional Camino path, is to go through Puente la Reina.

Each daily Camino stage can also be divided into stages. There is a typical general order to daily Camino routines (e.g., get up, get dressed, pray, read the Bible, have breakfast, walk, eat lunch, walk, check into the overnight accommodation, shower, eat dinner, rest, read, write, sleep). And some of these stages cannot or should not occur until some prior stage or stages have been realized. For instance, it would be difficult to get dressed before getting out of bed, and you can't take a shower until you've checked into your place of lodging. Also, it's better to eat breakfast before setting out to walk an extended distance. Earlier daily stages are necessary and/or beneficial to prepare a pilgrim to be able to accomplish or benefit from later ones.

Following the Path toward Deeper Knowledge of God

In this chapter, we'll reflect on the most general sequence of soul stages that provides the framework within which more specific routines (which we'll discuss in the following two chapters) can operate effectively. I'll discuss four general practical stages that define a soul pilgrim's path, starting with the path's first stage and then considering the next two stages pilgrims need to traverse to get to the last stage of their final destination.

Though I refer to these practices as "stages," they can also be considered to be repeatable routine patterns. That's because soul pilgrims will need to cycle through them over and over while on the trail toward deeper knowledge of God. Just as there's a typical general order to daily Camino routines, so there's a typical order to regular soul pilgrim routines. Both literal and soul pilgrimages include stages typically accomplished in the same order but with some variation as different and sometimes unexpected circumstances arise. And both types of pilgrimages involve the regular repetition of these routine patterns of sequential stages.

Here are the four stages in order: (1) asking, searching, and knocking; (2) dying and rising; (3) trusting and obeying; and (4) drawing near to God to taste and see that God is good. These four stages correspond roughly to the four traditional stages of the Christian mystical path we've been discussing. The first stage involves conversion—turning away from focus on oneself and toward the Lord in prayer to ask for what one needs on the pilgrim's way. The second has primarily to do with purgation—being cleansed of selfish desires and cultivating godly ones to be strengthened for the journey. The third can be thought of as a response to illumination—responding to the Spirit's teaching and guidance with trust and obedience. And the fourth culminates in union—practicing the presence and partaking in the goodness and love of God.

> **Soul Pilgrim Reflection Questions**
>
> Does it appeal to you to think of your walk with God in terms of a repeatable sequence of stages? Why or why not?

Asking, Searching, and Knocking

The first soul pilgrimage stage involves prayer. We need to start with prayer because the second stage involves dying and rising. What I have in mind is dying to oneself in order to rise to selfless life with God. But dying to oneself isn't easy (as my own experience indicates). As sinful, fallen human beings, our tendency is to put ourselves first. Soul pilgrims can't make progress on their pilgrimage toward deeper knowledge of God without relying on the power of the Holy Spirit. In order to deny ourselves and take up our crosses daily, we need to continue to ask the Spirit for help. We need to pray.

According to Luke, after Jesus had prayed in a certain place, one of his disciples asked him to teach them to pray. Jesus then taught them the Lord's Prayer. And after that, he told them the parable about the person who comes to a friend's house at midnight asking for three loaves of bread to feed a guest who had just arrived at his house. Jesus said that, although the friend was initially reluctant to get up and meet the request, the asker's persistence would eventually cause his friend to give him the loaves. Jesus then urged his disciples to follow this petitioner's example:

> So I say to you, ask, and it will be given you; search, and you will find; knock, and the door will be opened for you. For everyone who asks receives, and everyone who searches finds, and for everyone who knocks, the door will be opened. Is there anyone among you who, if your child asks for a fish, will give a snake instead of a fish? Or if the child asks for an egg, will give a scorpion? If you then, who are evil, know how to give good gifts to your children, how much more will the heavenly Father give the Holy Spirit to those who ask him! (Luke 11:9–13)

We soul pilgrims can be assured that God will give us help on our soul pilgrimage if we ask him to do so. He's promised to give us his very Spirit to guide us and provide for us!

Practicing this first stage will make it possible to participate effectively in the later stages. If we ask the Holy Spirit to help us, he'll assist us in our daily dying to self and rising to new resurrection life with Christ. And our implementing this ongoing Spirit-empowered pattern will give us what we need to trust God and obey him. As we continue to trust and obey God, we'll be able to draw closer and closer to him (through honest confession, single-minded devotion, growth in Christlikeness, and holy living). And as we do, we'll be in a position to experience God's goodness in intimate loving communion with him. Moreover, we can do all these things through Christ who strengthens us (Phil 4:13), since "God will fully satisfy every need of (ours) according to his riches in glory in Christ Jesus" (Phil 4:19) and again, "His divine power has given us everything needed for life and godliness, through the knowledge of him who called us by his own glory and goodness" (2 Pet 1:3).

Jennifer and I found that our success on the Camino depended on our regularly relying on others for help. From our initial research to our final day in Santiago, we needed frequently to depend on what others did for us. As I've already mentioned, we benefited from other people's contributions to our motivation to go, our selection of things to take with us, our decisions about how to plan our trip, and, once we were on the Camino, our ability to find our way and to secure the things we needed for the journey along the way. Without our continual asking for directions, searching for provisions, and knocking on the doors of our accommodations, we wouldn't have been able to complete our trip successfully.

An example of our *failure* to ask for help on one occasion will illustrate my point. We had heard that every evening at the *albergue* associated with the Church of Santa María in Carrión de los Condes there is a mass with singing nuns and a pilgrim's blessing. We wanted very much to participate in this event, and we knew we had only one opportunity to do so, since we needed to leave early in the morning for our next Camino stop in Lédigos. We arrived at the church at the time we thought the service was starting. Since we didn't see anyone, we assumed we'd gotten the time wrong and had missed the event. In our disappointment, it didn't occur to us to check with anyone there to find out if we were too early instead of too late. Instead, we trudged back to our hostal dejectedly—only to find out later the mass had taken place a short time after we left. We should have knocked on the door of the church in our search for the service and asked for assistance. We should have relied on others for help!

I'm finding the same thing to be true in my soul pilgrimage. Of course, I need to rely on fellow soul pilgrims in various ways (as all of us do—see chapter 9). Soul pilgrimage is a communal endeavor. But as we've been seeing, we soul pilgrims depend especially on God the Holy Spirit to make progress. And I have a growing awareness that my personal soul pilgrimage progress (or stagnation or regress) is a result of how much I'm actively persistent in pursuing God in prayer—or not. In my own experience, I'm confirming Jesus's words: asking leads to receiving, searching leads to finding, and knocking results in an open door. But failing to ask, search, and knock (as is unfortunately often the case with me) leaves me without the responses, resources, and opportunities I need on my journey of soul toward a closer connection with God.

In spite of my tendency to neglect this stage, some days I'm proactive about asking, searching, and knocking. Recently, after reading Dallas Willard's *Life Without Lack: Living in the Fullness of Psalm 23*, I chose to implement his advice about how to spend a day with Jesus. I started the day praying God would enable me to abide in Christ and walk in the Spirit until bedtime. And I continued to seek God in prayer off and on for most of that time. Though my vigilance waned toward evening, it was clear to me the quality of my experience with God was better than normal; I was more regularly in conversation with God, more disposed to act selflessly, more willing to trust and obey what I understood of God's word, and more in tune with God's presence and activity. It was sweet. And thinking back on the delights of that day makes me wonder why it can be so hard for me to live with the same degree of openness to God *every* day.

Soul Pilgrim Reflection Questions

Do you make it a daily practice to turn to God regularly in prayer to ask him for assistance, seek his will, and knock on the doors of opportunity to trust and obey him? If not, why not, and what can you do to become more prayerful? If so, do you find it challenging to persist in this practice?

Dying and Rising

The second stage is dying and rising. We need to engage in that practice to prepare ourselves for the third general soul pilgrim stage—trusting and obeying God. Soul pilgrims can realize and act on their need for the Spirit's help to enable them to trust him and obey him only if they engage in a regular practice of dying to themselves in order to rise to a trusting and obedient life with God. Dying to oneself means being willing to set aside one's will—one's agenda—when it conflicts with God's will. After Paul characterizes the fruit of the Spirit in his letter to the Galatians, he says, "And those who belong to Christ Jesus have crucified the flesh with its passions and desires" (5:24). What Paul means by "the flesh" here is autonomous human life—the human will when it is not subject to God's will. Soul pilgrims will find that the flesh, understood in this way, is such a problem on their pilgrimage they will need to make it a daily practice to crucify it. Once is not enough. Luke makes this clear when he quotes Jesus as saying,

> If any want to become my followers, let them deny themselves and take up their cross *daily* and follow me. For those who want to save their life will lose it, and those who lose their life for my sake will save it. What does it profit them if they gain the whole world, but lose or forfeit themselves? (9:23–25; emphasis mine)

Denying oneself and taking up one's cross involves both refusing to live on the basis of desires contrary to God's will and also working to extinguish those desires so they'll no longer tempt one to build one's own kingdom rather than God's. Jesus is the supreme example of such self-denial. He models it in his Gethsemane prayer: "Father, if you are willing, remove this cup from me; yet, not my will but yours be done" (Luke 22:42). Jesus's temporary human desire was not to have to suffer and die on the cross. But his ultimate will (his effective desire) was to submit himself trustingly and obediently to God's will. Jesus died to himself in order to live to God.

Walking the Camino day after day is hard work. It takes discipline. And that discipline involves self-control. Pilgrims need to resist their desire to sleep in every morning so they can instead start hiking before dawn to arrive at their daily destination by a reasonable hour. They also need to minimize their rest and refreshment stops when they get hot and tired—for the same reason. At the same time, selfless pilgrims will be sensitive to the needs of their fellow travelers; they'll be willing to change their plans in order to assist a companion on the road. Dying to one's own desires is necessary for progress and for community.

During our Camino, Jennifer and I learned we had to renew our resolve to be both diligent and flexible on a daily basis. Just because we got an early start one day didn't mean we had a "get up and go" feeling the next. And even if we managed to set aside a plan of our own to accommodate our partner's needs on one occasion didn't make us automatically self-sacrificial on another. Our need to die to our lazy and selfish impulses was ongoing. Fortunately, our repeated efforts to be conscientious and caring made it easier over time for us to deny ourselves for the sake of our quest and for the good of our partner. Regular deaths to self can become habitual and can contribute to the formation of Christlike character.

In my soul pilgrimage, I'm finding my personal agenda so deeply rooted in my psyche that it takes a deliberate effort each morning to reaffirm my commitment to God's agenda and to stick with that dedication throughout the day. My deaths to my self-centered desires need to be "daily"—not just in the sense of occurring every day but also in the sense of occurring *throughout* each day! Yesterday is a case in point. While driving to the college where I teach, I asked God to help me be attentive throughout the day to what he's doing in the lives of my coworkers and students (stage 1). As a result, I developed a desire to put God's kingdom first in my interactions with others on campus (stage 2). But only an hour later, I found myself so absorbed in getting through my personal to-do list that I was oblivious to whatever God may have been trying to show me about the role he wanted me to play in the lives of those around me. I wasn't in a position to trust and obey him (stage 3), simply because I wasn't aware of what he was calling me to do. And I wasn't positioned to rest in and enjoy his presence with me (stage 4), since I wasn't thinking about him at all.

Jesus not only provided a model of obedient death to his natural human desires through his endurance of temptations and his death on the cross; he also provided a model of victorious resurrection life by his rising from the grave, never to die again. And now that Jesus has been restored to life, he makes the power of his resurrection life available through the Spirit to soul pilgrims who are willing to die to themselves in order to live with and for him. In his letter to the church at Rome, Paul says, "If the Spirit of him who raised Jesus from the dead dwells in you, he who raised Christ from the dead will give life to your mortal bodies also through his Spirit that dwells in you" (8:11). The life Paul has in mind here is not mere natural biological life (*bios*) but instead supernatural resurrection life (*zoe*)—a life that will enable us to participate in the life of God, even when our mortal bodies are decaying and dying. Paul has this distinction in mind when he says this to the Corinthians:

> But we have this treasure in clay jars, so that it may be made clear that this extraordinary power belongs to God and does not come from us. We are afflicted in every way, but not crushed; perplexed, but not driven to despair; persecuted, but not forsaken; struck down, but not destroyed; always carrying in the body the death of Jesus, so that the life of Jesus may also be made visible in our bodies. For while we live, we are always being given up to death for Jesus' sake, so that the life of Jesus may be made visible in our mortal flesh . . . So we do not lose heart. Even though our outer nature is wasting away, our inner nature is being renewed day by day (2 Cor 4:7–11; 16).

And Paul shares with the church at Philippi his own story of coming to consider his accomplishments apart from Christ to be worthless compared to "the surpassing value of knowing Christ Jesus (his) Lord" (3:8). Rather than pursuing a right relationship with God on his own by striving to conform to God's law, Paul seeks a righteousness that comes from God through his trusting in Christ. By counting everything other than Christ as "rubbish," (v. 8), Paul models dying to himself. And he also models a desire to rise to new life. He says,

> I want to know Christ and the power of his resurrection and the sharing of his sufferings by becoming like him in his death, if somehow I may attain the resurrection from the dead. Not that I have already obtained this or have already reached the goal; but I press on to make it my own, because Christ Jesus has made me his own. Beloved, I do not consider that I have made it my own; but this one thing I do: forgetting what lies behind and straining forward to what lies ahead, I press on toward the goal for the prize of the heavenly call of God in Christ Jesus. (3:10–14)

Paul has provided soul pilgrims with an inspiring example of dying and rising through the power of Christ's resurrection life.

Jennifer and I experienced a purely natural version of the dying and rising phenomenon on the Camino every day. As I said above, our dying to ourselves consisted partly in our resisting various urges to delay our departure, slow down on the trail, or even stop frequently for rest and refreshment along the way. As a result of our resolve to stick to our rigorous schedule, we not only arrived at our daily destinations early enough to spend the afternoon and evening relaxing and recuperating, we also found ourselves the next morning with renewed strength, energy, and motivation for the journey ahead of us. And to the extent that we followed this pattern on a daily basis, our endurance and enthusiasm increased—thereby empowering us even more for the remainder of our trip.

I continue to hope and pray for a similar but supernatural pattern of this sort to increase in my soul pilgrimage. At this point my petitions are for a growing desire to prize God's program over my own. To the extent that happens, I'll be better able to pursue God's plan with confidence and enjoyment. I'll be more open to the resurrection life God offers. And I'll be better able to enjoy God more regularly and deeply.

Soul Pilgrim Reflection Questions

Whose agenda drives your daily routine? Yours or God's? Or some of each? What can you do to move gradually toward decreasing your focus on yourself and increasing your attention to God?

Trusting and Obeying

During the stage of asking, searching, and knocking, a soul pilgrim turns to God to request help for the journey. Some of that help will come in the form of decreasing self-preoccupation and increasing desire for service to and life with God—the purifying process of dying to self and rising to God. Pilgrims who go through these two stages will be in a position to respond to the Spirit's illumination of God's guiding word with trust and obedience. Some older soul pilgrims may remember the following hymn that affirms the importance of this stage:

> When we walk with the Lord in the light of His Word,
> What a glory He sheds on our way!
> While we do His good will, He abides with us still,
> And with all who will trust and obey.
>
> *Refrain:*
>
> Trust and obey, for there's no other way
> To be happy in Jesus, but to trust and obey.[1]

Notice the lyrics state that God will abide with those who trust and obey him and the refrain indicates that happiness in Jesus requires trust and obedience. In other words, this stage is needed to reach the fourth and final stage of drawing near to God to taste and see that he is good. Trust and obedience are needed for loving union and communion with God. And this is the soul pilgrim's ultimate daily and lifelong destination.

Trust and obedience are closely related. Just as asking, searching, and knocking are all forms of petition, and dying and rising are two necessary parts of one process, trusting and obeying are two sides of the same coin. If we trust God, we're willing to obey him. And if we obey God, we're showing we trust him. Trusting God involves knowing he loves us and will be faithful to bring about what's best for us. So, if we say we trust him but then hesitate to do what he says, we show by our failure to act we don't really trust him after all. Similarly, if we do what he says even when we're not sure whether we trust him, we show by our behavior that we actually do trust him after all.

As Jennifer mentioned in one of her journal entries, our Camino was a mix of the known and the unknown. It was a blend of the expected and the unexpected. Our pre-trip research provided us with general information about the Camino Francés. And our guidebooks and maps gave us more specific orientation and direction. So, to some extent, we knew what we were getting into and we knew what to expect. But as we set out on the path

---

1. Lyrics by John H. Sammis, 1887.

each day, there was a lot we didn't know and much we couldn't anticipate. We had never been to northern Spain before. And of course, we didn't have a crystal ball to see into the future. So, our pilgrimage necessarily involved trust—faith in various people we had never met (most importantly the authors who wrote the guidebooks, the cartographers who drew the maps, and the workers who set up the signs). It also involved obedience—conformity to their guidance and directions.

But even when we relied and acted on these valuable tools, things didn't always work out the way we thought they would. Sometimes we misunderstood the instructions. Other times the information was misleading or even mistaken. I already told the story of our getting off course for a while in the city of Ponferrada because our hotel proprietor had given us bad advice. On another occasion, there was a mismatch between our reading of an otherwise trusted resource and what actually happened to us. This disparity between our expectations and our experience occurred the sixteenth day of our Camino—the day we walked from Las Herrerías to Triacastela via the little mountain hamlet of O Cebreiro. We knew from the Michelin guide the stretch from Las Herrerías to O Cebreiro would be the longest climb with the most elevation gain of our entire trip: over five miles long and two thousand feet up. The map in the guidebook made it look like it was all mostly downhill from O Cebreiro to Triacastela (another thirteen miles). As Jennifer related in the journal entry at the beginning of this chapter, we were surprised to discover there were still a couple of steep climbs on that part of our hike (up to San Roque and then to Alto do Poio). What had looked like minor bumps on the map were actually challenging inclines.

Of course, the soul pilgrim guidebook is the Bible and the soul pilgrim guide is the Holy Spirit—both completely trustworthy. But soul pilgrims still have to be careful to understand correctly what God is saying to them through his Word and Spirit. That's another reason the practice of prayer and the posture of openness to God are crucial preparation for trust and obedience. If we ask God for direction, we can expect his guidance. If we set aside our plans in favor of his, we'll want to follow his lead. If we desire to put his will into practice, we'll be inclined to comply confidently with his teaching. And if we keep Jesus's commandments, we'll abide in his love (John 15:10a).

I'm currently at a point in my soul pilgrimage where it seems that what I don't know exceeds what I do. At this writing the world is still in the grip of the COVID-19 pandemic. Though scientists have developed vaccines and pharmaceutical companies have produced them, governments are facing serious logistical challenges distributing them. So, people can't be sure when they'll get them. In the meantime, countries around the world are enduring the economic fallout of the pandemic as a result of lockdowns, stay-at-home orders, and business closures. And in the United States, there is deep political division and racial unrest. We're faced with an unprecedented combination of health, economic, political, and social crises.

In the midst of these crises, the Christian church is hampered by government prohibitions of in-person indoor corporate worship. Though my local church has managed to carry on via video and outdoor services, there are many members of our congregation I haven't seen since the pandemic started. And it's challenging to carry out our mission as a result. But this is a time when the members of the body of Christ need to trust God for their own well-being and to obey his call to care for those who are suffering. Though circumstances are dire, the work of God's kingdom continues. But I find myself hesitant to trust God and reluctant to obey him. For one thing, COVID-19 prevention measures like social distancing make in-person service and ministry more challenging. But also, my desire for self-preservation tends to interfere with my readiness to respond to God's call. Perhaps you've experienced something similar.

Fortunately, the Spirit is available to help us. Even if we find ourselves not wanting or able to trust the Spirit (because of fear or doubt) or obey the Spirit (because of selfishness or pride), if we *want* the desire and ability to trust and obey, we can ask the Spirit to change our hearts accordingly. In the Gospel of Mark, we learn about a father whose son had an unclean spirit that prevented the boy from speaking, convulsed him, and dashed him to the ground. The father brought his son to Jesus and said, "if you are able to do anything, have pity on us and help us." Jesus answered him by saying, "If you are able!—All things can be done for the one who believes." And the father's response was, "I believe; help my unbelief!" (9:22–24). Though the father was initially unable to have full confidence in Jesus's ability to heal his son, he wanted to have such complete trust, and asked Jesus to help him believe. This father provides a good model for soul pilgrims to follow.

> ## Soul Pilgrim Reflection Questions
>
> Are you finding it hard to trust and obey God? If so, what steps can you take to secure the Spirit's help on this stage of your soul pilgrimage?

Drawing near to God to Taste and See That He Is Good

As I've been saying, the goal of a soul pilgrimage is closer union with God—ideally, intimate loving communion. But this ideal pilgrimage goal can't be *fully* attained by soul pilgrims if there's either any distance between them and God or if they have any uncertainty about their relationship with God. That's why the stage pilgrims must attain before this ultimate destination can be reached involves approaching God in a condition that will make secure intimacy with God possible. In the last chapter, we discussed how soul pilgrims need to overcome both active resistance and indifference to make progress on their journeys. They need to make the right kind of move in a Godward direction in order for God to be willing and able (without overriding their freedom) to move revealingly in their direction.

Such a pilgrimage move would involve a fulfillment of the divine promise recorded in the book of James: "Draw near to God, and he will draw near to you" (4:8a). The second half of the verse indicates what pilgrims need to do to enable this to happen: "Cleanse your hands, you sinners, and purify your hearts, you double-minded" (4:8b). Pilgrims can't continue their soul pilgrimages toward God when their hands are dirtied by sinful activities and their hearts are divided by devotion (even partial devotion) to counterfeit gods (idols).

James may have had Psalm 24 in mind:

> Who shall ascend the hill of the Lord? And who shall stand in his holy place? Those who have clean hands and pure hearts, who do not lift up their souls to what is false, and do not swear deceitfully. They will receive blessing from the Lord, and vindication from the God of their salvation. Such is the company of those who seek him, who seek the face of the God of Jacob. (Ps 24:3–6)

According to the psalmist, pilgrims who seek God's face and want to stand in God's holy place to see it will have to ascend the hill of the Lord; they'll need to draw near to God. But desires for such a direct encounter with God will remain unrealized unless they first refrain from wrongdoing (have clean hands), acquire a godly character (have pure hearts), refuse to worship and serve anyone but God (do not lift up their souls to what is false), and avoid being dishonest (do not swear deceitfully). Pilgrims who meet these conditions will receive both blessing and vindication from the Lord.

Christian soul pilgrims won't have to meet these conditions on their own. That's a good thing, since it would be impossible for any human being to do so. Soul pilgrims can depend on the guidance and provision of the Holy Spirit to enable them to satisfy each of these four conditions. It will be helpful to see how this can work by considering each of them in the reverse order from how the psalmist presents them.

Soul pilgrims can ask the Spirit to help them be honest—both with themselves and with God—about their weaknesses, deficiencies, and failings. Such honesty will require them to humble themselves and be sorry about their sin. As James says, "God opposes the proud, but gives grace to the humble. Submit yourselves therefore to God . . . Lament and mourn and weep. Let your laughter be turned into mourning and your joy into dejection. Humble yourselves before the Lord, and he will exalt you" (4:6–7; 9–10). God promises to reward honest, contrite confession with merciful forgiveness and cleansing: "If we confess our sins, he who is faithful and just will forgive us our sins and cleanse us from all unrighteousness" (1 John 1:9).

In addition, soul pilgrims can rely on the Spirit to enable them to worship and serve only God rather than any earthly treasure, idol, or counterfeit god such as money, power, prestige, or sensuality. This is an important step, because a pilgrim can experience intimate loving communion with God only when he or she gives God his or her complete devotion. As Jesus says in the Sermon on the Mount, "No one can serve two masters; for a slave will either hate the one and love the other, or be devoted to the one and despise the other. You cannot serve God and wealth" (Matt 6:24). Serving two masters is as impossible as sharing a marriage bed with more than one spouse. Perfect and lasting loving intimacy can't withstand divided loyalties and affections.

Next, soul pilgrims can work with the Spirit over time to cultivate a godly, righteous, Christlike character that will enable them to sustain their singleness of devotion to God and their dedication to God's will. Only living by the Spirit and being guided by the Spirit will enable them to manifest the fruit of the Spirit (love, joy, peace, patience, kindness, generosity, faithfulness, gentleness, and self-control; Gal 5:22, 25). Only the reliance on the Spirit will enable soul pilgrims to "be perfect as (their) heavenly Father is perfect" (Matt 5:48) so that they'll be able even to love their enemies and pray for those who persecute them (Matt 5:44).

And finally, as the Spirit continues to enable soul pilgrims to be honest, to worship God only, and to grow in Christlikeness, they can also walk with the indwelling Spirit of Christ in such a way as for the Spirit to enable them to "fulfill the just requirement of the law" (Rom 8:4), please God (Rom

8:8), and live as a result of putting the "deeds of the body" to death (Rom 8:13). What makes a pilgrim's partnership with the Spirit possible for these purposes is that "those who live according to the Spirit set their minds on the things of the Spirit" (Rom 8:5b).

The soul pilgrim destination can be characterized in terms of Psalm 34:8—"O taste and see that the Lord is good; happy are those who take refuge in him." The soul pilgrim's ultimate goal is to be united in a loving communion with the Triune God so intimate that he or she will be in a position to experience God's goodness without any intermediary—just as one can enjoy a delicious meal by putting food directly into one's mouth and savoring its flavor. Such an unmediated experience of God's perfect loving character will put soul pilgrims in a position to see for themselves that God is supremely good. And their ongoing experience of God's goodness and love will become a happy refuge for them. It will keep their souls safe and secure. And to the extent pilgrims are able to sustain their confidence that nothing "will be able to separate us from the love of God in Christ Jesus our Lord" (Rom 8:39), they'll be truly blessed. In his *City of God*, St. Augustine says true blessedness or felicity is "the product of two causes working in conjunction, the untroubled enjoyment of the changeless Good, which is God, together with the certainty of remaining in him for eternity, a certainty that admits of no doubt or hesitation, no mistake or disappointment."[2]

The four conditions required for the full attainment of this last soul pilgrim stage are like the four requirements for achieving the *Compostela*—certificate of completion—on the Camino de Santiago. First, pilgrims must be *honest* in saying they did the last hundred kilometers on foot or horseback (or the last two hundred kilometers by bicycle). Dishonest pilgrims may get a certificate, but they won't get the satisfaction of knowing their pilgrimage was genuine. Second, they must be motivated by *religious* (or spiritual) rather than recreational reasons for engaging in the pilgrimage. Their walk must have been for God rather than just for themselves. Third, they must be *disciplined* in their collection of two *selos* (stamps) on their *credencial* (pilgrim passport) each day of the last hundred (or two hundred) kilometers—preferably from churches, hostels, monasteries, and cathedrals (rather than town halls, cafés, etc.). They must govern their behavior in a way that conforms to Camino regulations. And finally (an implicit requirement), they must have a sufficiently good *character* to enable them to achieve this honesty, devotional orientation, and right action. Ideally, Camino pilgrims will be morally and spiritually fit as well as physically fit.

---

2. Augustine, *City of God*, 444.

I'm pleased to report that Jennifer and I satisfied all four conditions for earning our *Compostela*. However, I continue to struggle to live up to their analogues on my soul pilgrimage. Of course, I'm not expecting to earn, merit, or deserve closer union with God. And I have no hope of deeper communion with him by simply trying harder to be honest, worshipful, Christlike, and righteous. Rather, I continue to pray that the Holy Spirit would enable me to become progressively more open to his works of grace in my mind, heart, soul, and life. I know God does the work of transforming soul pilgrims. Our task is to surrender, submit, and yield to this work. And the means by which we can position ourselves best for this purpose are to ask, search, and knock, to die to self and rise to God, and to trust and obey. As the Spirit enables me to do these things, I hope and pray that I will more faithfully engage in the practices that enable pilgrims to ascend the hill of the Lord to enter his temple and behold his face (the practices of honesty, devotion, purity, and righteousness).

> **Soul Pilgrim Reflection Questions**
>
> Which of the four conditions for deeper union with God do you need to focus on the most? Do you need to be more *honest* with him about your failings? Do you need to set aside something in your life that is competing with God for your allegiance? Do you need to look more to Jesus as an example to follow? Do you need to make better choices about how to live and act?

Practice

Choose a day to implement the four-stage soul pilgrimage routine I've described in this chapter. Start the day by praying that the Holy Spirit will guide and empower you throughout the day. Ask the Spirit to identify a specific area in your life in which you need to die to yourself and your selfish agenda so you can rise to new life and put God's will first—by the power God used to raise Jesus from the dead. As you seek to surrender this area of your life to God, pray that the Spirit will enable you to trust him to empower you to sustain your resolve. Pray as well that the Spirit will energize you to obey God's will once you've prioritized it over your own. Ask the Spirit to help you do all these things with an attitude of humble honesty, sincere worship, openness to transformation, and commitment to righteousness. Finally, pray that all of these Spirit-guided and Spirit-empowered efforts would enable you to enjoy communion with God in such a way as to experience his loving goodness.

As you go through the day engaging in these soul pilgrimage stages, you may want to keep in mind what Paul says to the Romans:

> Therefore, since we are justified by faith, we have peace with God through our Lord Jesus Christ, through whom we have obtained access to this grace in which we stand; and we boast in our hope of sharing the glory of God. And not only that, but we also boast in our sufferings, knowing that suffering produces endurance, and endurance produces character, and character produces hope, and hope does not disappoint us, because God's love has been poured into our hearts through the Holy Spirit that has been given to us. (5:1–5)

Paul is describing a similar soul pilgrimage pattern that starts with a challenge like dying to self (sufferings) and ends with an experience of God's goodness (God's love poured into our hearts through the Holy Spirit).

8

The Practices I
What Can You Do Alone to Know God Better?

October 6, 2018: Alto do Poio to Triacastela (from Jennifer's journal)

"Mommy, where do the birds go when it rains?" The memory of our five-year-old daughter looking through the living room window comes to mind. As a winter storm raged outside, she missed watching the northern bobwhites flit between branches and light on the bird feeder.

We are soaking wet. As far as the eye can see, Jim and I are alone on the Camino. The other pilgrims seem to have flown away. Where did they go? How did they find shelter? An hour ago, a light rain became a torrential downpour. Now the rain falls so hard it resembles sheets of water. My glasses have become a blurry mess, limiting my field of vision.

We shelter ourselves under a tree and I tip my umbrella against the rain. We huddle over a map to get our bearings. Jim guesstimates we're an hour from our final destination. We gauge the distance to the next town. "We should be very close to the tiny town of Filloval," Jim says.

Let us find it soon. My grumbling stomach reminds me I'm hungry. I'm hoping for even a modest café in that town.

As we fling ourselves back onto the path, I wonder if the gray mass I see through the driving rain is a building. Perhaps the café we're hoping for?

"Yes," Jim confirms. He sees it too. We pick up our pace, practically missing a wood-carved sign on our right with the seashell symbol, welcoming us to Filloval. We run the remaining hundred feet in the downpour to reach the building—a café entrance indeed.

We duck inside to find several pilgrims waiting for the rain to stop. Jim and I drip water onto the floor, too wet to speak. The fare is meager. Jim arranges to purchase a slice of bread and a slice of cheese for each of us, neither of which is on the menu. How many times has his knowledge of Spanish paved the way for us? Once again, I say a silent prayer of thanks for his dedication to learning the language. While the proprietor retrieves our order, we consider waiting out the storm there.

"I'd like to beat nightfall," Jim says. "We must be within an hour of Triacastela."

"We can hardly get any wetter than we already are," I agree. Removing all our rain gear seems like an enormous undertaking to me. Especially because we'd need to put it all back on. The cheese and stale bread satisfy my hunger and renew my resolve. As we step outside, the proprietor mops up the pool of water we've left on his floor. With his other hand, he shuts the door behind us.

Back in the downpour, I wonder whether we could have prepared any better for the rain? Before setting out this morning we dutifully heeded the weather forecast and packed accordingly. We're using the ponchos, hoods, umbrellas, gaiters, and knapsack covers we brought. In spite of our soggy state, each of these items has served us well. I'm pretty sure the layer of clothing closest to my skin is still dry, but in my current state, it's hard to tell!

An hour later, a canopy of trees on the Camino opens out to a wider trail. Then as suddenly as the hard rain came on, it abates. And, after we round a bend five minutes later, the town of Triacastela comes into full view. The daylight diminishes, but we'll make it ahead of sundown. The sight of our destination releases a kind of permission within me. I realize the heaviness of wet fabric on my skin. My legs are burdensome weights, but they move me forward. When we reach the entrance to our *albergue*, the rain stops.

Later we enjoy bread, *pimientos de Padrón*, Galician soup, and a local red wine in a tented restaurant. The autumn evening air has a damp wood scent. It wafts into the eating area, creating a cozy atmosphere. We relax in the comfort of chairs, dry clothes, and full stomachs. We buy chocolate at a local market to take back to our room. Our swollen feet and aching legs remind us of a good day's work.

Our Camino Pilgrimage Story: Daily Practices

As we followed the signs posted on the Camino and also took advantage of resources for our journey provided along the way, we were continuously directed and empowered by these indicators and items to make gradual progress toward our destination: the cathedral at Santiago de Compostela. From the very beginning of our journey, and as time went on, we became more and more settled into regular daily patterns and routines that enabled us to get closer and closer to our goal. These routines involved four main tasks: (1) getting our bearings, (2) replenishing our supplies, (3) continuing to walk with the orientation and strength provided by these things, and (4) resting. And we would repeat each of these routines throughout the day on an "as needed" basis. With respect to task (1), we would periodically check our map, look at our guidebook, ask a local or pilgrim for directions, and/or look for Camino signs. With respect to task (2), we would routinely recharge our phones, put on our hiking clothes, repack our backpacks, buy food, refill our water containers, and get out our trekking poles. As for task (3), we would just keep walking (and talking and praying). And finally, task (4) involved stopping to rest our weary legs and feet, using a restroom (or a convenient hidden trailside spot), showering, and sleeping. A more general way to think of our pattern is this: "Prepare, Eat, Walk, Rest, Repeat!"

This simple daily pattern or routine helped us to keep our primary goal central in our minds, enabled us to set aside distractions that would have slowed us down and/or taken us off course, and empowered us to make good use of the Camino's guidance and provision. Of course, there were unexpected obstacles and delays that came up along the way. And these unforeseen occurrences disrupted our routine. An example is our inability to find a grocery store or restaurant open between 4:00 and 8:00 PM after walking eighteen miles to the city of Ponferrada. We were hungry and tired! Fortunately, after walking around town for a while, we came across a little shop where we were able to purchase bread, cheese, fish, and wine from a helpful and friendly merchant. Another example is the time I left one of our guidebooks at a store where we stopped to use the restroom. We walked another mile or so before I realized it was missing, and I had to leave Jennifer waiting for me while I backtracked to retrieve it. It was strange to retrace my steps against the tide of pilgrims all walking toward me—some glancing at me with quizzical looks. The Camino is unidirectional and I was going the wrong way! Fortunately, I found the book, and before too long we were back to our routine.

Daily Individual Practices for Soul Pilgrims

In both this chapter and the next we'll explore some routines soul pilgrims can learn to implement to facilitate their growing in knowledge of and intimate friendship with God. We'll look at some *individual* practices in this chapter and some *communal* practices in the next.

As we think together about the character and application of these practices, let's keep in mind that our ultimate goal in employing them is knowledge of God in the form of direct personal encounter with God. And this direct personal encounter with God is a goal we're striving to achieve, not just for a moment but for the course of our entire lives. Our soul pilgrim aim is to do what we can to make our relationship with God our central focus. So, one purpose for these individual practices is for our exercise of them to make our relationship with God more and more a priority in our lives.

But more than that, soul pilgrims should strive for the quality of their relationship with God to improve in such a way that it becomes a *deeper and stronger* friendship, companionship, and partnership over time. The desired result is that our relationship with God will become our most important relationship as well as our deepest and strongest relationship. What will make it our most valued relationship will be that we will love God more than anyone or anything else. What will make it a progressively deeper and stronger relationship is that our love for God will grow more fully and become more secure and stable.

As I pointed out in chapter 3, growth in personal relationships requires both spending time together and doing things together. That's why I've characterized a soul pilgrim's relationship with God as both a companionship (being together) and a partnership (doing things together). Ongoing companionship and partnership facilitate growth in mutual love and growth in mutual knowledge (though since God already loves and knows each of us maximally, we soul pilgrims are the ones who will grow in these ways). Both being with a person and doing things with a person provide opportunities for mutual self-manifestation that can contribute to direct personal knowledge of one's companion and partner. And as I said in chapter 3, these opportunities increase as both parties make themselves directly, communicatively, and lovingly available to each other.

We've seen that God will make himself available to soul pilgrims in these ways to the extent they make themselves available to God freely, humbly, trustingly, openly, willingly, and obediently. So, the primary purpose of the practices we'll survey in this chapter and the next is to enable soul pilgrims to grow in their willingness and ability to make themselves submissively available to God in these ways. Since our natural fallen sinful disposition is to be resistant or indifferent to God, our learning to engage in these sorts of practices on a regular basis is necessary for us to be able to overcome this fundamental sinful disposition and to acquire instead a basic disposition to surrender to God gratefully, enthusiastically, and persistently.

> ### Soul Pilgrim Reflection Questions
>
> As you look back over your life, what individual practices do you recall engaging in for the purpose of growing closer to God? Were they effective for this purpose? Why or why not?

Spiritual Virtues and Spiritual Disciplines

In a nutshell, the soul pilgrim practices we'll discuss in this chapter and the next will involve exercising our God-given intellectual, moral, and spiritual capacities for the purpose of acquiring and cultivating the spiritual "virtues" needed for knowing God and growing in the knowledge of God. A human virtue is a skill you can come to have by training. Acquiring a virtue is like learning to play tennis or guitar or chess. And just as you can become an excellent tennis, guitar, or chess player by regular, disciplined practice, you can improve your exercise of a virtue in the same way. But unlike the specialized skills required for excelling in sports, music, or board games, virtues are general abilities to live well as a human being—regardless of your particular job or hobbies. And *spiritual soul pilgrim* virtues are general abilities to know, love, and serve God and others. As we've seen in previous chapters, it's important to have this know-how but difficult to get it, keep it, and use it well.[1]

The general area of human life in which soul pilgrim virtues apply is friendship with God involving companionship and partnership. Excellent functioning in this area involves the kind of submissive openness to God I described above. We need to acquire and cultivate this virtuous or excellent functioning because in our natural fallen sinful state we're opposed to God—stubbornly rebellious enemies of God or at least self-centered people indifferent to God. This sphere of human activity (active friendship with God) is thus challenging (though as I argued in chapter 2, *possible*); it

---

1. My characterization of human virtues in this paragraph is based on the definition provided by Roberts and Wood: "a human virtue is an acquired base of excellent functioning in some generically human sphere of activity that is challenging and important." Roberts and Wood, *Intellectual Virtues*, 59.

requires the self-denial and self-sacrifice (dying to ourselves) involved in putting God's agenda ahead of our own (when ours conflicts with God's)—especially when God's agenda requires that we love our enemies. And this sphere of human activity is both general and important. It's the sphere of activity God designed *all* human beings for, and our ultimate human fulfillment, well-being, and happiness depends essentially and fundamentally on our being able to engage in it fully and eternally (as we saw in chapter 1).

In sum, we'll be discussing the use of our *faculties* (natural God-given innate capacities or abilities) in our engagement in certain *practices* (both individual and communal) in order to cultivate the *virtues* (acquired character traits) needed to achieve important *good results* (especially knowledge of God and Christlikeness). In drawing here on our thinking about these things (faculties, practices, virtues, and goods), we'll be seeking to develop a way of thinking about spiritual knowledge that we can use to regulate our efforts to know God and to grow in the knowledge of God by means of perfecting the virtues needed for this purpose.

And the practices featured can also be thought of as "spiritual disciplines." According to Dallas Willard, a "discipline" is "any activity within our power that we engage in to enable us to do what we cannot do by direct effort."[2] He uses playing a musical instrument as an example. For instance, mastery of the violin requires years of regular and sustained training and practice. The first time a person picks up a violin, he or she is unable to play it. But after ongoing disciplined practice, he or she acquires and eventually perfects the ability. A *spiritual* discipline is a discipline aimed at the cultivation and improvement of a spiritual activity—such as engaging in companionship and partnership with God.

Ben Patterson likens the practice of spiritual disciplines to the activity of spreading our sails to catch the wind of the Spirit (see John 3:8). He says of these disciplines that "by engaging in them we position ourselves to give the Holy Spirit maximum access." He goes on to say that, "the spiritual disciplines do for our souls what a camera shutter does for the film inside. Strictly speaking, cameras don't make pictures. Only light makes pictures as it gains access to the film in the camera. A spiritual discipline positions our soul to receive the light that changes us into the image of Jesus Christ."[3] Though this analogy is outdated due to the advent and current dominance of digital photography, it's nonetheless apt. It highlights how our spiritual transformation is a combination of our proper receptivity and God's gracious work in our lives.

---

2. Willard, "Living a Transformed Life," 32.
3. Patterson, *He Has Made Me Glad*, 25.

Willard and Patterson also agree that though a Christian's exercising of spiritual disciplines takes *effort*, it doesn't have the effect of *earning* God's favor. There's nothing we sinful human beings can do to merit God's love, forgiveness, mercy, and salvation. All these good things are gifts God gives us out of his unmerited grace. But we need to make the right kinds of efforts—even to *work* appropriately—to constantly put ourselves in a place or position to enable God to do his undeserved gracious work in our lives without God's needing to override our God-given freedom. And as I said above, we need to take steps to acquire the virtues required for us to be able willingly to receive and benefit from God's loving and healing efforts on our behalf in our minds and hearts. As Paul urged the members of the Philippian church: "Work out your own salvation with fear and trembling; for it is God who is at work in you, enabling you both to will and to work for his good pleasure" (2:12–13).

> **Soul Pilgrim Reflection Questions**
>
> As you think about the practices you identified in response to the previous soul pilgrim reflection question, would you say that any of them have resulted in virtues—settled and automatic dispositions or habits? If so, how do they compare in your experience with the practices that haven't?

The Four Individual Soul Camino Practices

In this chapter, I'll focus on four daily individual practices: the Prayer of Examen, walking in the Spirit, lectio divina, and contemplative prayer. These four practices (or disciplines) correspond roughly to the four physical pilgrimage practices that compose the daily Camino routine pattern I mentioned above in our Camino story and Jennifer illustrated in her journal entry: Prepare, Walk, Eat, and Rest. Though the Prayer of Examen involves evaluative reflection on one's day with the Lord, it also provides a basis to prepare for the next day living with God. And walking in the Spirit is the metaphorical equivalent of walking the Camino. Lectio divina, a prayerful way of reading Scripture, is at least in part a way of feeding on God's Word. Finally, contemplative prayer provides a means of resting in the presence of God.

These four individual practices can also be categorized roughly into the mystical stage categories of conversion, purgation, illumination, and union. That's because the Prayer of Examen involves conversion (or turning) from our self-centered plans to God's; walking in the Spirit includes purging us from the works of the flesh and enlivening us to manifest the fruit of the Spirit; lectio divina enables us to be illumined by the Spirit through prayerful meditation on God's Word; and contemplative prayer provides us with enjoyable rest in union with God. What all these practices involve is an openness to God's manifestation in our lives through the presence and activity of the Holy Spirit.

In addition, this four-practice cycle consists in specific ways to implement the general routine I discussed in the previous chapter. The Prayer of Examen is a means to Ask, Search, and Knock (ASK), walking in the Spirit involves dying and rising, lectio divina provides a basis to trust and obey, and contemplative prayer prepares you to taste and see. The following table provides a summary of all these relationships.

Camino Routine	Prepare	Walk	Eat	Rest
Mystical Stage	Conversion	Purgation	Illumination	Union
General Practice	ASK	Dying & Rising	Trust & Obey	Taste & See
Specific Practice	Prayer of Examen	Walking in the Spirit	Lectio Divina	Contemplative Prayer

The daily soul pilgrimage routine starts with preparation. We turn to God and ask him for guidance for the day after hearing from the Spirit about how we lived the previous day. Then we walk into the day open to the purging or cleansing work of the Spirit by dying to ourselves and rising to resurrection life with God as we attempt to walk in the Spirit moment by moment. At some point during the day, we pause to eat—to be nourished and illumined by a prayerful reading of God's Word, which we take in trustingly and live out obediently. At the end of our day, we rest in loving union with God in such a way as to taste and see his goodness through contemplative prayer.

Though I've presented these practices in a certain order to explain how they're related to each other, soul pilgrims should feel welcome to engage in them as needed and as the Spirit leads. I've experimented with different patterns. You may think it makes sense for you to start your day with lectio divina to feed on God's Word so you'll have the resources to walk in the Spirit throughout the day. And if you have some passages of Scripture memorized, you can continue to "chew" on them as you walk. Also, it may suit you to pause midday for the Prayer of Examen followed by contemplative prayer. You can take a "spiritual siesta." The important thing is to make each of these practices a part of your daily routine.

Jennifer and I met pilgrims on the Camino who regularly skipped breakfast in order to leave well before sunrise as soon as they woke up (they had done all their planning and preparation the previous night). They wanted to do most of their walking during the cool of the morning and they hoped to reach the *albergue* of their choice early enough to secure a bed before other pilgrims had claimed all of them. Once they arrived at their destination, they read, rested, and chatted with other pilgrims. The more religious of them would also attend an afternoon or evening worship service. Though their routine was different than ours (we always had breakfast before we hit the road and made it a habit to rest a bit and check our guidebooks midday), their days included the same general Camino practices ours did.

> **Soul Pilgrim Reflection Questions**
>
> Have you tried any of these practices before—or ones like them? If so, what did you think and feel about them? What is your initial reaction to any that may be new to you?

The Prayer of Examen

St. Ignatius of Loyola (1491–1556), the founder of the Society of Jesus or Jesuits (1540) and the author of *The Spiritual Exercises* (1548), considered his Prayer of Examen to be so important that he required the members of his religious order to pray it twice a day—at noon and at the end of the day just before going to bed. The primary purpose of the prayer is to review one's day in the presence of God in preparation for the next day (or the next part of the day). Soul pilgrims can use it as a means to be mindful about and grateful for the ways God was present with and active in and through them during the day. And they can employ it for the purpose of humbly discerning how they fell short of fully trusting and obeying God throughout that time. Thus, the prayer can provide soul pilgrims with a basis for both grateful praise and humble confession. It provides a regular divine-human "relationship check" in conversation with God. Consequently, it's like setting aside time to get your bearings on a literal physical pilgrimage. And once you have your bearings (Where have I been? Where am I now?) you can plan and prepare for the next stage of your journey (Where am I going and how will I get there?).

Engaging in this practice can facilitate soul pilgrims' daily "dying and rising": turning from their self-centered (and perhaps self-absorbed) dispositions, habits, routines, and agendas and converting to God's self-sacrificially loving will, agenda, plans, and way of life. It provides a crucial tool that can enable soul pilgrims to pay attention to and reflect on how their pilgrimage is going and what their next steps should be. Without this practice—or one like it—soul pilgrims will likely be insufficiently aware of the progress (or regress) of their friendship with God over time. And a deficit in this awareness will likely prevent them from moving in the right direction in the best possible way. But a daily practice of deliberate review, reflection, evaluation, preparation, and planning will likely facilitate forward movement toward deeper knowledge of and partnership with God. More than that, making Examen a regular exercise will help soul pilgrims grow in spiritual virtue—in the way that a muscle develops through physical exercise. As a result, they'll become more loving companions of God and more cooperative partners with God.

Over time, practitioners of Examen have come up with a number of variations of this prayer exercise. And soul pilgrims should feel free to formulate a method, in conversation with the Holy Spirit, that best suits their temperament, personality, circumstances, needs, and desires. St. Ignatius's original version features five steps: (1) awareness, (2) gratitude, (3) emotions, (4) noticing, and (5) tomorrow.[4] The acronym AGENT will help you remember these parts. And it will remind you that the prayer is designed to help you be more *active* in your growth as a soul pilgrim.

The awareness step involves pilgrims tuning in to the Holy Spirit's presence with them and asking the Spirit for illumination as they review their day to see when and where God was present to (or absent from) them and when and where they were present to (or absent from) God. Pilgrims engage in the gratitude step by thanking God for whatever they're grateful for as they recall and process the day's events. As for the emotions step, pilgrims should go over these events again to identify how they felt in each moment and then discern what these feelings might indicate about how God is working in them and how they may need to be more cooperative with God's work in their lives. The noticing step requires pilgrims to choose a specific part of the day or a feeling—one that stands out to them—in order to pray about it (by means of prayers of thanksgiving, confession, petition, and/or intercession). Finally, the tomorrow step is taken when pilgrims look ahead to the opportunities and challenges they're likely to face going forward. This is the point at which they should ask the Spirit to be present

---

4. These are my labels for Ignatius's ideas.

to them, to guide them, and to help them when the time comes for them to spend the next day walking in and with the Spirit.

I confess my own use of the Prayer of Examen has been sporadic. For many years, I've had a well-established habit of spending time with the Lord each morning in preparation for the coming day. After learning about Examen, I resolved to add it to my daily schedule. At first, I ambitiously planned to practice it both midday and right before going to bed. But I quickly discovered it was difficult enough to pause once each day for this holy time of review. And even that more limited frequency has proved elusive. I've become painfully aware how true it is that old habits die hard. In my case, once I've finished my morning devotions, my to-do list becomes my master—and even writing "Prayer of Examen" down as one of my tasks for the day doesn't guarantee I'll end up doing it.

But when I *do* pray this prayer, I'm richly rewarded. For a few moments I emerge from the river of Chronos (clock) time, which has been carrying me in its relentless flow. And I spend calm Kairos time—time to reflect on opportunities for decisive action in my soul pilgrimage—with the Holy Spirit. The benefits are many. I'm aware of God, grateful to him, sensitive to how I feel about my day so far, able to discern the significance of what I've done and what's happened to me, and open to God's guidance going forward. I continue to hope and pray my practice of this valuable spiritual exercise will become more regular.

Why were members of Ignatius's order so accomplished in this practice when my employment of it is still largely aspirational? And why did I do so much better with the preparation stage every day on my literal Camino pilgrimage than I do daily on my soul pilgrimage? I think the main reason is that in the Society of Jesus and on the Camino, pilgrims have a communal context that facilitates their pilgrimage practices. When everyone around you is doing the same thing, it's easier for you to follow suit. For this reason, even though the Prayer of Examen is an individual exercise, soul pilgrims would be well advised to find a community of others who are also practicing it. This community could be a local church fellowship, a small Bible study group, or an accountability partner (see chapter 9).

Soul Pilgrim Reflection Questions

Would you like to make the Prayer of Examen a daily habit? If so, when and where will you engage in it? And what will remind you to do it? If you'd rather not adopt this practice, what alternative type of

> prayer would you consider employing to get your soul pilgrimage bearings on a regular basis?

Walking in the Spirit

Paul tells the Galatians to "walk in (or 'by') the Spirit, and do not (or 'you will not') fulfill the desires of the flesh" (5:16; my translation). I include these parenthetical alternative translations, since there are multiple ways to interpret Paul's wording here in English. The NRSV uses the word *live* rather than *walk*. The Greek word is a form of *peripatein*, which literally means "to walk," but Paul is clearly using it metaphorically, so "live" is appropriate. Since soul pilgrims are on a pilgrimage, they are "walking" toward deeper knowledge of God. That is, they are living a life aimed primarily at attaining that destination or goal. And we have been talking about how soul pilgrims are accompanied by God the Holy Spirit on their journey. Soul pilgrims are walking together with God through life. And as they walk together, the soul pilgrim's task is to walk *in* and/or *by* the Spirit. In chapter 5, we saw that John 17 reports that Jesus prayed to the Father that there would be a relationship of mutual containment between those who believe in him and the Triune God. And Paul also tells his Roman readers that, "you are not in the flesh; you are in the Spirit, since the Spirit of God dwells in you" (8:9a). Soul pilgrims are in the Triune God, in Christ, and in the Spirit. So, they can walk, or live, in the Spirit.

But soul pilgrims should also walk or live *by* the Spirit. They should walk by means of the Spirit's guidance and provision. When they're led and empowered by the Spirit, they "will not fulfill the desire of the flesh." That is, they won't end up doing things harmful to themselves, hurtful to others, and dishonoring to God (the "deeds" of the flesh—the actions of people who follow their own path in their own power rather than God's path with God's power).

How do soul pilgrims walk by the Spirit? Paul says the way to walk by the Spirit is to "keep in step with" the Spirit. That's a good way to translate the Greek word *stoichein*, a form of which Paul uses in verse 25: "If we live by the Spirit, let us also *keep in step with* the Spirit" (my translation). The NRSV uses "walk" instead of "keep in step with." But the latter is more specific, and it helps soul pilgrims know *how* to walk by the Spirit. The word *stoichein* is used in contexts having to do with soldiers marching together in battle ranks following a leader. And of course, it's very important that soldiers walk in a straight line or row (*stoichos*) and that they march in the cadence or rhythm set by their leader. If they get out of step by walking to their own beat or in their own direction, they're likely to disrupt their company's ability to work together to achieve their leader's goals effectively. They could get hurt, they could hurt another solider, and they could dishonor their leader.

So how do soul pilgrims keep in step with the Spirit? They *attend* to the Spirit's directions, *ask* the Spirit for the power to resist their desire to go their own way (due, for instance, to their pride or fear), *rely* on the Spirit's provision (of humility and/or courage, for example), *trust* the Spirit, and *obey* the Spirit. In sum, they walk by the Spirit in trust and obedience—and as a result, they're purged (cleansed) of their sinful habits and strengthened in their godly ones. To switch the analogy, soul pilgrims walk by the Spirit by learning how to plug into the Spirit's energy source. And they learn, over time, to stay plugged in. They *abide* in Christ's Spirit and in his love. Still another analogy: soul pilgrims learn to breath properly while they walk by the Spirit: they breathe out their selfishness and breathe in the power to be self-sacrificially loving; they breathe out what could destroy them and they breathe in what will give them true life. And this analogy is appropriate, since the Hebrew and Greek words for "Spirit" (*ruach* and *pneuma* respectively) can also be translated "breath."

On the Camino, walking is the main activity. It's the primary means by which pilgrims make progress toward their destination. Of course, pilgrims need guidance to walk in the right direction. And they need energy to walk well. They also need regular refreshing pauses to remember why they're walking. That is, they need to prepare, eat, and rest. But walking is what gets pilgrims closer to their desired end. They engage in these other three activities in order to facilitate their forward movement. As Jennifer wrote in the journal entry that appears at the beginning of chapter 4, "My work today is to walk the Camino." And indeed, walking was our primary focus. And we enjoyed it!

I wish I could say the same for walking in the Spirit on my soul pilgrimage. Don't get me wrong. I *want* it to be my all-consuming passion throughout each day. I want to make practicing the presence of God and abiding in Christ while walking in the Spirit my main priority moment by moment. But the world (fallen cultural influences), the flesh (my old sinful self), and the devil (the enemy of our souls) constantly conspire to trip me up. As a result, I continue to think of this soul pilgrimage practice as something I aspire to do (I keep putting it on my daily to-do list) rather than something I am accomplishing (I rarely put a check by it at the end of the day).

Why do I struggle to make this practice a regular habit? Why have I been able for many years to start each day with a time of private devotion and yet spend the rest of the day inattentive to God—for the most part?

Though I've memorized 1 Thessalonians 5:16–18 ("Rejoice always, pray without ceasing, give thanks in all circumstances; for this is the will of God in Christ Jesus for you."), I've fallen short of putting it into practice. As a result, I've been missing out on an opportunity for deeper knowledge of God. And sometimes I feel I'm leading a double life: I'm a spiritual Dr. Jekyll in the morning and a selfish Mr. Hyde by the end of the day (but fortunately without the criminal behavior!). I've given God part of my day so far. But I hope and pray to become more willing and able to give him the rest.

I can think of two reasons I fall short here. First, I tend to be task-oriented rather than person-oriented. Second, when I'm engaged in my tasks, my attention is entirely absorbed by them—to the exclusion of everything else (I'm a bad multitasker!). What I need to do instead is to prioritize relationships over activities. And I need to see my activities as ways of serving others—God and the people in my life. I also need to practice being mindful of the Holy Spirit as I engage in these person-serving tasks. Would that involve multitasking? I don't think so. It would be like doing something with another human being. Just as Jennifer and I can walk and talk at the same time, I think soul pilgrims can engage in their daily activities while mindful of God. Sometimes that attentiveness will involve talking to God and other times it will take the form of just being aware that God is with them—even while they're talking to a fellow human being.

In spite of my many failures in this area, when I *have* succeeded in keeping in step with the Spirit for parts of my day, I've been richly rewarded. The reward comes primarily in the form of ongoing communion with God, but it also includes more meaningful connections with the other people with whom I interact throughout the day. The bottom line is that walking in the Spirit focuses my attention outward toward others rather than inward toward myself or downward toward my tasks. And when I *am* engaged in my tasks, I'm able to see them as instruments of service to God and fellow humans rather than as ends in themselves. As a result, I feel freer and more fully alive. As I reflect on my experiences of walking in the Spirit, I realize they involve living life the way God intends—giving oneself away to him and others for his glory.

The practice of walking in the Spirit is the primary locus of the kind of experimental practical theology I discussed in chapter 3. While soul pilgrims are walking in the Spirit, it may seem to them the Spirit is directing them to do something (such as share the gospel, spend time with a needy person, give money to a worthy cause, ask a friend for forgiveness, or work for peace and justice in a particular way). The pilgrim may have a number of reasons, based on factors difficult to identify and articulate, for thinking the *Spirit* is directing him or her to do this. The pilgrim may have a strong and persistent conviction it would be good or even obligatory to do this. And the pilgrim may think it unlikely he or she would have considered doing it without prompting from an outside source—given the pilgrim's characteristic tendency to be more self-absorbed. Additionally, the pilgrim may have an internal conscious experience of something best described as an encouraging "prompting" or "nudge" (or in the case of sensing a direction from the Spirit *not* to do something, a warning or caution of some kind). Finally, the pilgrim may be aware that the apparently Spirit-suggested action is just the kind of thing God would want the pilgrim to do on the basis of what God teaches in the Bible.

So, the pilgrim forms the hypothesis that God wants him or her to perform this action. And on the basis of this hypothesis, the pilgrim asks the Spirit for the resources to do so (e.g., courage, humility, self-sacrificial love) and the ability to trust that the Spirit will provide these supernatural resources. Then the pilgrim obeys. And on the basis of the outcome, the pilgrim may be able to confirm the Spirit did indeed call him or her to engage in this course of action. If so, the pilgrim will be better able to discern the Spirit's direction, trust the Spirit's provision, and obey the Spirit on the basis of this direction and provision going forward. If not, then the pilgrim may have learned something that will make him or her better able to discern the Spirit's "voice" in the future.

This practice will help soul pilgrims get to know God better. In particular, it will enable them to get to know God's values and purposes better by means of their participation with God in God's chosen projects. Of course, pilgrims will already know, at least theoretically, what God wants to happen in the world. The Bible is full of instruction about God's general will, purposes, and plans. But the advantage for pilgrims of walking in the Spirit in this experimental way is they can learn from experience by partnering with God what some specific ways are God wants his general goals to be implemented. And since God's agenda is driven by God's gracious and loving self-sacrificial nature, pilgrims will be inspired to transition progressively toward more other-oriented and God-directed attitudes and actions. Then a pilgrim's prayers will become at least as intercessory (praying for others) as they start off tending to be mostly petitionary (praying for oneself). As they walk in and by the Spirit, soul pilgrims should aspire to partner with God more constantly and less episodically, more actively and less passively, and more sacrificially and less selfishly. In short, they should strive to walk with the Spirit as Jesus did. And it will be instructive and motivational for them to continue looking for relevant examples in the life of Jesus as reported in the Gospels.

> **Soul Pilgrim Reflection Questions**
>
> Have you ever tried to walk in the Spirit in the ways I've been describing? If so, what was your experience like? Did you find it easy or difficult? Limiting or freeing? What steps can you take to make this practice a more regular and sustained dimension of your daily life?

Lectio Divina

Lectio divina ("divine reading") is a practice of reading the Scriptures for the purpose of deepening one's friendship (companionship and partnership) with God. Soul pilgrims shouldn't think of this practice as a *replacement* for careful study of the Bible. The aim of the latter is to discern the authors' intentions for writing what they wrote in the context in which they wrote it—a context that includes their intended audience. Rather, lectio divina is a devotional *supplement* to responsible exegesis. As a devotional practice, the emphasis of lectio divina is on a *conversation* with the Holy Spirit about what one is reading. And it's a conversation for the sake of illumination, spiritual nourishment, and ultimately, communion with God. Lectio divina provides an opportunity for soul pilgrims to enjoy a spiritual meal in the presence of their divine host. And it's a reminder of what the Israelites learned while they wandered forty years in the wilderness (and of what Jesus replied to the devil's first temptation): "One does not live by bread alone, but by every word that comes from the mouth of God" (Matt 4:4; see Deut 8:3).[5]

Though lectio divina can be practiced communally, it can also be employed privately and individually to provide soul pilgrims with an opportunity for deepening their intimate knowledge of (friendship with) God. Accordingly, it's best to find a relatively secluded place where you can take your Bible to be alone with God. Such solitude has many advantages, including the benefit of getting away from influences that tend to shape or form you in ways contrary to God's character and will and immersing yourself in the Word of God while in the presence of God. In this way, lectio divina provides soul pilgrims with a means to follow the wise counsel of Paul, who urged the Roman Christians not to be "conformed to this world, but (to) be transformed by the renewing of (their) minds, so that (they) may discern what is the will of God—what is good and acceptable and perfect" (Rom 12:2). Another advantage of being alone is you can read or recite the Scriptures you've selected aloud if you choose, a practice that could enhance

---

5. For an eloquent and extended meditation on reading the Bible for spiritual nourishment (with a discussion of lectio divina), see Peterson, *Eat This Book*.

your ability to fully enter in to your experience of them. The goal is for your appropriation of the verse(s) or passage to become as deep as possible—moving from your mind into your heart.

Christians have been practicing lectio divina for centuries. It was a regular monastic practice in the sixth century, when St. Benedict (c. 480–c. 547) founded his monastic order. Since it was developed at a time when Latin was the language used by the Western European church, the four stages or "moments" of the practice have Latin names: lectio, meditatio, oratio, and contemplatio. But English-speaking soul pilgrims may find it more helpful to use the labels reading, reflection, response, and rest, since these words capture the primary activity pilgrims engage in at those moments or in those stages. It's important to remember that, though "oratio" means "prayer," all four stages of lectio divina are meant to be forms of prayer.

If we practice the four in order, we'll start by reading some (relatively small) portion of Scripture slowly and prayerfully—asking for and listening to the Spirit's illumination. Then we'll prayerfully meditate or reflect on the verse(s) or brief passage—just as we might savor a bite of food in order to enjoy as much of its texture and flavor as we can. Next, we'll ask the Spirit for advice or direction on the basis of our prayerful reading and reflection. And finally, we'll simply rest in God's presence—no longer praying actively (for illumination, meaning, or direction) but instead passively enjoying the presence and activity of God the Spirit with us. And that's the point at which the practice of lectio divina merges into the practice of contemplative prayer (which I'll discuss in the next section).

I've said practicing lectio divina is like eating. Just as pilgrims on the Camino must eat and digest food regularly to be nourished and energized for their trek, so also soul pilgrims must read and absorb God's Word habitually to be sustained and empowered for their journey. As I said above, Jesus told Satan that humans live by "every word that comes from the mouth of God" (Matt 4:4). And Jeremiah told God, "Your words were found, and I ate them" (15:16). Peter invited his readers to be "like newborn infants" and "long for the pure, spiritual milk so that by it (they) may grow into salvation" (1 Pet 2:2). And Paul told Timothy to act in such a way as to be "a good servant of Christ Jesus, nourished on the words of the faith and of the sound teaching that (he has) followed" (1 Tim 4:6). Finally, Jesus told his disciples that "The Spirit gives life; the flesh counts for nothing. The words I have spoken to you—they are full of the Spirit and life" (John 6:63, NIV). Lectio divina enables soul pilgrims to ingest life from God's Word and Spirit.

On the Camino, Jennifer and I woke up hungry every morning. We ate breakfast at our place of lodging before heading out on the trail. And by midday, after walking for hours, we were famished. So, we would stop at a café or eat food we had picked up at a market. And after we arrived at our daily destination, we were always ready to eat again. For the most part, we didn't have to be hungry for long before we found a way to fill our stomachs. But as I mentioned at the beginning of this chapter, the day we arrived (later than usual) in Ponferrada, all the restaurants and stores were closed until 8:00 PM due to siesta. At that point, finding food became our sole focus. And even though we were tired of walking, we spent at least an hour roaming the downtown area until we found a small *tienda* open in an otherwise completely deserted marketplace. We were delighted. After taking our purchases back to our cramped hotel room, we feasted on them as if they were haute cuisine.

I wish my desire to consume the Scriptures on my daily soul pilgrimage were as consistently urgent as our regular craving for food on the Camino. I want to be more like the psalmist, whose celebration in Psalm 119 of God's Word reveals the many dimensions of his longing to treasure what God has said to humans. In his lengthy poetic prayer, he exclaims "Oh, how I love your law! It is my meditation all day long" (v. 97). And "How sweet are your words to my taste, sweeter than honey to my mouth! (v. 103). Then comes the well-known utterance that shows the relevance of his yearning to a soul pilgrimage: "Your word is a lamp to my feet and a light to my path" (v. 105). Another psalm indicates the life-changing power, for those who avoid "the path that sinners tread," of a practice like lectio divina: "their delight is in the law of the Lord, and on his law they meditate day and night. They are like trees, planted by streams of water, which yield their fruit in its season, and their leaves do not wither. In all that they do they prosper" (Ps 1:2–3).

As I look back at my life, I realize the times I've experienced the most joy in reading the Bible are times I've intentionally slowed down to reflect and respond—rather than just to read. In my experience, just as full enjoyment of a gourmet meal requires putting small portions of food into your mouth that you allow to linger on your tongue and then chew attentively and thoroughly, so also complete delight in God's Word involves reading limited passages of Scripture that you meditate on thoughtfully and extensively. And just as the pleasure in eating fine food is enhanced by talking about it with fellow diners, so also the satisfaction in reading divine discourse is amplified by conversing about it with the Holy Spirit.

What I've found is that *memorizing* passages of Scripture intensifies the effects of lectio divina on my mind and heart. When I rehearse verses over and over again for the sake of committing them to memory, the wonder of the Bible opens up to me as if I were entering a whole new world. I see God's Word in a fresh way. Each word seems to take on new power. And I feel as if I'll never be able to exhaust the richness of divine revelation. In those moments, I come to see why the psalmist likened God's Word to honey. The experience of savoring it in my mind and heart is genuinely sweet. And the lingering effects of dwelling on it provide ongoing resources for walking in the Spirit. As I said above, soul pilgrims can "snack" on remembered verses as they keep in step with the Spirit throughout the day. Lectio divina can also lead naturally to contemplative prayer, as we'll see in the next section.

> **Soul Pilgrim Reflection Questions**
>
> Have you experimented with different ways to read the Bible? Have you ever tried lectio divina—or something like it? If so, was it a positive experience? If it wasn't, what steps might you take to enter more deeply and prayerfully into God's Word?

Contemplative Prayer

Contemplative prayer (the fourth moment or stage in lectio divina) is an ancient Christian practice. More recently, the Roman Catholic Trappist monk Thomas Merton (1915–1968) characterized it as prayer "centered entirely on attention to the presence of God and to His will and His love."[6] Even though this type of prayer could be thought of as belonging to the practice of lectio divina, I've made it a separate discipline, since soul pilgrims can engage in it on its own, without first implementing the read, reflect, and respond steps of the prayerful approach to Scripture I sketched above. One reason for making contemplative prayer a distinctive practice is that it involves the cultivation of a passive interior silence, whereas the other stages of lectio all require a more active conversation with the Holy Spirit about the biblical text one is reading. The purpose of this inner quietness is to set aside time to obey God's command to "Be still and know that I am God" (Ps 46:10a).[7]

Life in today's world is often very full. Many people have a lot to do and they're often short on time because of their many commitments. Throughout the day, we can feel pulled in many different directions. Our lives can become fragmented and we can be easily distracted. In such circumstances, it can be easy to try to multitask to accomplish as many things as possible in a short amount of time. Those of us who become overly task-oriented can

---

6. Quoted in Pennington, "Thomas Merton," 50.

7. Teresa of Ávila calls this type of prayer the "Prayer of Quiet." Teresa, *Interior Castle*, 55–60.

begin to see other people—and God (when we think of God) as means to our ends rather than as infinitely valuable ends in themselves to be loved and enjoyed for their own sake. In the midst of such a frantic and self-centered life, contemplative prayer can become a wonderful countercultural—even subversive—practice. It can become a regular means for soul pilgrims to slow down, rest, and attend to the one reality that ought to be constantly at the center of our lives. It can be a way to recenter on the presence and activity of God in our lives. And in order for that recentering to be as fully realized as possible, contemplative prayer involves a method that conduces to an unmediated openness and receptivity to the Triune God.

The method is simple. You merely sit quietly for an extended time resting in the presence of God. Contemplative prayer involves being with God more than talking to God. It's more about communion than conversation. It's more an opportunity to enjoy him than to ask him for things or tell him things. It's like quiet time with a beloved human friend. Jennifer and I spent a fair amount of time during our Camino sitting or walking side by side without speaking. We just took pleasure in being together. We simply delighted in knowing and being known by someone we knew loved and accepted us. Of course, our love for each other is imperfect. But God's love for us in Christ is unconditional, complete, and eternal. He knows us fully and accepts us completely through the sacrifice of Christ on our behalf. And contemplative prayer involves humbly and appreciatively knowing and receiving that love.

When I've included this practice in my soul pilgrimage daily and for days on end each morning, I've found it easier and more natural to think fondly of God off and on throughout the day. When I've neglected it for an extended period, I've become less attentive to him and as a result, more distant from him. In my experience, contemplative prayer has been a powerful means of opening my life more fully to God. It's enabled me to become increasingly aware of the God who is always there. And this awareness has made it easier for me to abide in Christ (John 15:1–11) and walk in the Spirit (Gal 5:16).

But it wasn't easy for me to introduce this practice into my daily routine. And once I did, it was initially challenging to make it a habit. The reason it was difficult for me to begin engaging in contemplative prayer is twofold. I am a person who wants to be in control and to be productive. So, it was hard for me spend time (usually up to twenty minutes) doing nothing but resting quietly with God. Since I wasn't actively *doing* anything, I wasn't in charge of what was happening. Rather, I was practicing submission to the sovereign God. And of course, by its very nature, contemplative prayer involves refraining from trying to bring about any discernible results—at least results I have in mind and am striving to produce. The purpose of contemplative prayer is simply to be with God. Any possible fruit forthcoming from the practice is entirely up to him, incidental to the exercise, and likely to emerge mostly down the road in the form of gradually deepening intimacy with God.

And my experience of engaging in contemplative prayer was troubling at first. My attempts to quiet my mind to focus on God seemed to backfire. Instead of calm I got chaos. My thoughts kept bubbling up from a cauldron of unrest. Among the unwelcome intruders were anxieties about unfinished projects, worries about struggling friends, fears about an upcoming medical procedure, regrets for foolish decisions I had made, and doubts about my spiritual progress. I couldn't keep them from coming. My initial reaction was to think of my experiment in contemplative prayer as a failure. But on reflection, and after talking to others with similar experiences, I realized this outcome was inevitable. It's the natural state of my subconscious mind! I also came to see that my awareness of this fact provided me with an opportunity to get to know the darkness within me better. And that self-knowledge enabled me to be in a better position to partner with God in his project of transforming my thought life so I could eventually acquire a Christlike mind—a mind at peace and capable of resting in the contemplation of God.

Now that I've practiced contemplative prayer for a number of years, I've observed the fruit it's produced in my life. It's enabled me to know myself better. And it's helped me see the value of regular rest and sabbath. I've come to look forward to it as an oasis in my day—a time when I can slow down and know God. Over time, it's given me more peace of mind but also a more relaxed body—at least during the time I engage in it. Even more, contemplative prayer has planted in me a deeper longing to be with God. As a result of regularly resting in this way, I resonate more deeply with the psalmist, whose soul longs and thirsts for God like a deer longs for flowing streams (Ps 42) and whose flesh faints for God as in a dry and weary land without water (Ps 63). And as I said above, daily practice of this spiritual discipline makes it easier for me to remember God during the rest of the day.

As I've been saying, deeper union and communion with God is the goal of a soul pilgrimage. Contemplative prayer is the individual practice that focuses most directly on attaining it. Soul pilgrims who engage in this practice daily will experience a daily arrival at their soul pilgrimage destination. But the pilgrimage will continue the next day, since it's always possible to know, love, and enjoy God more deeply and to experience his love more fully.

While we were on the Camino, Jennifer and I spent time each day imagining together what it would be like to be in Santiago de Compostela. In doing so, we had a foretaste of our arrival there. But it wasn't a replacement for our actual entry into that city—and into the cathedral there to worship. In the same way, contemplative prayer can be a valuable soul pilgrimage way to spend time in God's presence and to grow in the knowledge of God. It provides a foretaste of the final realization of the ultimate soul pilgrimage goal—to know God intimately and directly and to enjoy secure and permanent union with God. This prayer practice can provide soul pilgrims with an experiential confirmation of what the psalmist says to God in Psalm 16: "You show me the path of life. In your presence there is fullness of joy; in your right hand are pleasures forevermore" (v. 11).

> ### Soul Pilgrim Reflection Questions
>
> Do you live a busy and hurried life in which it seems there isn't enough time to rest and enjoy others adequately—including God? Do you long to have a deeper ongoing loving communion with God? Are you willing to stop hurrying and take time out of your busy schedule to rest in the presence of God on a daily basis? Are you willing to try contemplative prayer?

Practice

Choose one of these four prayer practices (the Prayer of Examen, walking in the Spirit, lectio divina, or contemplative prayer). Try it out every day for a week. Then switch to another of the practices and try it out for a week. After a four-week cycle in which you've tried each practice, try gradually to build up to a regular routine in which you engage in each of these four practices every day.

9

The Practices II
What Can You Do With Others to Know God Better?

Friday, Oct 12, Santiago de Compostela (from Jennifer's journal)

"What a great view of the plaza!" I motion Jim to come to the window. After settling into our second-story room, we revel in a balcony view of a vibrant nightlife below. The Camino surprised us yet again today. On our last leg of the entire Camino, a torrential downpour consumed us. Instead of joining other pilgrims in front of the cathedral to celebrate the culmination of a long journey, we hightailed it to the Pensión Libredón in the historic center of the city.

Eight hours later, street lamps cast a shine on wet cobblestones as the rain relents, giving the stones a jewel-like quality in the dark. A throng of people moves below us on the Plaza de Fonseca. A thrum of voices rises to remind us we aren't alone. We're in the center of something exciting.

"I can't wait to see the city tomorrow," I say. "There's something magical about this place."

Saturday, October 13, Santiago de Compostela (from Jennifer's journal)

We climb many stairs to enter the magnificent cathedral. We slip inside where people have gathered for mass. A staggering number of pilgrims and other worshippers fill the inner cavity. Extended aisles surrounding the apse allow visitors to walk freely around the church interior without interrupting religious services. Even so, today there is standing room only. Jim and I separate out of a need to find space from which to view the Eucharist.

I find my place standing alongside a column, and immediately recognize some faces from the Camino in the multitude of pilgrims. I nod a greeting to Suzanna standing across from me, recalling her anguish at misplacing her passport in Viana. Other faces are ones we've met since arriving in Santiago de Compostela. I exchange a smile of recognition with the woman working the front desk at Pensión Libredón. Others unknown to me don't seem like strangers in this context. Collectively we fix our gazes in the same direction. We all belong here. Together we are a unique blend of pilgrims, tourists, and residents, worshipping together at this moment.

I hardly notice when eight men quietly make their way to the central dome area where a censer hangs from the ceiling. My eyes rest on the giant silver ball, one of the most representative symbols of the city. I recall Jim's nose in our guidebook last night, exclaiming with surprise about its dimensions.

"Can you believe the *Botafumeiro* is five feet in diameter and weighs one hundred thirty-five pounds?" he'd asked me.

"What's the point of using a giant incense burner?" I'd responded. "What purpose does it serve in the church?"

"The translation is *smoke expeller*," Jim had explained. "It serves as a physical manifestation of prayer."

Now I remember the men's red robes mark them as *tiraboleiros*, or incense carriers—another helpful piece of information we'd gleaned from our guidebook. But what are they doing here *today*? I'm puzzled. I'd checked the cathedral's online calendar this morning. I'd learned the *Botafumeiro* was not scheduled to swing today—a disappointment.

"October 13 is not one of the church's holy days!" I overhear a woman standing next to me whisper to the man beside her. "I mean, how could we possibly witness the *Botafumeiro* in use *today*?" she asks.

Her question is my own, so I lean in to hear the man's response. "Someone must have given a very generous donation for it to happen," he explains. Although his voice is quiet, his crinkled eyes and upturned mouth indicate his delight.

We watch the *tiraboleiros* position themselves to move the gigantic ball by a system of pulleys. Then, along with hundreds of others, I witness the *Botafumeiro* swing to spectacular heights, driven by the eight red-robed men. The sweet wood-scented smoke from the incense fills the cathedral with a heavenly fragrance, a symbol of the peoples' prayers rising to heaven. My senses are heightened in this holy place I now share with others who have made the same journey.

I locate Jim across the nave. Our eyes meet. We share this moment with each other and our fellow pilgrims. It is good to worship together.

Our Camino Pilgrimage Story: Communal Practices

Jennifer and I were glad to experience the Camino together. We partnered in planning the trip, walking the path, learning from our experience, and celebrating together when we arrived at our destination. And every one of these four stages involved our interactions with other people. Before we left home, we relied on others for information, equipment, advice, and encouragement. During our journey, we depended on local Camino residents for directions, accommodations, meals, and conversation. We were also enriched by other pilgrims we encountered who shared their plans, struggles, stories, and lives. And we joined other pilgrims in Santiago as we completed our journey in the Cathedral Square, received our *Compostela* at the Pilgrims' Reception Office, visited the Museum of Pilgrimage, and attended a worship service in the Santiago Cathedral.

Though most of our interactions with other pilgrims involved exchanges of the customary greeting "*¡Buen Camino!*" in passing, we had a number of more significant encounters. Of the many more meaningful social experiences, four stand out in my mind.

One (mentioned in Jennifer's journal entry preceding the Introduction) took place in Pamplona before dawn, when we set out from our hotel on our very first day to find the Camino. When we got to a walkway that looked like it might be our route, we hesitated, because we weren't sure whether to turn onto it. Before too long a lone pilgrim with a backpack and trekking poles came striding along the path. Seeing the confused look on our faces, he simply pointed one of his poles in the direction he was heading and said, "It's this way." Relieved, we turned and followed him.

On another occasion we saw a group of pilgrims standing around a fig tree beside the trail. One of them was plucking a plump ripe fig from a branch on the tree. When we paused to find out what was going on, the man with the fig looked at me, divided the fruit in two, and gave me half, saying, "*¡Buen Camino!*" as he did so.

A third event was more prolonged. At the Albergue La Morena in Lédigos, Jennifer and I shared a dinner table with a Catholic priest named James and an English teacher named Heidi. We shared food and wine as well as Camino stories and reflections. It was a nourishing and enriching experience of fellowship and communion.

Finally, one cold morning just outside of Astorga on the way to the mountain village of Foncebadón, we spotted a little chapel across the roadway. Another pilgrim couple—a man and a woman—were walking over to look at it. We did too. When we joined them just outside the building, we noticed that little signs featuring a "Pilgrim's Prayer" had been posted across the front of the church over the entryway. Each sign contained the prayer in a different language. When I saw the one in English, I turned to the man and said (in English, since he looked American), "I'm glad they have a pilgrim's prayer." Without skipping a beat, he said, "Why don't we all say it together?" So we did!

Communal Practices for Soul Pilgrims

Our Camino experiences with other pilgrims suggest four communal practices soul pilgrims can engage in with other soul pilgrims to assist each other on the path toward deeper knowledge of God. One of these practices is spiritual companionship, which involves meeting with at least one other soul pilgrim for spiritual direction, friendship, discipling, coaching, and/or mentoring. Another is partnering in Christian service, which can include acts of mercy, service projects, ministries, and missions of various kinds. Table fellowship is still another. It includes the practice of hospitality and of sharing life in the Word and Spirit together with other soul pilgrims. Finally, there is corporate worship, during which soul pilgrims collectively offer themselves in adoration, confession, thanksgiving, and supplication to the Triune God.[1]

As we'll see, each of these practices can help soul pilgrims grow in knowledge of God in ways not possible through the exercise of individual practices alone. For instance, a spiritual companion can help one discern the Spirit's guidance when one is struggling to figure it out for oneself. And working with others in Christian service can enable one to experience the

---

1. These four specific communal practices could be added to the table (in chapter 8) of Camino routines, mystical stages, general practices, and specific individual practices in a bottom row—in the order they're presented here.

active guidance and power of the Holy Spirit in the company of others who share that experience and can testify to its reality and efficacy. Table fellowship can provide opportunities for intimate exchanges of stories about what the participants perceive God to be doing in their lives. And pilgrims who eat together can also offer each other perspectives on what God's Word and Spirit are teaching them. Finally, in corporate worship pilgrims can encounter and experience God together in such a way as collectively to be in the best position to be receptive to the presence and activity of God the Holy Spirit in their midst. When our attention is focused directly on the Triune God, when we're most open to God's manifestation to us and influence among us, and when we're sharing this focus and openness with a number of other people, we can be in an optimal position to grow in our knowledge of God.

The four Camino vignettes I sketched at the beginning of this chapter illustrate these four communal soul pilgrim practices. In the first, a fellow pilgrim gave us needed guidance on the path. In the second, another pilgrim gave us a welcome gift. The third example featured our enjoyable communion at dinner with two other pilgrims. And the last involved an impromptu devotional offering with still two more.

In each case, others enriched our pilgrimage experience through companionship, service, fellowship, or worship. As a result, we were reminded that a pilgrimage is not merely an individual endeavor. We saw that even our private pilgrimage practices are part of a larger program. And this important truth applies to both the Camino and a pilgrimage of soul. As St. Augustine said, Christian pilgrims are members of a City—the City of God. And what binds us together is that we strive to put love of God above love of self.[2] The citizens of the City of God include both those "on pilgrimage in this mortal life" and those "eternally immortal in heaven."[3] In the language of Jesus, these two groups are members of the kingdom of God. And from Paul's point of view, they are members of the body of Christ.

Soul Pilgrim Reflection Questions

Does your soul pilgrimage include any of these four practices? If so, which one(s)? And to what extent do you think of your journey toward deeper knowledge of God a *communal* one?

---

2. See Augustine, *City of God*, 593.
3. Augustine, *City of God*, 463.

A Transformative Cycle

As we think about these communal practices, let's keep in mind that growing in our knowledge of God requires an ongoing cycle of both moral and intellectual transformation on the part of soul pilgrims. In order to be sensitively and appreciatively attuned to the presence and activity of God in our lives, we need to become more like God—more godly, more Christlike. When we experience ourselves undergoing specific types of moral changes, we'll be better able to recognize and discern those moral virtues in God. And when we experience those moral virtues in God, we'll be motivated to want to grow in those virtues ourselves. What I have in mind here is the continual interplay of the stages of illumination and purgation. The more we know God, the more we can see God's character. And the more we can see God's character, the more we're likely to admire and appreciate it. The more we admire and appreciate what God is like, the more we'll want to be like God, to emulate God. And the more we want to imitate God, the more we'll realize our need for the Holy Spirit to provide us with the strength to make that possible. Finally, the more we depend on God for help in this way, the more godlike we'll be. And our growing likeness to God (restoration of the broken image of God in us) will enable us to see God more and better going forward.

The efficacy of this moral-intellectual cycle is enhanced when we're also in the presence of other soul pilgrims who are undergoing the same sorts of transformations. We'll be able to witness their growth in and exercise of moral and intellectual character as they witness ours. And these mutual observations will contribute to our recognition of Christlike qualities and our motivation to become more Christlike. They'll also provide us with opportunities to see God at work in our fellow soul pilgrims—and this will help us to grow in our knowledge of God as well. They'll also facilitate opportunities for God to reveal himself to us indirectly—through other people.

For instance, suppose I witness another soul pilgrim engage in an act of genuine self-sacrificial love toward someone who has treated her poorly. I'm moved by her behavior, and I'm simultaneously motivated to emulate her. At the same time, I become more attentive to this virtue in others and better able to recognize it when I see it. And as the ability grows, develops, and strengthens, I cultivate the intellectual virtue of a kind of spiritual perception or insight that enables me to recognize occasions when the Holy Spirit is present and active in my life in graciously loving and compassionate ways—in spite of my tendency to neglect the Spirit's guidance and to fail to take advantage of the Spirit's empowerment of me. And when I perceive the Spirit's generosity on my behalf, I'm so humbly grateful for the Spirit's undeserved favor that I'm inspired to grow in self-sacrificially generous and compassionate love myself. And the cycle continues.

A similar cycle was evident in our Camino experience. Since we were journeying together, Jennifer and I were constantly learning from and being motivated by each other. And as a result, both of us grew over time in our acquaintance with the Camino and in our ability to navigate it well. The Camino had an ongoing impact on each of us. And we could see how our partner was being transformed and how we were being transformed by our partner. Jennifer's fascination with the age of the buildings we saw gave me new eyes to see our surroundings. And her enthusiasm for these ancient structures awakened a similar wonder in me. My delight in speaking Spanish with the locals impressed on her the value of knowing a foreign language. And when we met a French couple, she was emboldened to follow my example by conversing with them in their native tongue. I could give many more examples of ways in which our observations of each other created an ongoing round of changes to our minds and hearts.

On a soul pilgrimage, this transformative cycle is sufficiently general that we should expect to observe manifestations of it in each of the four communal practices I'll now briefly describe and discuss: spiritual companionship, Christian service, table fellowship, and corporate worship.

> ### Soul Pilgrim Reflection Questions
>
> Can you think of a relationship you have with another soul pilgrim in which the two of you help each other grow in knowing God and wanting to be like him? What's a specific example of how you've transformed each other?

Spiritual Companionship

In both the Bible and in Christian history there are examples of human relationships that have facilitated their participants' relationship to God. From the creation of Eve after God's declaration that, "It is not good that the man should be alone; I will make him a helper as his partner" (Gen 2:18) to the missionary collaboration between Paul and Barnabas—and then Paul and Silas—the Word of God affirms the importance of human companionship and partnership for our lives with God. In between these examples we find Abraham and Sarah, Moses and Aaron, Ruth and Naomi, David and Jonathan, Elijah and Elisha, and Priscilla and Aquila. In the Gospels, we also find Jesus sending out the twelve "two by two" (Mark 6:7) and seventy disciples as well—also in pairs (Luke 10:1). In Christian history, St. Augustine had his friend Alipius, and more recently, C. S. Lewis was friends with J. R. R. Tolkien.

It seems clear that God intends these "horizontal" human relationships to be an important means by which we can enjoy our "vertical" relationships with the Triune God (who is himself an eternal loving community of three persons). A passage in Ecclesiastes, which is often used at weddings, expresses some of the benefits of human relationships well:

> Two are better than one, because they have a good reward for their toil. For if they fall, one will lift up the other; but woe to one who is alone and falls and does not have another to help. Again, if two lie together, they keep warm; but how can one keep warm alone? And though one might prevail against another, two will withstand one. A threefold cord is not quickly broken. (4:9–12)

While toiling on pilgrimage, soul pilgrims who walk with companions will be able to enjoy each other's assistance, comfort, and protection. They can even also gain from the inevitable friction that characterizes close friendships: "Iron sharpens iron, and one person sharpens the wits of another" (Prov 27:17) and "Better is open rebuke than hidden love. Well meant are the wounds a friend inflicts, but profuse are the kisses of an enemy" (Prov 27:5–6).

When Jesus called people to follow him as his disciples (apprentices, students), he wanted not only to prepare them individually for life in the kingdom but also to form them into a loving kingdom community. He taught them to "love one another" as he had loved them (John 15:12). And he called them his friends (John 15:15). He also called anyone who "does the will of (his) Father in Heaven" his "brother and sister and mother"—members of his family (Matt 12:50). So soul pilgrims are fellow friends of Jesus and also brothers and sisters in the family of God. The practice of spiritual companionship presupposes both friendship and family as models for mutual pilgrim interaction.

Families with children include both hierarchical and egalitarian relationships. In hierarchical relationships, one person has a kind of authority over another, and in egalitarian relationships that's not the case. In healthy families, the parent-child relationship is hierarchical during the child's preadult years. In families with more than one child, relationships between siblings, at least when they're younger and the age distance between them is sufficiently great, tend to be hierarchical as well ("Johnny, obey your older brother while I'm gone."). In ideal circumstances, egalitarian friendships between siblings develop later in the adult years.

Friendships with people outside one's biological family can be either hierarchical or egalitarian as well. Although we may tend to think of such friendships as falling into the latter category, the example of Jesus, the Lord of the universe, calling his disciples (and by extension, other soul pilgrims) his "friends" shows that friendships in general can be hierarchical too. Indeed, as I pointed out in chapter 3, the author of the book of James says Abraham was "called a friend of God" (2:23).

These reflections on family relationships and friendships that are either hierarchical or egalitarian provide us with resources for thinking about the diversity of ways soul pilgrims can engage in the practice of spiritual companionship. Some of these ways involve hierarchical relationships and some involve egalitarian ones.

Among the forms of *hierarchical* spiritual companionships are spiritual direction, discipling, and mentoring (or coaching). In all those cases, one soul pilgrim who is further along in the journey toward deeper knowledge of God provides supervision, instruction, guidance, correction, and/or other similar types of assistance to soul pilgrims who are not as far along on the path. These relationships tend to be relatively asymmetrical and unidirectional. Their focus is on the nurture and cultivation of the directee, disciple, or mentee. The more mature partner may also have his or her own director, teacher, mentor, or coach.

Among the forms of *egalitarian* spiritual companionships are spiritual friendships and small spiritual life groups. The purpose of these relationships is to provide opportunities for mutual encouragement and accountability. Whether with just one other person or with ten or twelve, the relationships are mutual, symmetrical, multidirectional, and reciprocal. That is, each party fulfills the same roles in the relationship as each of the other parties does.

It would be good for soul pilgrims to engage in both a hierarchical and an egalitarian spiritual companionship. And it would be good for these relationships to be both intimate and regular. Elders in the faith (though not necessarily in biological years), on the basis of their advanced pilgrimage experience, can help soul pilgrims become more attuned to the presence and activity of the Holy Spirit. And the former can also assist the latter in becoming prepared for what they're likely to experience further along the trail. And spiritual peers, whether in pairs or in small groups, can share testimonies, confess their sins to each other, encourage each other, and hold each other accountable. In all these types of relationships, soul pilgrims can grow in their knowledge of God as God speaks to them through others and as they see God at work in others' lives.

Before, during, and after our Camino experience, Jennifer and I benefited from both hierarchical and egalitarian relationships. Of course, throughout this time, our egalitarian friendship with each other was the most important human resource for both of us. But we also had access to other pilgrims who helped us along the way. Initially, our other Camino friends were veterans of the Camino who answered our questions, told us their stories, alleviated our concerns, and encouraged us to go. Some of these were people we knew and others were "friends" we discovered on the internet who had posted their Camino reflections and advice. All these relationships were hierarchical, since they were with pilgrims who had already walked the Way of Saint James. While we were on the path, we had temporary friendships of both sorts. Though most of the pilgrims we encountered were also on their first pilgrimage and only as far along as we were, some had already walked the entire route at least once before, and were doing it again. After returning home, we've enjoyed both reminiscing with fellow *Compostela* earners as peers and educating prospective pilgrims as mentors.

My experience with spiritual companionship has been mixed. Years ago, when I was transitioning from Christian skeptic to soul pilgrim and yearning for guidance from an older and wiser mentor, I secured a spiritual director through a local group. We met for lunch at a nearby restaurant monthly for a while. He was friendly and helpful. But though he identified as a Christian, I learned more about Buddhism from him than about deepening my friendship with Jesus. My main takeaway from those encounters was the importance of theological compatibility for a spiritual companionship. One of these days I hope to find a soul pilgrim further along the path than I am who shares my general Christian perspective.

Though Jennifer is my primary spiritual peer, I've also found a satisfying, fruitful, and long-lasting spiritual friendship with a male colleague of mine. For nearly a quarter century, we've checked in regularly with each other through meetings, messages, and phone calls for accountability and encouragement. We've discussed books on Christian themes, exchanged emails about devotional works we've read together, confessed our shortcomings to each other, and urged each other to keep to the pilgrim's path. We've also shared life more generally going on trips together with our families, going out to eat, taking hikes, drinking beer, and engaging in silly banter. Years ago, we co-led a study trip in Europe. This friend and his wife are also members of the group with which Jennifer and I are currently regularly enjoying the practice of table fellowship (see below).

Over the years I've also met with a few male students looking for spiritual guidance. At first, I wasn't as comfortable in the mentor role as I was in that of a mentee or peer. I wasn't sufficiently confident in my degree of maturity, wisdom, and virtue to feel I had enough to offer others in the way of direction and advice. The first young man with whom I met grew into a devoted follower of Christ and faithful contributor to God's kingdom in spite of my clumsy and often misguided efforts on his behalf. A few years later, another student asked me to be his counselor for a Boy Scout "God and Life" award he was working on. This time, I felt emboldened by my first experience, and I offered him a list of expectations and challenges in our first meeting that seemed appropriate for the role he had asked me to play. Since he never showed up for another meeting with me and never explained his abrupt termination of our arrangement, I decided I must have come on too strong. Since that time, I've been striving to find a good balance between the timidity of my first experience as a mentor and the temerity of my second. But I've also learned effective spiritual direction is more about good listening than good advice and has more to do with relying on the Spirit than depending on oneself.

> ### Soul Pilgrim Reflection Questions
>
> Do you have any spiritual companions? If so, are you a mentee, peer, or mentor—or more than one of these? If not, which of your current relationships might lend itself to this practice?

Christian Service

Friendships grow not only through face-to-face encounter (companionship) but also through mutual concerned efforts to make a meaningful and positive contribution to others outside the friendship (partnership). Both internally oriented and externally directed practices of loving attention facilitate growth of intimacy between the participants in these practices. We've seen that this general principle is true of divine-human relationships. In this chapter, we're seeing how it applies to human-human relationships. The communal practices of spiritual companionship and Christian service are both essential components of a soul pilgrimage. Both are needed for growing in loving knowledge of God and of fellow pilgrims. A paradigm example of the complementarity of these practices is the human family consisting in a mother, a father, and at least one child. The entire family grows in loving intimacy through the ongoing face-to-face companionship of the wife and husband and their continual outward-looking partnership in nurturing their children.

I've personally experienced the power of participating, as a member of a team, in ministries and service projects that combined spiritual companionship and Christian service (in addition to elements of both table fellowship and corporate worship). I can think of four examples throughout my life that were especially noteworthy in their facilitation of my growth in knowledge of God.

In the first example, I was a high school student on a team consisting of members of our church's youth group. We had agreed to put on a weeklong vacation Bible school one summer at a church in a nearby city. In preparation for the week, I met with another team member for a period of time to pray together daily for God's equipping of the team and blessing of the Bible school participants through our ministry to them. During the team's week of work, I had a strong sense of God's presence and activity through our corporate planning, service, fellowship, and worship.

In the remaining three example experiences, I was also a member of a team that engaged in these practices together. In my senior year in college, I led a team that administered a vacation Bible school for a week in a small village in Ensenada, Mexico. Shortly after college, I worked on a team as a counselor at high school summer camp at Campus by the Sea on Catalina Island. And as an older adult, I went with a group of families from my home church to Ensenada for another VBS—but also to help build a basketball court for the village with which we were working. In every case, I had a palpable sense of God at work among all those who were involved.

As I think back on these occasions, it seems to me that there is a pattern common in each of them that facilitated my heightened experience of God's presence and activity. There was a shared anticipation among the team members that God's involvement would be evident as we served together. This expectation was created by the team's praying in advance together for divine assistance. There was also a mutual recognition among the team members of our inability, both individually and collectively, to meet the challenges we faced without God's help. This fostered in us a strong sense of dependence on God. Finally, our ongoing requests for God's empowerment made us especially attentive to signs of his presence and activity in our midst. And this increased attunement made it more likely that we'd witness these signs when they showed up. Though it's true that the same pattern can account for an individual's awareness of God when he or she is alone, its presence in a group can amplify its effects because of the members' communications with each other.

This group dynamic is illustrated by the experience of the two disciples who encountered the resurrected Christ on their way to Emmaus (Luke 24:13–35). At first neither of them knew it was Jesus because "their eyes were kept from recognizing him" (v. 16). But after they invited their new traveling companion to stay with them when they reached the village toward which they'd been walking, "their eyes were opened, and they recognized him" (v. 31a). Luke implies that this epiphany was due to the fact that when Jesus "was at the table with them, he took bread, blessed and broke it, and gave it to them" (v. 30). Then, after Jesus suddenly "vanished from their sight" (v. 31b), "they said to each other, 'Were not our hearts burning within us while he was talking to us on the road, while he was opening the scriptures to us?'" (v. 32). Surely their simultaneous joint recognition of Jesus was reinforced by their mutual spoken confirmation of what they had witnessed. And soul pilgrims today who already know that Jesus was resurrected can benefit from knowing that "where two or three are gathered in (Jesus's) name, (he is) there among them" (Matt 18:20). Such knowledge can provide them with a strong basis for being motivated to look together for signs of the Lord's presence with them.

Our Camino experience provides another analogy with Christian service as a soul pilgrimage practice. As I've been saying, this practice facilitates friendships between soul pilgrims and their friendships with God. But it also has the potential to draw those who are served into the soul pilgrim fellowship—a result that's mutually enriching for all involved. In the same way, many of our encounters with others on the trail not only enabled us to get to know them but also strengthened our bond with each other and our acquaintance with the Camino itself. These results occurred especially when there were acts of kindness or hospitality involved—whether we were the givers or the receivers. In addition to the vignettes I've already shared above, a couple other examples will illustrate this point.

When we arrived at the B&B Zaldu in Estella at the end of the second day of our hike, we discovered that the Correos delivery service had brought my suitcase but left Jennifer's behind. After a call to the service met with no answer and a full message inbox, I phoned the Hotel Rural Bidean in Puente la Reina where we had stayed the previous night and explained our plight to the friendly proprietor in halting Spanish. She confirmed that our missing item was still in the hotel basement and offered to contact Correos on our behalf to arrange for its transfer to our new lodging. We were relieved and grateful for her generous help and our good feeling added to our appreciation of the region through which we were traveling. We also had a renewed regard for each other. I was thankful for Jennifer's patient willingness to do without her suitcase for the rest of the trip if necessary. And she was pleased with my efforts to retrieve it.

Toward the end of our trip, when we were walking from Palas de Rei to Arzúa, we encountered a young man from Barcelona who was walking the last part of the Way while on holiday with friends. After we started chatting, it was apparent he was as eager to practice his English with me as I was to try out my Spanish with him. We settled on a compromise that involved the use of both languages by turns. This mutually beneficial exercise was a service to both of us. After a half hour or so of bilingual conversation, we parted with a bit more fluency in each other's native language as well as (given how I was feeling and the look on his face) appreciation for the warm good will of a stranger and increased satisfaction with our Camino experiences.

> **Soul Pilgrim Reflection Questions**
>
> How often do you participate in acts of service with other soul pilgrims? Do your experiences connect you more deeply to each other, to God, and to those you serve?

Table Fellowship

It's interesting to note that the Emmaus-bound disciples I mentioned above experienced their recognition of the risen Lord's presence with them while they were "at table" with him after he "took bread, blessed and broke it, and gave it to them" (v. 30). And this sudden realization was preceded by their "hearts burning" while Jesus "interpreted to them the things about himself in all the scriptures" (v. 27) during their walk. From their point of view in retrospect, there were subtle signs of the Lord's presence with them even before they came fully to see and appreciate them. What this example suggests is that the practice of table fellowship may have a special role to play in deepening soul pilgrims' corporate intimacy with each other and with God. Though spiritual companionship and Christian service provide opportunities for growing together in the knowledge of God—as indicated in the preceding sections of this chapter—table fellowship can create a context in which such an increase in knowledge can culminate in an especially vivid perception of God based on the preceding group experiences.

After all, that part of Christian worship called "communion," the "Eucharist," or the "Lord's Supper" is based on Jesus's last meal with his closest disciples. And the Lord's Supper is a central practice in Christian worship. Table fellowship can be thought of as a less formal version of that Christian sacrament. Furthermore, during this final meal with his companions, Jesus alluded to a time in the future when he would share this meal with his followers again "in (his) Father's kingdom" (Matt 26:29). And the "Heavenly" or "Messianic" Banquet has become a dominant image of life together with

God. Table fellowship can be practiced as a means to anticipate what communal life will be like when the heavenly kingdom has come in its fullness. And we saw in chapter 6 that Jesus told the church at Laodicea he was knocking on their door hoping they would invite him in to eat with them. Soul pilgrims who share together in the practice of table fellowship can confidently consider themselves to have opened the door to welcome Jesus to dine with them.

The central theme of table fellowship is *nourishment*. Of course, the physical food and drink provide nourishment for the body. But Jesus offers his Word and himself as nourishment for our souls. And soul pilgrims who practice table fellowship together can follow Jesus's example by lovingly and generously offering their words and selves to each other for mutual soul nourishment. They offer their words to each other through testimony, encouragement, exhortation, confession, and dialogue. They offer their lives to each other through listening to each other, serving each other, laughing with each other, crying with each other, and caring for each other. Table fellowship is a prime context within which the biblical "one another" commands can find their fulfillment. And when soul pilgrims love one another, forgive one another, pray for one another, and bear one another's burdens (among many other things), they'll be able to see God present and at work in one another as well.

Over the years, Jennifer and I have had the privilege and pleasure of being involved in three different long-term small fellowship groups—one in each of the three cities we've lived during our married life. In each case, we numbered ten to fourteen people and met together on a regular basis for study (of the Bible and a variety of Christian books), sharing, and prayer. In our current group, we also eat dinner together. This addition of a meal as part of our time together has added a valuable extra dimension that was lacking in our earlier group experiences (as rich as those were). There is something about breaking bread together around a table in the name of Christ that binds a group together in sacrificial love. It also helps that we rotate homes and food assignments from month to month. That way, everyone always has a contribution to make to the fellowship. And the host couple always leads the time of study, sharing, and prayer after the meal. Our conversations during these events range from the silly and hilarious to the sane and serious. Throughout our time together as a group, there've been plenty of opportunities for us to "rejoice with those who rejoice and weep with those who weep" (Rom 12:15).

Of course, there are many other models of table fellowship; ours is not the only viable approach. But all varieties include the common elements of sharing food for the body and food for the soul with a small group of fellow soul pilgrims. More specifically, all kinds involve face-to-face participation in an activity that combines the sustenance and enrichment of both biological and spiritual life. And all types provide an occasion for deepened knowledge of the Unseen Guest—or rather, Unseen Host—who is always present with those who gather in his name and welcome him to their table for the mutual sharing of food and lives.

At the beginning of this chapter, I mentioned an occasion when Jennifer and I shared a meal with a Catholic priest named James and an English teacher named Heidi. That was the closest we got to engaging in the practice of table fellowship on the Camino. While we shared food and wine, we talked about our Camino experiences as Christians who were seeking to deepen our relationship with God during our pilgrimages. And James talked about opportunities he had had to share the gospel with nonreligious pilgrims along the way. We also reflected on spiritual lessons we were learning from various Camino experiences—such as our discovery that the simplicity that comes from packing light frees us up to focus more on God and other pilgrims. And we agreed that slowing down to a walking pace (as opposed to racing through the Camino on bicycle) made it easier to attend to the beauty of God's creation—including our fellow pilgrims God created in his image.

> ### Soul Pilgrim Reflection Questions
>
> Do you belong to a fellowship group that meets regularly for the nourishment of your bodies and souls? If so, in what specific ways does this group help you to grow in your knowledge of God? If not, what people in your life can you identify who may be interested in forming such a group with you?

Corporate Worship

Just as contemplative prayer is the apex of individual soul pilgrim practices, corporate worship is the pinnacle of corporate soul pilgrim practices. That's because the purpose of both is simply to set aside all other activities in order to offer oneself fully to the Triune God in an attitude of humble and receptive adoration. Both practices require the practitioner or practitioners to fully attend to God in his presence and activity with them. One difference between the two practices is that corporate worship is more *active* than contemplative prayer is. Whereas the latter requires one to "be still and know that (he is) God" (Ps 46:10), the former requires worshippers to join together in active praise, adoration, confession, thanks, petition, intercession, and engagement with God's Word both read and preached.

And corporate worship, in virtue of principally involving one's complete focus on the Godhead, also differs from each of the other communal soul pilgrim practices. Though there are moments during corporate worship when worshippers attend temporarily to each other (such as during the passing of the peace, the sharing of testimonies, and the announcements) and to the world God calls them to serve (such as during the announcements, the offering, and the sermon), the main purpose of this practice is to direct oneself to God in the presence of others who are also worshipping him. Though one is also mindful of God when practicing spiritual companionship, Christian service, and table fellowship, these latter three practices require one to keep fellow human beings more in the center of one's awareness. Corporate worship is the most God-centered activity humans can engage in together.

This maximal conscious directedness to God makes corporate worship, like contemplative prayer, a practice that is the most likely to deepen one's capacity for communion and union with God. And the advantage of corporate worship over contemplative prayer in this regard is that the former involves other members of the body of Christ. As a result, it provides an opportunity for the highest possible foretaste of the kingdom of God in all its fullness. At its best, corporate worship offers soul pilgrims an experience that anticipates arriving at their desired destination: an ongoing state of enjoying God together forever. Of course, there is an important sense in which this goal is never fully achieved. No matter how much soul pilgrims have deepened their knowledge of God, there will always be more of God to know (and more to know about God). As I pointed out in chapter 1, the unicorn in Lewis's *The Last Battle* says about Aslan's country (heaven), "I have come home at last! This is my real country! I belong here. This is the land I have been looking for all my life, though I never knew it till now . . . *Come further up, come further in!*"[4] (italics mine).

Corporate worship comes in a wide range of varieties and styles. But there are typical commonalities in spite of these differences. One way to articulate these similarities is to employ the Christian mystical conversion–purgation–illumination–union pattern we've been using. If we think of conversion generally as the practice of turning from self to God, then we can see the call to worship as an invitation to engage in that practice and the affirmation of faith (by means, for instance, of the Apostles' Creed) as a way of expressing our confidence in God rather than ourselves apart from God. And the part of corporate worship that most closely resembles purgation is

---

4. Lewis, *The Last Battle*, 196.

confession of sin and the spoken assurance of God's forgiveness and cleansing. Illumination can occur through both listening to the reading of Scripture and attending to the sermon or homily. And communion, the Lord's Supper, or Eucharist provides an opportunity for focused union with God as does the heartfelt and grateful singing of psalms, hymns, and spiritual songs. The latter emphasizes giving God praise and the former highlights receiving the gift of God's praiseworthy presence.

Since corporate worship may be the most familiar Christian practice among the readers of this book, it may be helpful to emphasize the importance of being deliberately mindful and prayerful in one's participation in it. I've found it challenging over the years to be fully mentally, emotionally, and spiritually present during worship services. The routine general structure of the service can become an obstacle to complete involvement—in spite of the variation of specific worship contents such as themes, prayers, songs, Scriptures, and responsive readings. This problem is especially acute when it comes to more consistently regular liturgical aspects of worship such as the recitation of the Apostles' Creed, the praying of the Lord's Prayer, and the response to the reading of God's Word ("This is the Word of the Lord"—"Thanks be to God!"). I have found it helpful to prepare for worship in advance by praying that God would enable me to be actively attentive and responsive to the Spirit throughout the service. And during worship, when I find my mind wandering (as I often do), I try to prayerfully return my focus to the Triune God via the liturgical vehicle in use by the congregation in that moment. The similar discipline of returning to single-minded attentiveness to God when distracted by one's thoughts during individual contemplative prayer can contribute to one's ability to sustain one's concentration during worship.

When a service of corporate worship is both designed wisely and engaged in fully, it can be a powerful tool for the Holy Spirit to use in the ongoing process of spiritual formation. Through the practice of this important corporate discipline, soul pilgrims can find themselves gradually transformed into the likeness of Christ. They can experience the restoration of the image of God in them—the image in which they were made but which was distorted as a result of sin. And this ongoing restoration or redemption can empower them to be more loyal in their spiritual companionship, more giving in their Christian service, and more loving in their table fellowship. But all the essential general elements of corporate worship need to be included, and the worshippers must humbly and prayerfully make use of these elements as they receive God's loving gifts of mercy and grace and respond to God by humbly and gratefully offering themselves back to him. And this ongoing cycle of giving and receiving will become both the soul pilgrim's path and his or her destination.

While we were on the Camino, we visited various chapels, churches, and sanctuaries—places where corporate worship takes place. Though the architecture and artwork were different from what we were used to, we often experienced a quiet sense of reverence that made us want to linger in those buildings designed for communal devotion. On one occasion before we arrived in Santiago de Compostela, we attended a small service in which a mix of locals and pilgrims gathered to honor their Creator and Redeemer together. Though they were strangers to us (and us to them), and though we had a hard time following the Spanish spoken by the priest and sung by the parishioners, we sensed a deeper connection with the congregation. We were joined together by the ancient practice of Christian worship—a practice that transcends place, culture, and language. A practice that can satisfy the deepest hunger of each human soul. A practice that will lead to union with the God who came to be with us forever through Christ and his Spirit.

> ### Soul Pilgrim Reflection Questions
>
> Do you see your Christian worship experiences as opportunities to draw closer to God and fellow Christian worshippers? What can you do to make corporate worship a more meaningful part of your soul pilgrimage?

Practice

Choose one of these four corporate practices (spiritual companionship, Christian service, table fellowship, or corporate worship). Try it out every week for a month. Then add another of the practices and try it out every week for another month in addition to the one you have already established. After a four-month cycle in which you have tried each practice, try gradually to build up to a regular routine in which you engage in each of these four practices every week. Unlike the exercise involving individual practices in the previous chapter, this one involves a weekly rather than a daily habit. The main reason for that difference is that the corporate practices require other people, and you will need to find other soul pilgrims who are both willing and able to join you. And you will need to figure out a schedule together that works for both (or all) of you.

Conclusion

A Prayer for a Deeper Friendship with God (A Camino Prayer)

Dear Lord and Guide of the Soul Camino,

    Help me to see that knowing you is more worthwhile than anything else I can experience;

    Help me to believe you have made it possible for me to know you—and will keep doing so;

    Help me to understand how knowing you is different from knowing about you;

    Teach me what I can know about you that will enable me to learn how to see you in my life;

    Teach me how to recognize the signs of your presence with me on the soul pilgrim's path;

    Teach me to discern your provision through your guidance and empowerment of me;

    Enable me to find and follow the path that leads to deeper and better knowledge of you;

    Enable me to engage in practices that improve my capacity to walk and work with you;

    Enable me to do things with other soul pilgrims that facilitate our communion with you.

    I pray all these things to the Father who provides the Soul Camino, through the Son who is the Soul Camino, by the Spirit who leads and equips me to walk the Soul Camino,

    Amen.

Bibliography

Aquinas, Thomas. *Summa Theologiae*. https://www.newadvent.org/summa/.
Aristotle. *Aristotle's Nicomachean Ethics*. Translated by Robert C. Bartlett and Susan D. Collins. Chicago: University of Chicago Press, 2011.
Augustine. *City of God*. Translated by Henry Bettenson. London: Penguin, 1984.
———. *Confessions*. Translated by Henry Chadwick. Oxford: Oxford University Press, 1991.
———. *On Christian Doctrine*. Translated by D. W. Robertson Jr. New York: Macmillan, 1958.
Brierley, John. *A Pilgrim's Guide to the Camino de Santiago (Camino Francés): Saint Jean de Port—Santiago de Compostela*. Glasgow: Kaminn Media, 2018.
Bright, Bill. *Have You Heard of the Four Spiritual Laws?* San Bernadino, CA: Campus Crusade for Christ, 1965.
———. *Would You Like to Know God Personally?* Orlando: Bright Media Foundation and Campus Crusade for Christ, 2014. https://www.cru.org/content/dam/cru/how-to-know-god/knowing-god-personally.pdf.
Butler, Alban. *Butler's Lives of the Saints*. Edited by Herbert J. Thurston and Donald Attwater. Westminster, MD: Christian Classics, 1990.
Clark, Kelly James. "Rocks, Persons, and Gods." https://www.academia.edu/6761967/Rocks_persons_and_gods.
Descartes, Rene. *Meditations on First Philosophy: With Selections from the Objections and Replies*. Translated and edited by John Cottingham. Cambridge: Cambridge University Press, 1996.
Gottman, John M., and Nan Silver. *The Seven Principles for Making Marriage Work*. New York: Three Rivers, 1999.
Grahame, Kenneth. *The Wind in the Willows*. New York: Sterling, 2007.
Hass, Peter Traben. *Centering Prayer: A One-Year Daily Companion for Going Deeper into the Love of God*. Brewster, MA: Paraclete, 2013.
Ignatius of Loyola. *The Spiritual Exercises of St. Ignatius*. Translated by Louis J. Puhl. New York: Vintage, 2000.
James, William. *Varieties of Religious Experience: A Study in Human Nature*. New York: Random House, 1902.
Lewis, C. S. *The Last Battle*. New York: HarperCollins, 1984.
———. *The Problem of Pain*. San Francisco: HarperSanFrancisco, 2001.
Melchert, Norman. *The Great Conversation: A Historical Introduction to Philosophy*. 4th ed. Boston: McGraw-Hill, 2002.

Michelin. *Michelin Guide to Camino de Santiago*. Nanterre, France: Michelin Editions des Voyages, 2018.

Nietzsche, Friedrich. *Beyond Good and Evil*. Translated by Marianne Cowan. Chicago: Henry Regnery, 1955.

Ortberg, John. *If You Want to Walk on Water, You've Got to Get Out of the Boat*. Grand Rapids: Zondervan, 2001.

Packer, J. I. *Knowing God*. Downers Grove, IL: InterVarsity, 1973.

Pascal, Blaise. *Pensées*. Translated by A. J. Krailsheimer. New York: Penguin, 1966.

Patterson, Ben. *He Has Made Me Glad: Enjoying God's Goodness with Reckless Abandon*. Downers Grove, IL: InterVarsity, 2005.

Payton, James R. *Irenaeus on the Christian Faith: A Condensation of "Against Heresies."* Cambridge: Lutterworth, 2012.

Peale, Norman Vincent. *The Power of Positive Thinking*. Hoboken, NJ: Prentice Hall, 1952.

Pennington, M. Basil. "Thomas Merton and Centering Prayer." *Studia Mertoniana* 2 (2003) 49–60.

Peterson, Eugene. *A Long Obedience in the Same Direction: Discipleship in an Instant Society*. Downers Grove, IL: InterVarsity, 1980.

———. *Eat This Book: A Conversation on the Art of Spiritual Reading*. Grand Rapids: Eerdmans, 2006.

Rea, Michael C. *The Hiddenness of God*. Oxford: Oxford University Press, 2018.

Reed, Jessica. "Should Only Those Following God Embark on a Pilgrimage?" *The Guardian*, September 5, 2012. https://www.theguardian.com/commentisfree/belief/2012/sep/05/god-pilgrimage-camino-santiago-atheist-dilemma.

Roberts, Robert C., and Jay Wood. *Intellectual Virtues: An Essay in Regulative Epistemology*. Oxford: Clarendon, 2007.

Sammis, John H. "Trust and Obey." 1887.

Smedes, Lewis B. *Union with Christ*. Grand Rapids: Eerdmans, 1983.

Smith, James K. A. *How (Not) to Be Secular: Reading Charles Taylor*. Grand Rapids: Eerdmans, 2014.

Taylor, Charles. *A Secular Age*. Cambridge, MA: Harvard University Press, 2007.

Taylor, James E. *Introducing Apologetics: Cultivating Christian Commitment*. Grand Rapids: Baker Academic, 2006.

Teresa. *Interior Castle*. West Valley City, UT: Walking Lion, 2006.

Tolkien, J. R. R. *The Lord of the Rings*. Houghton Mifflin Harcourt, 2012.

Underhill, Evelyn. *Mysticism: A Study in Nature and Development of Spiritual Consciousness*. New York: Dover, 2002.

Westminster Assembly. *Westminster Shorter Catechism*. https://www.shortercatechism.com.

Willard, Dallas. *The Great Omission: Reclaiming Jesus's Essential Teachings on Discipleship*. New York: HarperOne, 2006.

———. *Hearing God: Developing a Conversational Relationship with God*. Downers Grove, IL: InterVarsity, 1984.

———. *Knowing Christ Today: Why We Can Trust Spiritual Knowledge*. New York: Harper-Collins, 2009.

———. *Life Without Lack: Living in the Fullness of Psalm 23*. Nashville: Thomas Nelson, 2018.

———. "Living a Transformed Life." In *Renewing the Christian Mind: Essays, Interviews, and Talks*, edited by Gary Black, 11–53. New York: HarperOne, 2016.

———. *The Spirit of the Disciplines: Understanding How God Changes Lives*. San Francisco: HarperOne, 1999

Scripture Index

Genesis
2:18 — 175

Deuteronomy
8:3 — 162

Job
42:5 — 80

Psalms
1:2–3 — 164
16:2 — 51
16:11 — 51, 168
19:1 — 38
24:3–6 — 142
34:8 — 124, 144
42 — 167
46:10 — 184
63 — 167
84:5 — vi
119:97 — 164
119:103 — 164
119:105 — 164
139:1 — 50–51

Proverbs
27:5–6 — 176
27:17 — 176

Ecclesiastes
4:9–12 — 176

Isaiah
11:9 — 18

Jeremiah
9:23–24 — 17
15:16 — 163
22:15–16 — 17
24:7 — 18

Hosea
6:1a — 16
6:3 — 16
6:6 — 16

Jonah
1:17 — 89
2:19 — 89

Matthew
4:4 — 162, 163
5–7 — 96
5:17–48 — 97
5:20 — 96
5:23–24 — 112
5:44 — 143
5:48 — 60, 97, 143

SCRIPTURE INDEX

Matthew (continued)

6:8	51
6:24	143
6:25–33	105
6:33	105, 115
7:13–14	124
11:27	94, 100
11:28–30	123
12:50	176
13:13	89
14:25–32	63
16:1	89
16:3	89
16:4	88, 89
18:20	181
19:26	57
26:29	182

Mark

1:15	93
1:17	93
6:7	175
9:22–24	141

Luke

9:23–25	136
10:1	176
11:9–13	133
15	125
18:1	118
18:9–14	115
22:42	136
24:13–35	180
24:16	181
24:27	182
24:30	181, 182
24:31a	181
24:31b	181
24:32	181

John

1:1–2	100
1:3	100
1:14	80, 100
1:18	100
3:16	14–15
4:24	50
6:44	94
6:63	163
8:19	19
8:31–32	19
10:14–15	65
10:30	100
10:38	100
11	57
11:25	89
14:7–9	100
14:16	101
14:16–17	104
14:17	19, 101
14:26	19, 101
15:1–11	19, 166
15:10a	140
15:12	176
15:13	59
15:14	60
15:15	52, 57, 176
15:26	94
16:8–11	94
16:12–15	84
16:33	19
17	20, 158
17:3	9, 15, 18, 24
17:20–24	19
17:21	103
17:23	103
17:25	24
20:28	81
20:29	81

Acts

1:5	93
1:8	93

Romans

1:18b	38
1:19–21	39
1:19–20	51
2:14–15	51
5:1–5	146

7:15	98
7:19	98
7:22	98
7:23	98
8:4	97, 143
8:5	97
8:5b	144
8:6	97
8:7–8	98
8:8	143–44
8:9a	158
8:11	137
8:13	98, 144
8:16–17	102
8:23	23
8:39	144
12:2	162
12:15	183

1 Corinthians

2:10–13	101
2:45	94
13:12	22, 27

2 Corinthians

4:7–11, 16	137
5:7	50

Galatians

3:27–28	19
5:16–17	123
5:16	158, 166
5:22–23	99
5:22, 25	143
5:24	99, 135
5:25	158
5:25–26	99
6:2	123

Ephesians

1:17–19	102
3:18–19	20

Philippians

1:7	19
2:12–13	153
2:19–30	59
3:8	29, 137, 138
3:10–14	138
3:10a	20
3:14	29
4:6	116
4:7	116
4:13	134
4:19	134

Colossians

1:9–10	20
1:10	27

1 Thessalonians

5:16–18	160

1 Timothy

1:17	50
4:6	163

Hebrews

1:3	80
4:15	52
11:1	36
12:1–2	122

James

2:23	52, 177
4:6–7, 9–10	143
4:8	142

1 Peter

2:2	163

2 Peter

1:2	21, 39

2 Peter (continued)

1:3–4	125
1:3	21, 39, 134
1:4	21
3:18	27
3:18a	127

1 John

1:9	143
3:24	102
4:1–6	90
4:7b–8	54
4:19	51
5:20	15

Revelation

3:15–32	119

www.ingramcontent.com/pod-product-compliance
Lightning Source LLC
Chambersburg PA
CBHW031427150426
43191CB00006B/426